Taking Social Research to the Larger World

Taking Social Research to the Larger World

Edward B. Harvey

CSPI ✹

Canadian Scholars' Press Inc.
Toronto

Taking Social Research to the Larger World
by Edward B. Harvey

First published in 2005 by
Canadian Scholars' Press Inc.
180 Bloor Street West, Suite 801
Toronto, Ontario M5S 2V6

www.cspi.org

Canadian Scholars' Press gratefully acknowledges financial support for our publishing activities from the Ontario Arts Council, the Canada Council for the Arts, the Government of Canada through the Book Publishing Industry Development Program (BPIDP), and the Government of Ontario through the Ontario Book Publishing Tax Credit Program.

Library and Archives Canada Cataloguing in Publication

Harvey, Edward B., 1939–
    Taking social research to the larger world / Edward B. Harvey.

ISBN 1-55130-255-1

    1. Harvey, Edward B., 1939– 2. Social sciences—Research—Canada.
3. Social policy—Research—Canada.   4. Applied sociology—Canada.
5. College teachers—Ontario—Toronto—Biography.   6. Consultants—Canada—Biography.   7. Social scientists—Canada—Biography.   I. Title.

H59.H37A3 2005   301'.072'02   C2004-906130-5

Cover design and typeset by Zack Taylor: www.zacktaylor.com.

05   06   07   08   09   5   4   3   2   1

Printed and bound in Canada by AGMV Marquis Imprimeur, Inc.

This book is dedicated to the many students and research assistants who joined me in the work to make the tools and understandings of social science relevant to practical problems and policy issues.

Table of Contents

Acknowledgements

When I first developed the idea for this book in June 2003, I had a discussion with Jack Wayne, president of Canadian Scholars' Press Inc. (CSPI). I had known Jack for many years as a colleague in the University of Toronto Sociology Department. I instinctively felt that Jack would relate to the approach I wanted to take and that his company would be the very best place for the project.

Jack soon introduced me to Althea Prince, the managing editor of CSPI. Althea's wonderful intellect and consistent enthusiasm has been a sustaining force. She and Jack are a great team to work with.

I also want to express my very great thanks to Rebecca Conolly, CSPI's manager of book production. Her creativity and professionalism made the final putting together of the book a totally positive process.

I am also indebted to Megan Mueller, the CSPI editor with whom I worked most directly. Megan was always available, supportive, and consistently constructive in her comments and guidance.

Others who helped include Maureen O'Neil, a long-time friend and former Ontario deputy minister, who discussed social policy with me; my former student, Richard Liu, who now works with me on various policy files; and Jill Given-King, who over the years has helped me produce several books and consulting reports. I also want to record my special thanks to Nels Granewall, a good friend and fellow Victoria College student during my time. When Victoria College became the University of Victoria, Nels embarked on a long and distinguished career in the university's Office of Alumni Affairs. On countless occasions he graciously took the time to answer my questions on various aspects of college history. I also want to acknowledge with thanks the generous assistance provided to me by Jane Turner, university archivist at the University of Victoria, and Lara J. Wilson, associate archivist, in accessing historicial documents and photographs pertaining to Victoria College.

I developed the step-by-step outline for the book while enjoying the warmth of a Provençal summer. I wrote most of the book surrounded by the snow of an Ontario winter.

I also want to thank my wife, Lorna Marsden, who took time from her demanding schedule to sit by the fire and listen to me read the results of a day's writing. As usual, her comments were insightful, incisive, and invaluable.

Edward B. Harvey
Toronto, 2004

Foreword

When Ted Harvey asked me to write a foreword for his book *Taking Social Research to the Larger World*, I was delighted to participate for three reasons.

Number one: I learned more about my friend Ted by reading the manuscript, which is constructed like a finely braided rope, intertwining Ted's personal, university, and private-sector lives.

Number two: I have great respect for Ted and his peers, who have made significant contributions to public policy processes through applied social research, setting policy directions, and solving not just current, but future problems as well. Ted, in many ways, was ahead of his time in his use of demography to identify public challenges (a method later popularized by David Foote).

Number three: Writing the foreword gave me an opportunity to reflect on my own time in public life and on some of the broad policy challenges we faced, as well as on a number of the actions we took to address the issues that faced Ontario.

Politics presents many challenges. One is always confronted with today's crises, exacerbated by an aggressive press and an institutionalized opposition, whose only intention is to embarrass the government and to prove it unworthy. Fortunately, these challenges usually pass, and the real stuff of governing continues: setting policy directions to engage the real (not the imagined) problems, which do not disappear; rather, left unattended, they compound.

When our band of idealists was elected in 1985—some say by accident—we brought with us the strong view that government was not in itself inherently evil, inherently inefficient, or inherently an impediment to the average person having a good life. Rather, government was an expression of the collective will that could represent the positive in all of us; it could represent people's hopes and aspirations as we all strive for the ultimate objective of equality of opportunity for all Ontarians.

It has always been my belief that the strong can look after themselves. It is not the role of government to represent either large business or big unions—they have both made a meal of taking their share of power. Rather, our responsibility was to speak for people who did not have large institutions to support them—people who were dispossessed or unable to fight for their own interests. Our job was to fight for our children's interests and for those without lobbyists. We represented the wheels that didn't squeak.

In spite of relative prosperity in Ontario at that time, it was obvious to me that a number of structural challenges faced the province. We set out with an incredibly competent group of ministers and bureaucrats to attack the problems. Indeed, I look back and say with some pride that I don't think there has ever been a finer cabinet assembled in Ontario's history—though I know I am biased—either with a greater sense of purpose or sense of nationhood, who were prepared to challenge the status quo and bring lasting solutions and lasting changes of approach to some of Ontario's greatest problems.

At the core, it was absolutely vital to keep Ontario's economy competitive in an increasingly globalized context. The world was changing rapidly, particularly at that time with the increased market dominance of Japan and the Far East, as well as competition from the United States. We were involved in discussions about a trade agreement that would fundamentally alter our competitive base: when finally implemented, it took 300,000 industrial jobs out of Ontario's economy in the first two years. It was imperative that we create a highly knowledge-based, research-oriented, high-technology economic base to compensate for the more commodity-based economy that had been our heritage.

At the same time, we had to deal with a dramatically changing workforce, with new immigrants entering into it, as well increasing numbers of women who wanted to participate fully in all that Ontario had to offer. Many Ontarians were coming forward to participate in the political, economic, and social life of a country without walls or barriers. We had to build the spaces, the places, the atmosphere, and the institutions to accommodate all of the talent in this diverse province. We wanted to build an inclusive, not exclusive, club.

It was obvious then, and it is increasingly obvious now, that our health care system had to be revamped and changed in order to accommodate the massive pressure that was being put on it—the pressure of aging populations, new diseases, new technologies, and increased demands. The current model was not sustainable in all respects, and changes had to be made.

The degradation of the environment also had to be addressed; we needed to find new ways to deal with the despoiling of our lakes, our air, and our forests, as well as the issue of garbage. Not to dramatically oversimplify the solutions to any of these problems, but it was clear that without a world-class education system that embraced the concept of lifelong learning, we would not have the human resources nor the leadership to solve the problems that we were facing, not just in Ontario, but in Canada. We needed to find our place in the world.

No less a critic than Lori Goldstein, a former *Toronto Sun* editor—not exactly a liberal tabloid—told me that ours was the most active legislative agenda he had seen in his many years covering Queen's Park. We engaged the brains and credibility of people like Ted Harvey to assist us by way of consultation, research, and advisory councils on health and technology, and we worked hard to involve a whole new generation of people in finding solutions.

But study and consultation are no substitute for action.

We adopted an extraordinarily active agenda, introducing groundbreaking legislation in such areas as freedom of information, pay equity, employment equity, human rights, Native affairs, welfare reform, and environmental reform (from new air quality controls to the introduction of the blue box recycling program, which has since been adopted in many cities around the world).

An innovation agenda funded centres of excellence, research capacity, entrepreneurialism, and education for new approaches toward a knowledge-based economy. In addition, the health system was looked at in detail by the Premier's Council on Health, bringing new imagination to managing health care.

While maintaining this level of activism, the government was able to balance the budget—the first government to do so in almost 20 years in Canada.

It is not as if all of the above reforms have stood the test of time, but it wasn't for a lack of effort or failure to deal fundamentally with the problems. None of these initiatives would have been possible without people like Ted Harvey and the new discipline and knowledge he brought to social research, to understanding the problems, and to finding solutions to complex issues.

Individuals like Ted, who possess the experience, the flexibility of mind, and an understanding of the future, combined with the subtlety to work with all the constituents in both the public and private sector to advance the cause, were absolutely essential to these reforms.

People with a great social conscience are vital to the process of finding solutions. I am very grateful to have had the opportunity to work with Ted Harvey. He is one of those individuals who has always had an understanding of not only where the world is going, but also where it *ought* to go.

David R. Peterson
Toronto, 2004

CHAPTER ONE

Introduction

After World War II, Canada embarked on a journey of exceptional economic growth and social change. Unlike the devastated Europe and Asia, it had escaped material damage during the war. There was still a price to be paid, however, as tens of thousands of Canadians were killed or wounded in the service of their country. My eldest brother, 17 years my senior, served in the Royal Canadian Air Force and lost his life when his plane went down in 1943.

Canada's wartime economy made a relatively quick and effective transition to a peacetime economy. The war years had been characterized by many privations and consumerism had been placed on hold. As a result, after the war, there was a great deal of pent-up demand in the domestic economy. Put in less technical terms, people wanted to start consuming again, and big-ticket items like automobiles and appliances were high on the list. The factories that had been producing weapons of war responded accordingly.

The economy was also stimulated by the high rate of post-war family formation. Simply put, people got married and had children—lots of children. By 1951, Canada's total fertility rate (live births per 1000 women) rose to 3.5 (in 1936 it had been 2.7); by 1956, it increased to 3.9. In 1961, it was 3.8.[1] This was the making of the "baby boom." It was a period of great optimism. Economic growth was translating into job growth. People felt that the war to bring lasting peace had been fought and won. It seemed like a good world to bring children into—which, in the moral climate of the times, generally meant being married first. In 1951, the median age at marriage for men was 24.8; the corresponding age for women was 22.0. By 1961, the median age at marriage was 24.0 for men and 21.1 for women.[2] All of this household-forming activity contributed directly to even more economic growth.

Apart from the rebirth of consumerism and the emergence of the family formation boom, the post-war world faced a massive task of reconstruction. Compared to the aftermath of World War I, there were many more programs after World War II designed to restore the defeated countries to have functioning economies that would be inclined toward the development of stable democratic institutions. Initiatives like the Marshall Plan reflected lessons learned from post–World War I economic destabilization in Germany and the rise of fascism. Canada's rich endowment of natural resources experienced increasingly strong demand as world reconstruction proceeded. The situation was further enhanced by the fact that there were fewer competitors than is the case nowadays.

Strong domestic demand and strong external demand produced sustained economic growth while inflation remained low. During the 1950s and the 1960s, the real after-tax purchasing power of Canadians doubled—a period of income growth we have not experienced since. Even with stable income taxation regimes, governments in Canada experienced huge increases in revenues. Substantial amounts of this revenue found their way into massive investments in both physical infrastructure (highways, airports, public buildings, etc.) and social infrastructure (health, education, social security, and other government programs). The spirit of the times was reflected in the views of great Canadian leaders like Clarence Decatur (C.D.) Howe, who, when questioned about such expenditures in the House of Commons, said shrugging, "What's a million?" (a lot in the 1950s), and got on with the job of nation building. Howe's enormous energy and take-charge style earned him the nickname "Minister of Everything."

The economic growth transformed many aspects of Canadian society. People began to move to the cities; the initial reason was employment, but as time passed, lifestyle considerations became increasingly important. As Canadians found themselves with increasing disposable income, their appetite for services grew. The service sector expanded accordingly—an important part of the white-collar employment revolution so brilliantly analysed by C. Wright Mills.[3] Most service jobs were non-union and many were part-time. The growing availability of this type of work signalled the beginnings of greater female labour force participation, a major trend of the second half of the twentieth century.

The 1950s and 1960s are often described—at least for countries like Canada—as a "golden era" in economic terms. The politics of nostalgia promises that if we do "the right things," we can get back to that condition. This is an incorrect view. That particular phase of the Canadian experience was the consequence of a combination of circumstances not likely to be repeated in the future. It gave the country a great deal in terms of expansionary initiatives and new horizons. It also established expectations that became increasingly difficult to meet after 1973 as new and serious challenges emerged—including the energy crisis, stagnant economic growth, and high inflation.

* * *

I was born a few years ahead of the baby boom. This—coupled with earning a doctorate while still in my twenties and entering university professorship and consulting in 1966—proved to be a continuing advantage.

For various reasons, some of which I discuss in this book, I had come to a fairly early realization that Canada was going through a major transition, that getting as much education as possible was a good idea, and that because of the rapid growth in social policies and programs, there would be a strong demand for people trained to help shape this ongoing process.

In summary, this is what the book is about. It is an account of my career, past and present, which has always—since its very beginning—combined university professorship with applied social research and policy-oriented consulting to both the public and private sectors. It is not about some workaholic tendency to keep overly busy. It is about trying to build bridges between what we learn, teach, research, and write about in university social science departments and the practical, pressing needs of jurisdictions outside the university.

Part of the book deals with selected specifics of the applied, policy-oriented social research projects I have been involved in over the past 38 years. But in order to understand this material, it is necessary to have some knowledge of the formative experiences and relationships that led me to take this career path. In this sense, the book is partly a memoir and partly an examination of how and what one can do with applied, policy-oriented research understandings and techniques.

Apart from this introduction, the book is organized in three sections. Part I contains four chapters and examines the preparatory experiences that led me to become a university professor and entrepreneurial businessperson in the consulting industry. It deals with the period from 1958 to 1967, during which I completed my bachelor's, master's, and doctoral studies and also lived in Europe for a year. This was the human capital formation phase of my life.

Part II contains five chapters, the first of which deals with a seven-year period beginning in 1967, when I accepted a position with the University of Toronto, and ending in 1974, by which time I had become a full professor and a department chair and had incorporated my consulting practice. In effect, the chapter is concerned with how I established and consolidated my career path as a professor and consultant. The next chapter examines the three guiding principles that enabled me to manage that career path over the ensuing three decades.

The final three chapters of Part II observe a less chronological approach than the preceding ones. They examine aspects of my consultancy work in the three broad areas in which I have participated—royal commissions and task forces, governments and the broader public sector, and the private sector. These three chapters are intended to provide a feel for what it is like to do applied, policy-oriented social research in each of the different areas of activity.

In order to accomplish this goal, I describe various projects for which my consulting group was engaged. Like everyone else who pursues this type of work, I have had my share of disappointments arising from proposals that were not successful. This has been the case in all three of the broad sectors in which I have worked and is the natural course of events in a competitive industry. I managed to succeed, in part, by always having more than one proposal out in the field at any given point in time. Other management strategies I used included keeping up with the trends, putting together strong teams, learning from those unsuccessful proposals and—above all—moving on.

Part III of the book contains a single concluding chapter, in which I set out my views on the prospects for applied, policy-oriented social research and strategies for achieving the full promise this field of work holds.

* * *

My wife, Lorna Marsden, and I have been married for over 40 years. At points in this book, I refer to aspects of our jointly shared experience. In doing so, it is not my intention to offer an account of her own life and times. As a woman of major accomplishments—senator of Canada, university president, and a board director of many public and private sector organizations—she is more than capable of writing about such matters herself, when and if she chooses to do so.

Part I

Preparatory Experiences

This part of the book contains four chapters that deal with the preparatory experiences that led to my becoming a university professor and entrepreneurial businessperson. It covers the period from September 1958 to August 1967, the nine years during which I completed my undergraduate and post-graduate studies at three universities—with one year out for work and travel in Europe.

Chapter 2 revisits my 1958–61 undergraduate studies at Victoria College (now the University of Victoria) and a highly formative period in Europe between 1961 and 1962. Chapter 3 deals with my post-Europe time at the University of British Columbia—1962–64—during which I finished my bachelor's degree, completed a master's degree, and was accepted to doctoral studies at Princeton University. In Chapter 4, I reflect on the two years I spent in residence at Princeton while pursuing doctoral studies and go through the various activities that culminated in my successfully completing the general examinations in May 1966. The final chapter of this section deals with the following year (1966–67), during which I worked full-time as an assistant professor of sociology at the University of Western Ontario while simultaneously completing and successfully defending my doctoral dissertation, the final hurdle in the Princeton experience.

First and foremost, these nine years constituted an intense period of human capital development or, to use a less technical term, becoming educated. But it was also a period of considerable social capital development—my development of social skills and understandings—as a result of my experiences in Canada, Europe, and the United States. It was also a time during which I developed a clear view of what I wanted to do in my career. The core of this vision was to take the insights and methods of sociology, combine them with other disciplines such as demography and economics, and address practical problems in both the public and private sectors. Although the university would be an important base for my work, I realized that I would work in other institutional settings as well. To use a distinction coined by sociologist Alvin Gouldner, I intended to be a "cosmopolitan," not a "local." My interest lay in boundary-spanning activity, not in supporting disciplinary hegemony.

CHAPTER TWO

Starting University
and Discovering Europe

The University of Victoria in Victoria, British Columbia, Canada, came into being on July 1, 1963. Prior to that it was known as Victoria College and, under that name, had a distinguished 60-year history of providing instruction at the university level.

When I arrived at Victoria College in September 1958, the institution had two main components: a Faculty of Arts and Science and a Faculty of Education. At that time, Arts and Science was offering the first two years of the B.A. degree. The Faculty of Education offered the first two years of the B.Ed. degree. The College had an affiliation agreement with the University of British Columbia (U.B.C.) in Vancouver under which U.B.C. recognized Victoria College coursework and counted it toward U.B.C. degrees.

In that era, there was something of a tradition in Victoria of young, university-bound people doing their first two years at the college and then "going across the water" to complete their degrees at U.B.C. Victoria College, although small compared to U.B.C., enjoyed a good academic reputation and was situated in a physically pleasant setting. There were also obvious economic advantages to living at home, at least for part of one's post-secondary education. All of these factors figured in my decision as I set out to enroll in Victoria College's Arts and Science program.

I had attended a comprehensive high school in Victoria. It had a strong academic stream but also offered a great many vocational courses in subjects such as shop (all male) and typing/secretarial skill development (almost totally female)—all of this very much in keeping with the powerful sex-role stereotyping of the times. Although I was in the university-bound stream, the nature of the school enabled me to meet a great many different kinds of people. I had an English sports car that required constant

Edward B. Harvey, off to a high school graduation event.

fixing, and the guys in the shop classes were invariably helpful, even though they (really quite gently) poked fun at my esoteric vehicle. (Their idea of automotive nirvana was a hot-rodded Ford or Chevy.) I managed to learn some useful things about crankshafts, carburetors, and ring jobs. I also learned something about how very bright people—who could have been engineers or scientists—got streamed into blue-collar jobs because of their working-class origins. I developed an early skepticism about school guidance counsellors and their role in reproducing "the social order." As for meeting (and sometimes even understanding) many different types of people—that proved to be a lifetime advantage.

My pre-university work included Grade 13 or senior matriculation, mainly known in Canada today for the "double cohort" problems created by its recent (2002–03) phasing-out in Ontario. The Grade 13 work I did wasn't exactly university, but it certainly wasn't high school either. The program was highly structured. Two advanced English courses were mandatory (literature and composition/grammar), and then one chose from other courses that had to include a foreign language, mathematics, and a science course. I ended up taking French, mathematics, physics, and chemistry. It was all useful preparation for university, particularly learning grammar the hard way and developing something of a quantitative and scientific perspective.

The 1958–59 year at Victoria College represented a turning point in the college's history. Enrolment far exceeded expectations. Arts and Science saw a 14.5 percent increase, while Education was left to deal with a staggering 50.9 percent increase. Dr. Harry Hickman was the principal of the college. His doctorate—from the Sorbonne—was in French literature, and demographic projections and the analysis of social trends were not his province. In this, he was much the same as the vast majority of university administrators during the era. With 20/20 hindsight, what was happening—particularly in Education—was the growing awareness among young people embarking on university studies of the future demand for teachers that the post-war baby boom generation would create. More generally, an increasing number of us were becoming aware that Canada was changing. The country was industrializing and urbanizing. Jobs—and job requirements—were beginning to change. It's important to remember that this was an era when a person with a high school diploma could get a decent job. Going to university was still seen as being for the few rather than the many.

This was reflected in the social makeup of Victoria College. First, even in a small place with only a few hundred students, there was a great gulf between Arts and Science and Education. Students in Arts and Science were much more likely to come from upper-middle-class backgrounds than students in Education. Preparing for a job was generally not a high priority for the typical Arts and Science student—particularly in the first couple of years. The Canadian economy was enjoying an extended period of growth and job creation. There was a prevalent feeling among my classmates that "something would happen." The general expectation was that it would be something good. The goal of going to university was to expand one's mind, meet people, and have a good time. This probably sounds elitist and hedonistic. It was. By way of contrast, students in Education were less likely to enjoy the socioeconomic circumstances that supported intellectual and experiential experimentation and a relaxed view of the job market. The demand for teachers was such that it was possible to get a teaching job after just two years in the program. The prevailing ethic was "get in, get through, and get out." There was relatively little social interchange between the Arts and Science and Education students.

There was also a substantial demographic difference between the two faculties. The 1958 Victoria College freshman class in Arts and Science had 326 students, 70 percent of whom were male. The proportions in the Education freshman class were reversed: 22 percent were male and 79 percent were female. At that point in history, we were still at the front end of the baby boom, and the initial impacts of this demographic phenomenon were occurring in the earlier grades of the school system. Women were much more likely to be elementary school teachers than men. The enrolment numbers reflected the reality of this occupational gender pattern.

Also, these enrolment figures were for the start of the year. I remember a number of students who received "the B.A.C. degree," which was the prevailing abbreviation for "Bounced at Christmas." It was the equivalent of being "sent down" at Oxford or Cambridge. A less draconian penalty was a "pull up your socks interview" with Dr. Hickman. I managed to avoid both these perils.

It wasn't all that difficult to become distracted from one's studies. Victoria College, apart from the usual sports, had a great many clubs—the Players Club, the Poster Club, the Jazz Club, the Chess Club, the Science Club, the Radio Club, the Philosophy

Club, the Listening Club, and many more. There were also three political clubs: the Progressive Conservative, Liberal, and C.C.F. (standing for Canadian Commonwealth Confederation, fore-runner to the NDP). I became involved in the Players Club, the Jazz Club, and the Liberal Club. This last one proved to have a lifelong influence. The purpose of all this social activity, of course, was to build social capital and, as I went on in life, I more and more realized how difficult it is to apply your intellectual capi-tal effectively without a measure of social capital. In retrospect, I think it was an effective strategy as long as one was able to maintain a sense of balance between studies and socializing. It worked for me. I met many people, some of whom I still know. It also provided the broader context for the personal development that comes with the opportunity to have social association with others, to talk with them (including having spirited arguments), and generally develop the skills of social relations. Heavy analysis aside, it was also fun.

In 1958, only a small proportion of Canadian high school graduates went on to university (community colleges didn't exist at that time). Enrolments were beginning to increase (particularly in education), but that was from a relatively small base, numerically speaking. There were various reasons for this. As I have already mentioned, it was an era when high school diploma recipients could get decent jobs. Young people married young. The great increases in female post-secondary educational participation and labour force participation were still ahead of us. Although there were a handful of notable exceptions (I married one of them), the majority of young women I knew in the Victoria College Arts and Science stream were not there with the goal of preparing for a lifelong career. This observation is not intended in any way to disparage marriage and raising children. It is simply a comment on the demographic realities of the times and on the powerful emphasis that 1950s values placed upon marriage, having lots of children, and carefully observing traditional sex-role differences. For those who wanted to, it was not an easy value system to escape—particularly in a smallish city (population about 60,000) such as Victoria.

* * *

Several factors were involved in my going on to post-secondary studies. A major consideration was my being in the university stream in high school. At the time, the educational system was very rigid and highly bureaucratic. If you weren't in the university stream and later decided you wanted to go, it took an almost impossible amount of determination and additional coursework to make that happen. This was long before the era of "flexible curricula" and "mature student arrangements."

Apart from that crucial consideration, there was peer pressure. My closest friends were going to university, and I very much wanted to be part of that scene. I enjoyed being exposed to new ideas and learning, but I wanted to have a good time with the friends I had and to meet new people as well. I never had any doubt that, for me, university was the best place to do that.

Although my friends and I may have on occasions been less than serious in our behaviour, that didn't prevent us from taking ourselves very, very seriously. We stayed up half the night talking about ideas, morals, and (with the ingratitude of youth) how "boring" Victoria was. We were convinced that there was a larger and more interesting world "out there." In a much more sketchy way, we also had the sense that more education was somehow the key to provide access to all that. From a distant perspective of age and experience, I think our young instincts about education were essentially correct.

Although I criticized and complained about Victoria as much as any of my friends, if not more, I actually drew on many assets of the community and my situation that gave me a good start in life. First, it was difficult—for a middle-class kid like me—to get into really serious trouble. I had a stable and very private home life. My two older siblings had left home, and I inherited the top floor of my parents' house in Victoria. It became a sanctuary for the books and the L.P. ("long-playing") records I cherished. Adequately, if not exactly elegantly, furnished, the sitting room had a view—on a clear night—of the lights of Port Angeles, a small U.S. city some 20 miles across the waters. It was also a place where I could entertain friends, thanks to my relatively tolerant parents.

In 1958, less than 12 percent of the Canadian population had television sets. My parents resisted the seductions of the flickering screen for many years after that. In 1958, I had a good radio and Hi-Fi system, as it used to be called, and I was a C.B.C. (Canadian Broadcasting Corporation) addict. For me, the C.B.C. in those days was a window on the world beyond Victoria. Programs like C.B.C. *Stage* gave insights into the lives of sophisticated folk in Toronto and even more unimaginable venues like New York and London.

I also listened, almost religiously, to C.B.C.'s *Wednesday Night*, which was the corporation's evening of high, and often innovative, culture modelled after the B.B.C.'s *Third Program*. It brought a mix of music, drama, and commentary that was unapologetically elitist. I doubt if the C.B.C. management of the day cared if perhaps only 200 people were listening. *Wednesday Night* was invariably introduced by James Bannerman, whose educated and refined voice conjured up images of distant places with deep cultural and intellectual assets. Much later, I learned that "James Bannerman" was but one of the many pen-names of John Charles Kirkpatrick McNaught, an author, critic, and broadcaster born in Toronto in 1902 and educated at Upper Canada College and the University of Toronto. He was, I think, perfect for the part.

In the second half of my high school career, my extracurricular reading was considerably more influenced by C.B.C. listening than by the school program. Regular C.B.C. offerings like *Books in Review* were highly important, but there were others as well. I followed up my "leads" at the Victoria Public Library. I got to know one of the librarians quite well. She was probably in her late thirties (although one's judgement of age at sixteen is less than good). In retrospect, I realize what a remarkable person she was. One week I'd be asking questions about Marshall McLuhan and Lawrence Durrell. Next week it was Sigmund Freud and Ernest Hemingway. Then I'd move on to Barney Rosset and *The Evergreen Review*. She never treated me like a child, a dilettante, or worse. Instead, she patiently helped me find things, made helpful suggestions, and proved to be an insightful guide to the wonderful world that lives in books.

Before I went off to university, she gave me a copy of *The Esquire Book of Manners for Young Men*, which included a wide range of practical information on various topics such as "how to make conversation on a date." It's easy to mock this type of publication, but I found it useful and was genuinely touched by the gift.

There were two other Victoria institutions I frequented. One was the Greater Victoria Gallery of Art; the other was the Victoria Chess Club. The art gallery was located in Spencer House, the stately former home of the Spencers, a family that had made its fortune in the department store business. Over the years, the gallery has been greatly expanded with modern additions, but the original Spencer House remains an integral and effective part. In the 1950s, the fact that the gallery was a single—albeit large—house gave it a kind of intimacy and sense of accessibility. Virtually all the staff were volunteers. I found them welcoming and interested. For me, it was the foundation of a lifetime strong interest in Canadian works of art.

As for chess, I played it in the high school club and took it seriously enough to get hold of the annotated games of various grandmasters—like Alekhine, Capablanca, and Lasker—and study their moves. I then went on to other books that dealt specifically with opening, middle game, and endgame strategies. My math teacher was the staff member who looked after the club, and he encouraged me to play in the "downtown club." I greeted this suggestion with some trepidation—it seemed like the big leagues to me. However, I put on my best jacket and tie (grandmaster Alekhine had always dressed with elegant perfection for his famous matches!) and appeared at the club next Friday evening. I was greeted—if that's the right word—in the lobby by the elderly and severe-looking Mr. Moody, whose walking stick seemed as if it might double as an offensive weapon. After hearing me out and carefully scrutinizing my tie, he decided to err on the side of charity and let me in. I became a regular.

Although structured tournament play against the clock was very different from the high school club, my initial anxieties rapidly gave way to pure enjoyment. My original fears that everyone in "the downtown club" was a "genius player" soon evaporated. It was like everything else in life: there were a few very strong players, some not-so-good players, and a great many in-between.

I managed to make the "A" team. In that group, there were three players who stand out in my memory. One was Mr. DeHavilland—no one ever called him anything else—who, at what must have been the age of eighty, combined a mercurial temperament with exceptionally erratic play ranging from brilliant to totally inept. Although I didn't have a clue about such things at the time, I now suspect that his periodic aberrations may have had something to do with how much claret he had consumed with dinner. He would sit in his well-tailored three-piece suit, walking stick held between his knees, make his moves in a quick and seemingly offhand way, and then sit back and glower at his opponent unnervingly. After I had been coming to the club for about a month, I learned that he was the father of Olivia DeHavilland and Joan Fontaine, who (despite their different last names) were sisters and well-known Hollywood actresses.

The second player was Len, a man in his early seventies at that time. Born into an East London working-class family, he had immigrated to Canada in his twenties and had pursued a long career as a blue-collar steam engineer. Despite a large inventory of nervous tics and mannerisms, he was an extremely steady player who delivered consistently strong results. I played against him in several tournaments and learned from this experience the importance of making incremental gains, consolidating one's position at strategic points, and always planning ahead to the endgame, where victory or loss often hangs on a very slender thread. I never heard Len, or anyone else, use his last name.

The person I most enjoyed playing chess with was Dr. Simon Marinker. Dr. Marinker was born in Paris in 1913 to Polish parents who had eloped from Warsaw to France in 1910. When I met him, he was around forty-five or forty-six and serving as chief of surgery at Victoria's Royal Jubilee Hospital. He generally came to the club in the evening, after a long day at the hospital. With his fine mane of dark hair, neatly trimmed moustache, and well-cut suits, he was a dapper figure. Appearances aside, however, Dr. Marinker had an ingrained courtesy and warmth of personality that made him everybody's friend. He was also a powerful chess player.

We started to play against one another and, after a game, he was always prepared to analyse the contest, reflecting on good moves and bad moves, winning strategies, and losing strategies. He was a fine teacher as well as a distinguished surgeon. After four months, we were pretty evenly matched.

When he eventually retired from medicine, he went on to write and publish books, including his three-book trilogy, *Beyond the Citadel*, and an utterly fascinating historical novel titled *Assassination, Preparations & Consequences*.[4]

Dr. Marinker was the only member of the club with whom I kept in touch. I remember a telephone conversation with him when he was well into his eighties. I asked him how he was. With his invariable good cheer, he gave me his physician's self-assessment: "Still ambulatory. Long-term memory fine. Short-term memory shot."

As I became involved in my university studies, I gave up chess and have never returned to it. It was simply too time-consuming. Beyond that, I could also see that it had a certain addictive potential. Having said that, I'm very glad I learned it and played as long as I did. It taught me that certain things can bring people together in a positive way despite large age and life differences. And it also taught me—even though it's "only a game"—some things about strategy and planning that proved very useful in my later consulting business and investment activities.

In summation, then, several factors combined and propelled me toward university studies. Being in the university stream in high school was obviously a factor. Although there were things about high school I didn't like (some authoritarian and/or un-inspiring teachers, regimentation, etc.), I generally liked both qualitative and quantitative subjects and wanted to keep on learning. What my friends were doing was also highly impor-tant. We all influenced one another a great deal, particularly in a relatively small, class-stratified community. Having a stable home life and the freedom to pursue outside interests helped enormously. I already mentioned that my parents were tolerant. During his long life, I never once heard my father utter a racist or religious slur—a practice far too commonplace in those days. He was socially conservative about some things (such as wearing a jacket and tie, being polite, working for a living, honouring the community), but on the large and abstract moral issues I suspect he was a liberal—or at least an iconoclast about dogma and other "received wisdom." He kept journals for most of his adult life, and I read these after his death. The writing was articulate and interesting but quite unrevealing—a characteristic, I think, of Anglo-Saxon men of his generation. I have already said enough about the outside interests I was able to pursue. They were invaluable. As for the librarian, the art gallery volunteers, the C.B.C., Dr. Marinker, and all the others, I still think of them with admiration and affection. Finally, I had the sense—shared by many—that the times were changing and that higher education was going to be an increasingly important part of making one's way in the emerging Canada.

* * *

I have already made some comments about the programs and demographics at Victoria College. But what was my life as a student like?

When I arrived at the college in September 1958, it was still almost five years away from becoming the University of Victoria and moving to the new Gordon Head Campus. During my time, Victoria College was located on the Lansdowne Campus, a physically beautiful seven-acre site surrounded by a desirable residential neighbourhood and about a 10-minute drive from downtown Victoria.

The campus was dominated by the Young Building, an early twentieth-century structure in the late Renaissance Italianate Revival style with an imposing 95-foot high clock tower. Not surprisingly, "The Tower" was the name of the Victoria College yearbook.

A campus like Lansdowne and structures like the Young Building were well suited to a small institution with a stable enrolment. But increasing enrolment pressures—there was an unexpectedly large increase in 1958—made it clear that those days were fast disappearing. Such challenging problems were nowhere in my thoughts on the bright September morning I parked my British racing green M.G. sports car in the college lot and went off to get registered. I was very excited about what I was doing and totally convinced that it was the appropriate course of action, but I had only the vaguest ideas of where it would all lead.

The approach to Victoria College with the Young Building in the background. Drawing by Edward Goodall, c. 1959.

From the very start, I liked the university experience. The courses were interesting, and the pace at which one was expected to work was considerably faster than what I had experienced in high school. Because I had senior matriculation, I was able to take many second-year Arts and Science courses. This meant that I wasn't much affected by the enrolment increases, which had their main impact on first year courses and the Faculty of Education in particular. My classes were small (unbelievably small by today's undergraduate instruction standards), which unquestionably

An idyllic setting: students outside Victoria College's landmark Young Building, c. mid-1950s.

contributed to higher-quality learning experiences. Among other things, small classes fostered student discussions and created far more opportunity for individualized contact with professors.

During my time at the college, I specialized in social sciences and English literature and writing. The former was good preparation for the path I ultimately took to doctoral studies, professorship, and building a consulting business. The latter was a great help to my constant writing and publishing activity. By the time I had completed the third year of my B.A., I was convinced that—given the way Canada was evolving—"the social sciences would have important applications to industry" (the words I used in a 1961 discussion with my mistakenly skeptical future brother-in-law, who was a historian).

My friends and social activities at this time tended to be centred around artists, people who wrote or wanted to write, and individuals with entrepreneurial and innovative tendencies.

I met Michael Morris, now an internationally recognized Canadian artist, at Victoria College. At that time, Michael was actively painting, much of his work influenced by Herbert Siebner, an abstract expressionist artist who had immigrated to Canada from Germany in 1954. Siebner said of his paintings, "As I look back over my work, I like the ones best where I never found out why I did them."⁵ I became fascinated by abstract expressionist painting and worked at finding out more about its exponents, including Canadian-born Jean-Paul Riopelle (never imagining that one day I would have the good fortune to own some of his work). Abstract expressionism fitted well with my questioning of conformity and tradition.

Michael invited me to his Christmas party, and it was at this event I met Lorna Marsden, who was in her first year of study at Victoria College. We started to see one another regularly. I think our respective parents thought this was all right, although I suspect Lorna's father worried a bit about my racy car! Our parents were less sanguine when, several months later, we decided to get married and live and work in Europe for a year. We were awfully young—even by the "age at marriage standards" of the time. However, since we are still married more than 40 years later and throughout that time have systematically fostered one another's life and career development, I rest my case. Almost needless to say, our parents became reconciled to all this decades ago. It would appear that sometimes young people do know what they're doing.

Among other non-academic activities, I wrote for *Stylus*, the college's literary magazine, and kept the company of Allan T.J. Cairns, a Victoria College English professor and world traveller, and two fellow students—John Simpson and Ivor Alexander—who were active in the literary life of the college. Tragically, Allan died in 1988 of brain cancer at the much too early age of fifty-seven. He was a wonderful professor, friend, and mentor. I

Edward B. Harvey's MG TC sportscar parked in front of the Pacific Ocean, Victoria, c. late 1950s.

remain in regular contact with John and Ivor, two loyal friends for life.

The "wildest" thing I did during my time at Victoria College was co-managing a jazz club in Victoria for more than a year. My partner in this enterprise was Garry Nixon, an entrepreneurial fellow student then and now a tax accountant in Vancouver. At the end of the 1950s and the beginning of the 1960s, Victoria was not exactly a lively place, but it did have a jazz club known as The Scene. This waterfront establishment was located on Wharf Street, about a five-minute stroll from the venerable Union Club and the famous Empress Hotel.

I liked modern jazz (Paul Desmond, Charlie Parker, Cal Tjader, Charles Mingus, etc.) and used to visit the club from time to time. When I first discovered The Scene, it was being managed by a newly minted lawyer, Wally Lightbody (who also played the saxophone). One evening, Garry Nixon and I visited the club and fell into conversation with Wally. He told us that he had been offered a job with a well-established but somewhat stodgy law firm in town. Apparently, the senior partner had sternly counselled him that involvement in a jazz club was not "seemly" for a rising young legal talent. By the end of the conversation, we agreed to buy the club charter from Wally for one hundred dollars. Since this included the furnishings and a piano, it was truly a bargain basement price—even by the standards of the time.

Garry helped his parents run the Fox Cinema in Victoria, so he knew something about the entertainment business. I was reasonably good with organizational planning and financial management generally. We both agreed that the club had been an underutilized asset because of its exclusive reliance on a small coterie of local musicians. We proceeded to do what nowadays would be called a "market scan." In our case, it consisted of talking to people we thought might know something and trying to identify a viable entertainment policy for the club. The results were highly divided. About half the people thought we should continue doing what had worked in the past. The other half thought Victoria was starved for younger-audience type of entertainment and was ready for "big-name" jazz offerings.

Garry, who was a rather more flamboyant character than me, wanted to commit totally to the big-name policy. I argued for a mixed approach, contending that we couldn't afford to alienate the local musicians, since "big names" weren't always available or affordable and, even worse, were not always dependable. We ended up pursuing the mixed strategy. We brought in many more musicians from Vancouver, including the outstanding A1 Neill Quartet, which often worked in the East Coast "hard bop" idiom pioneered by the brilliant duo of Charlie Parker and Dizzy Gillespie. We picked up on the "reading poetry to jazz" movement that had drifted up from what Barney Rosset's *Evergreen Review* immortalized as the "San Francisco Scene."[6] One of the persons who read was Anthony "Tony" Emery, a professor of English at Victoria College who had a few months earlier instructed me in the complexities of Chaucer. I think his staider colleagues in the English Department were a bit shocked.

Encouraged by the success of these innovations, we decided to "bet the farm." At the dawn of the 1960s, Charlie Mingus was considered to be one of the best—perhaps the best—bass player in modern jazz. Now leading his own quintet, he had worked often with luminaries like Charlie Parker and Dizzy Gillespie and was the bass player on the now legendary 1953 *Jazz at Massey Hall* performance of the Charlie Parker Quintet.

Issue 2 (1958) of *Evergreen Review* with an incription to Edward B. Harvey written by the *Review*'s publisher, Barney Rosset (1998).

Charles Mingus in concert, Victoria College, 1961.

(The original recording of the concert is now a collector's item.) Long-distance negotiations at the beginning of the 1960s didn't enjoy the contemporary advantages of electronic mail and cheap telephone rates. I finally tracked down Mingus's agent in New York. He'd never heard of Victoria (not really surprising) and wanted to know how much snow we had. (Answer: none.) Several more telephone conversations were involved, but it turned out that "yes, the Quintet would be touring the U.S. west coast in five weeks' time" and "yes, Mr. Mingus would be prepared to perform in Victoria." The fee seemed astronomical but backing out now would have been a total admission of defeat.

We needn't have worried. Mingus played to standing room-only audiences and was held over. We also staged a concert in the packed auditorium of Victoria College. Even after paying all our bills, we were miles ahead financially. As for meeting someone like Charlie Mingus at that stage of life, well—that wasn't quantifiable.

We kept the club going, brought in other "big names" as well as local talent, and somehow kept up with our studies. The fact that people in their early twenties don't need much sleep helped. As time went by, it became clear that both Garry and I were going on to other things. We sold the club to someone wanting to cash in on the emerging fad for "beat generation coffee houses." Apart from the fun involved, which was considerable, the whole experience taught me a lot about running a business.

During the same academic year that witnessed the Charlie Mingus concert, the Victoria College auditorium was once again filled for a speech by the national Liberal leader and Leader of the Opposition, the Honourable Lester B. Pearson. I had been involved with the "Young Liberals" for two years and was excited about the Liberal leader's visit. I had been to various earlier "Young Liberal" events, including a presentation by Arthur Laing, who served with distinction as leader of the Liberal Party in British Columbia and later in several federal cabinet posts and, ultimately, as a senator. I was impressed with his ideas, his generosity with his time, and his totally non-patronizing way of dealing with a group of young people who, to be frank, didn't know all that much about the intricacies of the political and policy process.

I became convinced that a federal Liberal government under Mr. Pearson would be best equipped to strike a viable balance between economic growth and the development of supportive social programs for health, education, and income security—the sort of Canada Pierre Elliott Trudeau later spoke of as "the just society." I still haven't decided which was more interesting: being a Liberal in politically polarized British Columbia or being a Liberal in a university sociology department.

* * *

Lester B. Pearson, speaking at Victoria College, 1961.

How would I sum up my time at Victoria College? Educationally, it was a good place, but not as challenging as U.B.C. and a great deal less challenging than Princeton. Also, a fairly high proportion of Victoria College professors didn't have doctorates, but that was not unusual in smaller institutions in Canada at that time. I feel these limitations were more than compensated for by small classes and the opportunities for close interaction with professors and fellow students. The relatively small size of the college and the commitment of the administration to supporting student clubs and other activities provided important opportunities for building social capital. I met many people (most importantly, my life companion) and learned how to work with people with different interests and values and how to debate and argue in a constructive way. Victoria College was a good beginning to the rest of my life.

* * *

After Victoria College, but before the University of British Columbia, Lorna and I went to Europe to live and work for a year. She had travelled in Europe before. It was my first trip.

We both worked, and I was lucky enough to get a job, in London, as a researcher with the Encyclopaedia Britannica. The work gave me access to major libraries at the British Museum, the University of London, and the London School of Economics. The cosmopolitan culture of London was, in a word, fantastic. Through some contacts, we were able to locate very decent, affordable accommodation. We were also able to buy a car—another M.G.—and drove all over England and, in the summer, around France and Spain.

Going into all the details of the year abroad would require another book, or at least another two or three chapters, and that is not the purpose of the present work. I'll sum up by saying that, in retrospect, I think the decision to take a year away from studies was an excellent one. Speaking for myself, the year broadened my horizons greatly and gave me a deeper perspective on the advantages and disadvantages of life in Victoria. I developed a better sense of what life there had given me but also realized that the time had come to move on. My job with the Encyclopaedia Britannica strengthened my research and writing skills. And, with no disrespect to the Victoria College Library, discovering the British Museum Reading Room, the University of London libraries, and other collections was a real eye-opener. Overall, the year was a great maturing experience and couldn't have come at a better time. I was not a weak or negligent student at Victoria College, but I wasn't always as serious or focused as I might have been. As Lorna and I prepared to return to Canada and the University of British Columbia, I felt a clarity of focus and a strength of purpose that exceeded anything I had previously experienced.

CHAPTER 3

Establishing the Foundations for Doctoral Studies

Lorna and I returned to Canada by ship, arriving in Montreal in late August 1962. We wanted to drive from Montreal to Vancouver in order to see the country—something we hadn't done before—and also save money. Lorna had the opportunity to make the cross-country trip with some relatives, but since that was the last seat in the car, I had to make some other arrangements. I telephoned a number in a Montreal newspaper and connected up with two Englishmen who were ferrying a car from Montreal to Vancouver for a company engaged in the transporting business. We met and, after a brief conversation, it was evident they would welcome a third driver. One of the two was Phillip Malim, who was taking a half-term off from his studies at Oxford to explore "the colonies," as he jokingly put it. The other was Patrick Davis, whose uncle had designed the Davis Escape Hatch, extensively used on British and other Allied Forces submarines during World War II. (I learned this much later, I should add.)

Malim and Davis proved to be very congenial travelling companions. Thanks to the shared driving arrangements and the car—an almost new Chrysler V8—we made the trip in five days without breaking any speed limits and also managed to see a lot of Canada.

Once in Vancouver, Phillip Malim—an enthusiastic outdoorsman—started making plans to travel to the Peace River Valley and points north. Patrick Davis's plan was to work in Vancouver for a few months, buy a motorcycle, and set off for South America in the spring. He was an interesting and pleasant person, and Lorna and I kept in touch with him until his departure. A card that finally caught up with us two years later advised that he had survived the trip, enjoyed it enormously, and had now "bitten the bullet" and joined the family firm.

Lorna and I found an apartment near the U.B.C. campus, got registered, and quickly hunkered down to our studies.

* * *

I was taking courses required to complete the final year of an honours B.A. and, in order to complete one of my majors, took three courses in sociology. I found two of these offerings absolutely fascinating: Industrial Sociology, taught by Martin Meissner, and the Sociology of Work and Occupations, taught by Kaspar Naegele. The third course, the Sociology of Religion, taught by Werner Cohn, was a dispiriting experience for at least two reasons. First, the material was poorly organized. Second, Professor Cohn's method of delivery involved him sitting in front of the class, sometimes with his feet up on the desk, and rambling on. I invariably sat next to Wayson Choy—now well known as a leading Canadian author[7]—and we struck up the kind of friendship that sometimes results from being co-sufferers. I must confess that we also occasionally exchanged critical comments on Professor Cohn's pedagogical style. I'm sure some of my students have done the same for me over the past 38 years.

Martin Meisnner's Industrial Sociology course had about 20 students and was taught seminar-style. Martin had immigrated to Canada from Germany after World War II. He was genial, highly knowledgeable, and analytically incisive. He made a concerted effort to involve all students in the seminar dialogue. I had a special interest in the course he was teaching as a result of my work experience. Like most university students, I had worked at various jobs to pay for tuition, books, clothes, entertainment, and—in my case—a weakness for sports cars requiring esoteric maintenance. One of these jobs was with the Water Rights Licensing Authority of British Columbia. In B.C.—then and quite possibly now—a lot of people did not have access to piped municipal water. This meant relying on wells and diverting streams or pumping water from lakes. A person wanting to obtain water in this way had to go through a lengthy application process that included a site inspection. I did whatever I was required to do, which ranged from handling application-related correspondence to accompanying the water rights engineers on inspection tours.

Although I was a low-level employee, the diversity of the things I was given to do enabled me to develop something of an overview of the organization's process and decision-making procedures. In effect, then, I was also a "participant observer," to borrow a term from sociological research methodology. My observations led me to become increasingly fascinated by how irrational various aspects of organizational practice were and by the extent to which small-"p" political considerations shaped the decision-making process.

I developed a project proposal based on these experiences and submitted it to Professor Meissner. He was enthusiastic and pointed me to various readings that would provide a conceptual and analytical context for my work. The paper was a success and set the direction for my master's and doctoral dissertations. I will return to this later in the chapter.

Kaspar David Naegele was born in Stuttgart, Germany, in 1924. With his parents, he moved to England in 1937 and, shortly afterward, to Canada. He was an undergraduate at McGill University and then went on to complete a master's degree at Columbia (1947) and a doctorate at Harvard (1952). He began his teaching career at Harvard and then went on to the Department of Anthropology and Sociology at U.B.C. in 1954, rising to the rank of full professor in eight years' time.

The Sociology of Work and Occupations course had a substantial enrolment—about 80 students. Dr. Naegele had a reputation on campus as a brilliant, quietly charismatic professor who could hold students spellbound with his lectures. Although the course was taught classroom-style, he broadened the base of participation by inviting various students to give lectures on their work and occupational experiences.

I wrote a paper on the occupation of jazz musicians based on my earlier experience co-managing the club in Victoria. I framed my analysis using literature from the sociology of work and also studies of social deviance. I undertook to analyse and explain aspects of the jazz musician occupational culture, particularly its "in-group" and conformity-rejecting characteristics. Dr. Naegele gave the paper an A+ and wrote "please see me" on the face sheet.

Kasper D. Naegele, in his University of British Columbia Office, 1964.

I saw him in his book-lined, orderly office. It was my first conversation with him. Many more followed. In one of these I mentioned the research job I had done with the Encyclopaedia Britannica while in England. He asked me if I would like to work for him as a research assistant. My answer, of course, was yes.

I had never met anyone whose mind worked like Dr. Naegele's. He combined rigour, flexibility, and great imagination. He was part artist and part scientist. His intellect was luminous and inspiring. Much of the work he gave me to do dealt with the health professions. This proved to be invaluable preparation for my later policy research for the Royal Commission on Pharmaceutical Services and the Ontario Medical Manpower Commission. Dr. Naegele also started lending me books by Emile Durkheim, Max Weber, Talcott Parsons, and other foundational thinkers of social science.

One evening I was working late in Dr. Naegele's office, organizing some material for him, when he put his head in the door and asked me if I'd like to have a beer at the Faculty Club. In those days at U.B.C., invitations for undergraduate students to the Faculty Club just didn't happen.

We discussed the merits of German beer for a couple of minutes and then he asked me what I was intending to do after graduation. I had been planning to write the Department of External Affairs examinations, do the interviews, and get into the Foreign Service. I knew two other people who had done this, and I felt I had a good chance. Dr. Naegele was a good listener. He was pleasant and supportive of my plans. Then he said, "It might be worth staying here another year and doing a master's degree. It wouldn't take long. You could use the summer to take a post-graduate course, keep on reading, do some research ...." I told Dr. Naegele that I usually worked in the summer, confessing that last year's summer travels around France and Spain had been a pleasant exception. He simply smiled and said, "I don't think we'll have any trouble finding you financial support." I walked out of the Faculty Club in a daze, and it certainly wasn't because of the one glass of beer I had very slowly consumed.

* * *

I graduated with my B.A. in June 1963 and, one week later, learned that I had been awarded the University of British Columbia Industrial Relations Summer Fellowship in the amount of $1250—a lot of money in those days. In addition, I continued to work as a research assistant for Professors Naegele and Meissner, gaining a great deal of substantive knowledge but also learning how to manage research projects through to on-time completion with successful results—key ingredients of the consulting business. On top of all that, Dr. Naegele connected me up with Douglas Denholm, the executive director of the British Columbia Pharmaceutical Association. Doug Denholm wanted various studies, including surveys, carried out to learn more about the conflict many pharmacists experienced over being, on the one hand, businesspeople and, on the other hand, health professionals.

Despite my youth and my having only a B.A. degree, Dr. Naegele's obviously generous appraisal had convinced Denholm that I could do the job. It was my first consulting mission and, in July 1963, it produced my first professional publication, "The Professions and Sociology: Some Implications for Pharmacy."[8] It also led to many other things, which I will revisit later in this book.

Lorna and I celebrated our increasing financial well-being by moving into a new apartment. It was the upper half of a fine old house on Vancouver's 12th Avenue and included a garage to house the M.G. we had bought in England and subsequently shipped to Canada. The house was owned by a Mr. Gartshore, a grey-haired, jocular, and convertible-driving bachelor who owned a chain of coffee shops in Vancouver. Mr. G., as he liked to be called, had two wonderful qualities in a landlord: he was invariably cheerful and he left us alone. For our part, we always paid the rent punctually. It was a good relationship—one that lasted up to time we left for Princeton. As for the apartment, it had a large sitting room with a fireplace, a study with a fireplace, and a dining room you could actually entertain people in. In a word, it was terrific—for that stage of our lives.

In one of those strange coincidences of life, the man who lived across from us—on the other side of the alley behind 12th Avenue—had an M.G. sports car exactly like mine that he was rebuilding from scratch. (I should add that these cars are now collector's items with $60,000 price tags.) Don Pollock was a middle-aged man with a large inventory of technical knowledge and skills that went well beyond automobiles. He was also a remarkably generous person and gave me the kind of ongoing advice and assistance that kept my own M.G. in prime operating condition.

* * *

Despite all the work to be done, the summer of 1963 in Vancouver was really quite wonderful. It didn't rain much and there was time for various social events, including visits to The Cellar jazz club and connecting up again with Al Neill, who had played with his quartet at The Scene in Victoria.

I also took a summer post-graduate course in political sociology with Lionel Tiger, who had arrived at U.B.C. via McGill (B.A., M.A.) and the London School of Economics (Ph.D.). Lionel was young, charming, and wonderfully bright. With his consistent encouragement and insightful guidance, the course enabled me to refine the perspective I was developing on the political dimensions of organizational decision making and change.

Lionel's companion, Virginia, was the essence of Montreal *chic*. (I'm convinced no one at U.B.C. had ever seen anything quite like her dark green leather suit!) We saw them from time to time at parties and jazz events. I don't think either of them even knew how to spell the word "stuffy."

* * *

I entered the M.A. program in sociology at U.B.C. in September 1963. Having already completed one post-graduate course helped me to move ahead quickly. In addition, my summer research activities—both as a research assistant and as a research consultant to the British Columbia Pharmaceutical Association—had been helpful to my general preparation and also, in some cases, directly pertinent to my planned M.A. dissertation on decision making and change management in organizations.

My M.A. studies were highly intensive, lasting just under nine months from mid-September to the end of May 1964. I worked mainly with Kaspar Naegele and Martin Meissner, but I did have some involvement with two other persons in the program. One was Reg Robson, the head of the Small Groups Laboratory in the department; the other was Cyril Belshaw, a senior professor of anthropology.

* * *

Kaspar Naegele took the lead in guiding my continuing theoretical/conceptual development. This took place in two settings. The first was a course in sociological theory that included fourth-year undergraduate students specializing in sociology and M.A. program students (of whom there were only five!). Professor Naegele took us through key works by Max Weber, Emile Durkheim, and Vilfredo Pareto. The class then went on to explore how these foundational thinkers had been drawn upon by Talcott Parsons in his groundbreaking 1937 book, *The Structure of Social Action*.[9] During his long career, Parsons was the acknowledged intellectual leader of Harvard's Department of Social Relations, the department in which Kaspar Naegele completed his doctorate in 1952 and where he had worked closely with Parsons. With these foundations in place, the class went on to examine more recent theoretical work by Parsons, such as *The Social System*,[10] and other social theorists, including Robert K. Merton and Georg Simmel.

Throughout the course, Kaspar Naegele maintained a clear focus on how different types of theoretical perspectives could be evolved and synthesized to carry the discipline forward to higher levels of understanding and explanation. He also showed how theoretical resources focused the research process and, in turn, how research outcomes helped to reshape and reformulate theories. This dynamic between theory and research was a central theme in Robert K. Merton's writings, a body of work with which Kaspar Naegele had engaged with considerable enthusiasm as an M.A. student at Columbia University, Merton's intellectual home at the time (and, indeed, for much of his illustrious career).

The course was demanding but in all respects an excellent experience. It served as solid preparation for my doctoral studies, which were soon to follow at Princeton. But even more important, the way Kaspar Naegele taught it, the course was not a collection of "great names" with an associated set of ideas. Naegele breathed intellectual vigour into theory and showed it as a dynamic tool to foster enquiry and explanation. I learned, among other things, that before one could begin to use the tools of social research to investigate issues (including practical issues in the operation of societies, institutions, and organizations), one had to have a clear conceptual analysis to focus and guide one's work.

The other setting in which I worked with Kaspar Naegele was the master's seminar. This was held between 9:30 and noon every Thursday morning in a charming seminar room—it featured leaded glass windows—located on the upper floor of what used to be U.B.C.'s main library building. In my recollections of it now, it reminds me of Massey College. The cloistered sense was augmented by the fact that there were only five M.A. students (one of whom, regrettably, dropped out early in the process). At this point in time, the U.B.C. sociology M.A. program was absolutely in its infancy—hence the small numbers.

In the theory course, Kaspar Naegele had followed—without being even remotely didactic—an obviously carefully thought out strategy for presenting the material in a sequential, developmental way that would help students see connections and build understandings upon understandings. His goals in the master's seminar were quite different. He wanted to develop an ongoing dialogue; to foster this outcome, we were asked to prepare and make presentations. Another goal was to assist us—in both conceptual and practical ways—to make effective progress on our dissertations. He wanted to investigate intellectual issues and explore our intellectual talents and capacities—to engage us in thinking and working theoretically as part of an ongoing process of the intellectually examined life.

For me, the seminar felt as if I were having a personal dialogue with Naegele. Various sociological works and issues were discussed around the table. But it was clear that he wanted to lead us to some new and imaginative ways of thinking, such as the types of analysis that are possible when one combines perspectives from sociology with psychology and even psychoanalysis. We examined various works by Sigmund Freud, including his writings on the psychology of art, literature, love, and religion.[11] We moved on to many other works, including *Man against Himself* by Karl Menninger,[12] *Asylums* by Erving Goffman,[13] and *Consciousness and Society* by W. Stuart Hughes.[14] For me, the single greatest intellectual revelation of the consistently thought-provoking seminar was an exploration of a collection of papers by Erik Erikson on identity and the life cycle (published as a special issue of *Psychological Issues* in 1959).[15] I found this body of work the very essence of the analytical intersection between social forces and psychological development, and it continues to be a powerful influence in my understanding of the life journey.

One of the students in the seminar, Greig Paul, became a personal friend. Greig was unquestionably bright, but a number of seemingly intractable personal problems prevented him from realizing his full potential. He was locked in an unending conflict with his father—a senior banker—whom he regarded as authoritarian and rigid. He had an equally uneasy relationship with his mother. His girlfriend, Wendy, a young woman born to considerable privilege, had zero interest in Greig's various social justice causes; not surprisingly, the relationship came to an end—but in a protracted and painful way. Despite these difficulties, Greig was periodically capable of truly imaginative thought and, when not sunk in depression, was great fun to be with.

* * *

Martin Meisnner took the lead in guiding my M.A. dissertation to an early and successful completion. This was helped by the fact that—before I had formally enrolled in the M.A. program—I had developed a concept for the dissertation that both Meissner and Naegele approved. It was to be a study of organizational decision making and change management based on a case study methodology. It was designed to build on earlier work I had done with Meissner in Industrial Sociology, Tiger in Political Sociology, and various research assistant-related projects.

I already had some contact networks in Vancouver, and that was exceedingly helpful to the process of identifying possible case studies. In addition, my ongoing work with the B.C. Pharmaceutical Association had given me a growing sense of how to operate in the world of business and the professions. Four general principles emerged as key to gaining the access required for organizational case studies: (1) credible sponsorship and something of a "track record"; (2) a businesslike manner and appearance; (3) unvarying adherence to the highest standards of discretion and confidentiality; (4) ensuring that the work ("the study") would provide something actually useful to the participating organization. These principles were equally important to creating and successfully operating a consulting business now over three decades old.

While my M.A. was moving forward, Martin Meissner continued to direct me to new research and readings in industrial relations, industrial economics, and research methods generally. Meissner's broad and inclusive views fostered in me an enthusiasm for interdisciplinary work. This proved a great asset in many subsequent consulting missions for the private and public sectors, where the problems to be solved are almost invariably complex and multi-factorial and, in my experience, never unidisciplinary.

All of this was helped by the fact that Meissner and Naegele appeared to like and respect one another, something that is not always the case—as many graduate students have found to their own detriment—in university life.

* * *

I did not take a course with Reg Robson, the head of the Small Groups Laboratory at U.B.C., but I did serve as assistant on one of his projects that involved considerable statistically oriented data analysis. Robson was an astute and highly capable practitioner of quantitative analysis. I soon discovered that taking courses in statistical methodology and actually using the techniques in research were two different things. Although Robson was rigorous and demanding, he was also supportive and very good at explaining complex techniques in the context of practical, understandable events. The project afforded an opportunity for further growth and development, and I learned a number of things useful to social research in general and the consulting business in particular. I learned the very real limitations of rhetoric and ideology when dealing with "hard-nosed" people and the considerable importance of being able to offer up data, numbers, plausible and practical explanations, and clear proposals for further/future action. I also learned a great deal about that most important part of any consultant's "tool kit": the focus group.

* * *

When I did my M.A., and to this day, sociology and anthropology were organized in a joint department at U.B.C. In practical terms—as far as I was concerned—this meant that my M.A. coursework was required to include a course in anthropology. This presented no problem to me. I had read works by various anthropologists, including Margaret Mead, Ruth Benedict, and Franz Boas. I found the material and the anthropological frame of analysis highly interesting.

At this point in my student career, I was already on the path that would be a career-long journey: the application of social research to practical problems in the private and public sectors. A graduate-level course in applied anthropology seemed interesting, so I enrolled. The offering was taught by Cyril Belshaw, who had received his full professorship of anthropology in 1961. Belshaw was born in New Zealand in 1921 and started his career serving in the Colonial Service with responsibilities in the British

Solomon Islands. He obtained his M.A. extramurally and then went on to the London School of Economics, completing his doctorate in 1949.

There was no doubt that Belshaw was a highly capable anthropologist. Indeed, when I first met him, his important book, *Under the Ivi Tree: Society and Economic Growth in Rural Fiji,*[16] had just made its debut. As for his teaching, Belshaw had a stiff and almost bureaucratic style that made it difficult to appreciate the material being presented. I was determined to do well in the course and, at the end of the day, was able to do so. But it was a hard slog.

Belshaw and his wife, Betty, were kind enough to invite Lorna and me, along with other graduate and senior undergraduate students, to an April 1964 end-of-term party at their pleasant house near the U.B.C. campus. The evening proceeded in an essentially formal sort of way until, just as it was drawing to a close, Belshaw produced a long "log drum"—an artifact acquired during his service in the Solomon Islands. Divested of his jacket and tie, he proceeded to sit on the floor and beat the drum with a frenetic energy that was amazingly at variance with the staid classroom presence I had come to know.

During the 1978–79 academic year, Cyril Belshaw was on sabbatical leave. He passed part of this leave in Switzerland, accompanied by his wife, who was working on a biography of Katherine Mansfield, a New Zealand fiction writer. On January 15, 1979, while she and her husband were making a side trip to Paris, Betty Belshaw vanished without a trace. On March 28, 1979, a woman's body—badly decomposed and placed in a number of plastic bags—was recovered from a deep valley near Le Sepey in Switzerland. The Swiss authorities launched an extensive investigation in the course of which they wished to have further discussions with Cyril Belshaw. By this time, however, Belshaw had returned to Canada, and the Swiss authorities discovered that extraditing him was not a possibility. They pursued the alternative of sending two police officers to Vancouver to question him. Allegations surfaced that Belshaw had altered his wife's dental charts—the ones that he had earlier supplied to the Swiss authorities. On November 11, 1979, Cyril Belshaw arrived in Paris to attend a conference. He was immediately arrested and was incarcerated in a Swiss prison for several months while trial proceedings were prepared. The lengthy and complicated trial resulted in a verdict that Belshaw be acquitted "by reason of doubt." He returned to Vancouver and resumed his duties at U.B.C. until his retirement, a few years later, in 1986. As might be expected, the matter caused considerable discussion and discomfort at U.B.C., in Vancouver, and in related academic circles generally. It was also written about considerably at the time and, more recently, in Howard Engel's 2001 book, *Crimes of Passion.*[17]

* * *

During my M.A. year, I had regular meetings with Kaspar Naegele. One of these, which took place during the third week of October 1963, dealt with my proposed presentation for the master's seminar and my progress on some research assistance work I was doing for him.

After we had discussed these matters, he leaned back in his chair and said, "We don't have that much time." I thought he was referring to one of the deadlines I had to meet. I soon discovered otherwise.

What he had on his mind was my applying to various graduate schools to pursue doctoral studies in sociology. He went on to say that the work I had been doing "made it clear" that I could successfully follow this course of action—if I "wanted to." A lengthy conversation ensued in which we exchanged our views and perceptions of how Canadian society was changing. The nation was becoming increasingly urban and industrial. More and more, technology would shape society, organizations, and the nature of work. Highly trained people—Ph.D.s, in a word—would be required to help shape and guide these complex processes of change. The post-war baby boom, coupled with rising societal expectations, would place unprecedented pressure on universities. The demand for university professors would be huge. In sociology, people with an analytical understanding of organizational and institutional process and a strong command of research methods would have a particularly promising future.

This was not the first time I had discussed these kinds of issues with Kaspar Naegele, but it was the first time they had been so directly related to my own career decision making. Naegele and I had essentially the same view of what was happening in Canada. Since returning from Europe, I had become increasingly aware of and interested in the mix of transforming forces: social, economic, demographic, technological.

I felt positive and optimistic about the direction in which Canada was going. This was easy to do in the prevailing context of strong economic and employment growth and high levels of government investment in social and physical infrastructure. I could see—it would have been difficult not to—that universities were in an expansionary mode. I also realized that the sort of practical, policy-oriented social research that interested me would become increasingly important to the nation's institutional and organizational operations. The idea of writing the Foreign Affairs examinations was rapidly leaving my mind.

As soon as my interest became clear, Naegele moved directly to issues of process and strategy. Transcripts would have to be organized and appropriate referees selected. I would have to prepare statements of interest, which Naegele kindly offered to review for me, an offer I enthusiastically accepted. Then we turned to the question of the choice of universities to which I should apply. He suggested Harvard, Princeton, Yale, Michigan, and McGill. I was more than happy to defer to his judgement and spent the next several days getting all the material properly organized.

* * *

My M.A. year at U.B.C. was a time of many other developments as well. I mentioned earlier the economic growth and social and physical infrastructure expansion that characterized the 1960s. These conditions gave rise to feelings of optimism in general and had some particular effects on young people attending university. Based on my experience as a graduate student during part of the 1960s era, I would say the following: first, financial support was much more available than it is today, so there was little need to accumulate crushing debt; second, I—and some of my graduate student colleagues—knew that the baby boom was right behind us and would propel us forward for the rest of our careers. Being born shortly before the "demographic explosion" was a significant economic advantage for people in our situation. Most of us didn't worry about getting jobs and good jobs at that.

This relative lack of economic hardship and optimistic outlook for the future gave rise to other priorities and values, such as the pursuit of self-exploration, a theme that strongly characterized 1960s life and culture. This pursuit took several different forms. The 1960s witnessed the emergence of a revolution in sexual attitudes and behaviours, facilitated in part by the availability of inexpensive and highly effective oral contraceptive pills. The recreational use of drugs—notably marijuana and, to a lesser extent, hallucinogens like LSD—became more prevalent during the era. The rallying cry of recreational drug use gurus like Harvard's Timothy Leary was "turn on, tune in, and drop out." New forms of cultural expression emerged in many fields, including art, music, writing, and film. In early 1960s Vancouver, it started to become possible to see films by avant-garde European directors like Ingmar Bergman, François Truffaut, Michelangelo Antonioni, Jean-Luc Godard, and Federico Fellini. Compared to other North American cities like New York, San Francisco, and Toronto, Vancouver was still pretty "cut off" in those days. Those of us who saw these films, and we were an increasing number, found them highly influential in their depictions of very different moral systems and ways of life.

For people who had grown up as teenagers in the 1950s, a much more conservative decade, all of this presented a very sharp contrast. It is perhaps not surprising that many promising young people "went off the rails" in the 1960s. I knew a few of them. They were unable to successfully negotiate a viable transition from the constraints of a 1950s upbringing to the rapid change and much more fluid social and cultural arrangements of the 1960s.

Lorna and I had an active social life and an interesting circle of friends in Vancouver. Analysing society and seeking certain types of social change continued to be our central interest while, at the same time, we enjoyed exploring the new developments in music, films, painting, and writing. We were able to experience many of the opportunities for personal exploration and development offered by the 1960s without "going off the rails." Was this because of good luck? Was it because of good management? I think it had much more to do with the fact that being at university gave us the chance to encounter some really good minds and develop a frame of reference. This frame of reference enabled us to analyse and understand—at least up to a point—the turbulent changes even as we were deeply caught up in those changes. And the changes were emerging very rapidly, although more rapidly for men than for women.

* * *

The optimism and positive energy of the 1960s experienced a shattering setback when, on November 22, 1963, an assassin's bullet killed President John F. Kennedy in Dallas. I heard the news on the radio while I was parking my car in front of Thea Koerner House—the Graduate Student Centre at U.B.C. I had been planning to meet some friends. Instead, I drove back to our apartment, where Lorna and I spent the next three days glued to the television set. The decade of the 1960s recovered its energy and momentum, but it was never quite the same again for many of us.

* * *

In April 1964, I received letters of acceptance from Princeton, Harvard, Yale, Michigan, and McGill—all with tuition waivers and generous scholarship support. In a state of considerable excitement, I sought out Kaspar Naegele. He first read the letters carefully. Then we had a lengthy and systematic conversation about the options. Naegele suggested that, from the viewpoint of expanding my perspective, it would be to my advantage to pursue my doctoral studies outside Canada. I required no convincing on that point—the year in Europe had made me very aware of the advantages of international experience. The discussion then turned to the relative merits of the four universities in the United States.

The fact that Naegele had studied at Columbia and Harvard, and later taught at Harvard, had left him very well connected to the eastern U.S. "sociological elite." (Indeed, I realize that his letters of reference were a crucial factor in the fortuitous outcome of my various applications for doctoral study.) In short, Naegele

Kennedy assassination, November 22, 1963.

knew many of the people at the U.S. universities in question. He knew their work, their orientation to the discipline, and how they would likely respond to the kind of work I wanted to do. The discussion narrowed down to Princeton and Harvard—a tough decision, for both institutions were at the highest level of excellence. Princeton got the nod. First, it was smaller than Harvard and would provide more opportunity for the sort of individualized attention I appeared to thrive on. Second, the Princeton program was extremely flexible, modelled in part after Oxford and Cambridge. One could take courses. Or one could simply read. Or one could do both. In addition, one could take courses from various departments of the university. This appealed to me greatly because of my increasing desire to combine the perspectives of sociology, economics, and demography for the purposes of my work. At Princeton, the bottom line was presenting yourself, in two years' time, for a series of written general examinations. If you passed these, you could go on to your dissertation. The conversation ended with my thanking Naegele for all he had done. He simply smiled and said, "You'll have a good time and learn a lot."

* * *

For Lorna and me, the summer of 1964 was the last few weeks in Vancouver, a city we have revisited countless times but have never again called home. It was a busy time. We were both working (I was still doing research assistance work for Naegele and Meissner and consulting work for the B.C. Pharmaceutical Association), and there were preparations to be made for the move to Princeton, which was at the other side of the continent.

We packed up various possessions for cross-country shipment using a number of different containers, including an amazingly capacious old "steamer trunk" dating back to the days when people travelled in the grand style by ship across the Atlantic. Certain other things—including the monstrously large 1950s TV set with its flickering green screen—we bequeathed to various friends. This seemed only fair. After all, much of what we owned had been given to us by friends when it became time for them to move on.

There were also many social events, some of which had a bittersweet quality, as we reflected on the probability that we would be unlikely to see many of these friends again anytime soon.

Because Lorna and I both wanted to have the possibility of working in the United States, we decided to apply for green cards, which would confer on us all the benefits—and obligations—of being permanent residents who, in due course, could become citizens of the U.S.A. There was a tremendous amount of paperwork involved, and we both found ourselves dredging up a lot of information about our past activities and family histories. Apart from visa photographs, R.C.M. Police clearances, and x-rays for tuberculosis, I remember with particular distaste being subjected to a Wassermann test to prove I was not syphilitic. But, at the end of the day, we were granted the coveted green cards.

Our friend Greig Paul had been accepted for doctoral studies at McGill and had decided to drive from Vancouver to Montreal. Greig had a very unusual car—an N.S.U. Prinz— which was manufactured by a Czechoslovakian firm that also produced sewing machines (a fact that led to some less than kind jokes about Greig's vehicle!). The car was very small, had a two-cylinder/two-cycle engine, and probably got 200 miles to the gallon. This economy was achieved at the cost of certain performance limitations. However, on a flat road with a good tailwind, the N.S.U. could reach highway speeds.

After a number of discussions, we decided that we would drive "convoy style" from Vancouver to Toronto—Lorna and I in the M.G. and Greig in the N.S.U. Prinz. We would then go on alone to Princeton, New Jersey, while Greig continued on to Montreal.

We left Vancouver in mid-August on one of those bright, remarkably clear days you sometimes get on the Pacific Coast. Our state of mind can only be described as ambivalent. At the last minute, we realized that we had failed to pack up three paintings we had acquired in England. (I shudder to think how much the pictures are now worth as they hang in our Toronto house.) The M.G. didn't have a trunk, just a small space behind the two leather bucket seats. It was, of course, a ragtop, and you couldn't lock the doors. We put the paintings in the small space behind the seats. During the nine-day journey, the car was left in a wide variety of settings. Nothing ever happened. When people talk about "a kinder, gentler era," they're not entirely wrong.

CHAPTER 4

Princeton

Our "convoy-style" drive across Canada ended in Toronto. Greig Paul set out for Montreal and McGill University while we continued on to Princeton.

En route we stayed at a motel in rural Pennsylvania. It was a spectral sort of establishment, and the proprietor seemed downright odd, at least to us. In retrospect, I think we were doubtless under the influence of Alfred Hitchcock's 1960 movie, *Psycho*. In any event, at 2:30 a.m., Lorna and I were wide awake and imagining the worst. We packed up and departed at some speed. For the sake of propriety, I should add that we had paid in advance.

We arrived in Princeton the next evening, just after sunset. The town seemed quite beautiful and was reminiscent of Cambridge with its "dreaming spires." We found a pleasant place to stay and, fully recovered, went to the sociology department the next morning.

The fall term had yet to start, so many faculty members were still away, engaged in research, writing, and other projects. We were met by Professor Mel Tumin, whose work I had read during my studies at U.B.C. Tumin was a genial and welcoming man. He gave us a tour of the department, provided various types of background material, and put us in touch with the university housing people.

The housing staff were equally helpful. Princeton had accommodation for married graduate students. Located on a piece of land called Butler Tract, the housing was less than a 10-minute walk from most university buildings, was heavily rent-subsidized, and was well-maintained by the university. There was also a waiting list. We signed up and were told that it probably wouldn't take too long to get a unit. Meanwhile, we were given a list of other rental accommodations that had been vetted by the university. We started our search.

Holder Hall, Princeton University, a fine example of Princeton architecture.

Within two days, we located a cottage that was part of a larger country property about a 10- to 15-minute drive to the university. It had a living room, dining room, kitchen, bedroom, and bath. All the windows overlooked attractive New Jersey countryside and it was very quiet. The landlord, Mrs. Purdy, was a short, somewhat stout, and eminently practical "country woman." We took her straightforward manner as a good sign and entered into a month-to-month rental arrangement. The rent was about twice that of a university unit but, compared to other non-subsidized rental properties, was very good value.

The possessions we had shipped from Vancouver arrived safely and, amazingly, nothing was broken. We were fully set up and operational in about a week.

* * *

According to the U.S. census for the year 2000, the Township of Princeton had a population of just over 16,000 and covered a geographical area of about 16 square miles. In keeping with the classic "town and gown" syndrome, the population increased between September and May as a result of the student influx.

Princeton University was founded in 1746 and plays a highly significant role in (some would say "dominates") town affairs. The Graduate School, which I attended, was a relative newcomer by Princeton's patrician standards, having been founded in 1900.

During my time in residence at Princeton (1964–66), the university was even smaller and more elite than it is today. The undergraduate program did not become coeducational until the end of the 1960s. On January 11, 1969, a 24–8 show of hands vote by the trustees of the university decided to admit women as undergraduates. The Graduate School was officially coeducational, but it wasn't until 1964 that the first woman received her doctorate. In 1964, Princeton had only 12 Black students; by 1966, that rose to 41, and four years later stood at 318. In 1994, the university introduced an official diversity policy, and much has been done since that time to recruit students who are African Americans, Hispanic Americans, Asian Americans, and Native Americans.[18] Throughout American society, the 1960s were early days for the civil rights struggle and the women's emancipation movement.

* * *

In keeping with long-established practice, 10 new students were admitted to the Princeton sociology department in 1964. The number of applicants was said to be 60 times greater than the number of those admitted. The 10 of us chosen were all male. Two were Canadians—myself and Michael Levin, who went on to become a professor of anthropology at the University of Toronto.

Compared to graduate student culture at U.B.C., Princeton was much more intense and intensely competitive. That was perfectly congenial to me. I was there to work hard and my goal was early completion.

The program was very demanding. Course syllabi prescribed heavy doses of reading; if you didn't keep up, you were soon hopelessly lost. Incoming students were also encouraged to give early attention to "defining their fields," meaning the four areas in which they would present themselves (in two years' time) for written general examinations, which had to be passed in order to proceed to one's doctoral dissertation. In addition, there was a language requirement and a statistics and methodology requirement. I found it a useful strategy to look at copies of earlier general examinations and use them as at least one guideline to "field definition and development."

The competitive spirit was fuelled by the fact that, at no time, did faculty give the slightest clue about "performance expectations." This was quite deliberate, of course, and designed to foster an environment in which each student would make a maximum effort to achieve his or her full capacity.

This demanding situation was counterbalanced in a number of ways. First, professorial support was excellent and always available. (I had heard horror stories about large state university graduate schools where there were corridor-long lineups outside professorial offices. That never happened at Princeton.) Second, there was a comfortable, book-lined study room in Green Hall, home to the sociology department. Also, there were lockable carrels in Princeton's magnificent Firestone Library. Finally, there was Valerie Ayer, Sociology's departmental secretary. Valerie was born in 1936 and was the daughter of A.J. Ayer, the legendary Oxford philosopher.[19] Valerie's mother, Renee, had divorced A.J. and married Stuart Hampshire, a distinguished philosopher who had left Oxford to teach at Princeton.

Elegant in dress and demeanour, highly efficient in running the departmental office, and possessed of a caring character, Valerie showed me innumerable kindnesses and helped in countless ways. She became a personal friend of both Lorna and myself. Perhaps because she was an Englishwoman living in America, she understood the perils of social dislocation. She invited us to various events with family and friends, occasions that were uniformly enjoyable. Tragically, Valerie died in 1981, suddenly and unexpectedly, of Hodgkin's disease. She was only 45.

Princeton worked hard to combine scholarly excellence with social integration. The frequent colloquia held in Green Hall were a case in point. Persons would come from other institutions to talk about their ideas and research. The sociology department

Valerie Ayer, Princeton, 1966.

faculty and graduate student turnout was generally close to 100 percent and the level of engagement was high. Faculty did not dominate the dialogue. Students were encouraged to be vigorous participants. On some occasions, these events would be followed by receptions and dinners. It was both collegial and congenial.

One evening early in the first term, we sociology graduate students (and "significant others") were invited to a reception in a fine old house owned by the university. Surrounded by antiques and oil paintings dating back to Princeton's founding, we were served martinis in crystal glasses! I noticed an early original manuscript by Albert Einstein lying casually on a George III mahogany tripod table. Daily, I was developing a better understanding of the style and nature of northeastern U.S. elitism.

* * *

When I arrived, Charles Hunt Page was the chair of the Princeton Department of Sociology. In his book *Fifty Years in the Sociological Enterprise: A Lucky Journey*,[20] Page writes about Princeton's "star-studded faculty" in sociology. And, indeed, the faculty members I worked with proved to be a highly talented and capable group of people.

In my first term, commencing September 1964, I took courses with Page and with Richard F. Hamilton, who had just arrived at Princeton from Harpur College in the State University of New York system.

My course with Page fell under the rubric The Sociology of Knowledge, which he interpreted in a broad way, allowing the inclusion of a wide range of questions and issues. I was interested in certain internal conflicts within Canadian society, notably a growing tendency toward a political separatist movement in Quebec. This, of course, was some time before the murder of Quebec cabinet minister Pierre Laporte by a separatist "cell" and Prime Minister Pierre Elliott Trudeau's invoking of the War Measures Act. My paper was to be an investigation of the intellectual and structural foundations of Quebec separatism in Canada, and I would travel to Montreal to gather original source materials and do some interviews. Page was enthusiastic and gave me a free hand.

My coursework with Richard Hamilton was in the area of political sociology. I told Hamilton about my earlier research and M.A. dissertation work, as well as my strong belief that much of what happened in organizations was political in nature rather than "rational process." Hamilton was intellectually quite a contrarian and the idea appealed to him. Starting off with R.M. Cyert and J.G. March's important work, *A Behavioral Theory of the Firm*,[21] I developed an analysis of organizational politics that was to become the conceptual foundation for my Princeton doctoral dissertation, *Structure and Process in Industrial Organizations*[22]—and, subsequently, the guiding perspective for dozens of consulting missions I carried out in a wide range of organizational settings.

The two men could not have been more different. Hamilton had a stiff—almost prim—manner but was undeniably brilliant. Page was a Hemingwayesque character (there were wild rumours of his having had a torrid affair with Hollywood actress Tallulah Bankhead!) with an expansive and avuncular intellect. Both were a fine introduction to sociology at Princeton.

By mid-October 1964, I was totally caught up in the program. When not attending seminars (all classes were small), colloquia, or other academically oriented events, I read all the time. Apart from trying to do well in the courses I was taking, I was seeking to identify my four "fields" for the future general examinations and, looking even further forward, developing a doctoral dissertation strategy. It was not a normal existence but, then, Princeton was not a normal place.

At the end of October 1964, Lorna and I received some very good news. We had been assigned married student accommodation in Butler Tract. Each unit looked exactly the same with its white clapboard siding and dark green roof. Each of these bungalow-style houses comprised two dwelling areas, one on either side of a structural wall that divided the unit in half. Each of these apartments had a kitchen, living room, two bedrooms, and a bathroom. There was a front door, a back door, and some grass—which the university cut. The layout of every unit was exactly the same. If you'd seen one, you'd seen them all.

Despite this lack of architectural variability, Butler Tract had many significant advantages. The rental rate was about 50 percent below market levels, the university did the maintenance, you could walk just about everywhere, and you could participate in the Butler Tract social life. I have heard it said that students who are under the greatest pressure have the wildest parties. I believe Butler Tract generally supported that proposition.

One month after we had moved in, I was sitting in the bedroom that had become my study (working, of course) when I heard a crackling noise coming from the coat closet in the front entrance hall area. I investigated. Smoke was drifting down from the closet ceiling. I shut the door to deprive the fire of oxygen, telephoned the Emergency Services, and got out of the house. The fire department arrived in less than five minutes—another small-town advantage. Fortunately, the fire moved upward, effectively destroying a large section of roof and the chimney. The downward damage was limited to a few items in the coat closet.

In addition to my Princeton University scholarship, I also had support from the Canada Council. One of the council's rules was that support recipients must take out insurance on their personal property. Like most young people, I wasn't very insurance-oriented and thought it all a bit silly. However, a requirement is a requirement, and I took out a policy with the well-known Canadian insurance brokerage house, Marsh & McLennan. It turned out the fire was caused by faulty wiring. Since there was no blame on our part, we were fully covered. My attitudes toward insurance changed.

The university immediately moved Lorna and me into another unit and then proceeded to completely refurbish our former home. We were back in six weeks with what was now the nicest unit in Butler Tract. However, I don't recommend this approach to getting renovations done. Having said that, the whole episode was not really very disruptive, mainly thanks to the university's supportive attitude and fast action.

We liked our new unit so much we started going to country sales to get some additional furniture. We bought a turn-of-the-century, solid oak secretary desk—which I refinished as a healthy alternative to constant mental work—and a solid cherrywood chest of drawers. Both of these items are in our Toronto house today. When people see the desk in the main sitting room, they regard it as a valuable antique and I guess it is now. We paid $14 for it.

* * *

About a month before the fire, I travelled to Montreal in connection with the Quebec separatism paper I was doing for Charles Page. I also saw my friend Greig Paul, now at McGill. He was very unhappy about the program. I sat in on two seminars and could see why—there was no spark. Then I visited his bug-infested accommodation in the McGill "student ghetto." I suggested he apply to Princeton. He did.

* * *

The second term of my first year at Princeton began January 1965. I was gratified to find that I had done well in the papers for Page and Hamilton. Frankly, I don't think Charles Page was much interested in Canada or the country's sociopolitical peculiarities, but he felt I had done thorough and imaginative work.

Personally, I had found the work on Quebec separatism eye-opening. Both Lorna and I were becoming more engaged with the issues, and this elevated awareness shaped both our political and intellectual outlooks. In some instances, it also influenced our work, as in our 1979 co-authored book, *Fragile Federation*.[23]

As for the other paper, Richard Hamilton gave me detailed feedback: written and oral; critical and constructive. It was enormously helpful. I asked him if he would serve on my dissertation committee. He agreed but advised me that I would require a senior professor to lead the enterprise.

I signed up for three second-term courses. The first was Richard Hamilton's Industrial Relations and the Social Order. Hamilton took every sociological proposition and turned it around, asking why the opposite interpretation/conclusion couldn't be true. I found it a very productive intellectual strategy, particularly at that stage of my career.

The second course was Research Methods with Charles Westoff. Westoff, who received his Ph.D. from the University of Pennsylvania in 1953, was a distinguished demographer who came to Princeton in 1962. In addition to his demanding professorial duties, Westoff rapidly became associate director of Princeton's Office of Population Research. As well, he agreed to become the chairman of the Sociology Department, starting in the spring term of 1965. To this day, Charles Westoff remains importantly involved in demographic research, writing, and leadership.

I took the course for several reasons. First, Westoff had an excellent reputation. Second, given the nature of my work—past, present, and planned—I had a very strong interest in continuing to learn as much as possible about statistics and methodology from the best people. In addition, the Princeton program had a requirement that I successfully complete a statistics and methodology qualification.

The Research Methods class was small and we sat around a seminar table in the Office of Population Research. Westoff had an easygoing manner that downplayed his intellectual powers and driven nature. He was an outstanding teacher who made the most complex and abstract techniques understandable by relating them to practical—and interesting—research problems.

In doing this, he from time to time talked about research and consulting missions with which he was engaged. I found the discourse fascinating. It further strengthened my view that fields like sociology, demography, and economics (preferably in various types of combinations) could make a large contribution to the world of practical affairs.

One day, Westoff took us to Princeton's data management and computer centre. As I watched a high-speed IBM card sorter in operation (remember, this was 1965!), I experienced a revelation. I could see how automated approaches to data management and analysis were a hugely important tool to large-scale research and the building of information-centred business. My ongoing involvement with computers and computing began in earnest that morning. It has been a lengthy journey, going from huge, vacuum tube machines requiring refrigeration plants to cool them to the high-powered laptops of today, smaller than an attaché case.

The third course I took was Contemporary Sociological Theory with Wilbert E. Moore. Moore received his doctorate from Harvard in 1940, as one of Talcott Parson's "first generation of Ph.D.s," as Charles Page put it. He was a prolific scholar and author, writing almost every day. I had read many of his works during my U.B.C. period and was much impressed by his rigour and lucidity. He was held in the highest regard by members of the profession, an esteem reflected in his election, in 1966, to the presidency of the American Sociological Association.

In the year I arrived at Princeton, Moore resigned his professorship to become a sociologist at the Russell Sage Foundation in New York City. He continued as a part-time lecturer in sociology and unquestionably remained a powerful and influential presence in the department. Among other things, Wilbert Moore was an eminent industrial sociologist. He was well aware, via Kaspar Naegele, of the work I had done and of my future plans. In an early meeting, he told me that notwithstanding his heavy responsibilities at the Russell Sage Foundation, he could and would work with me. He became a great mentor and supporter.

* * *

Wilbert E. Moore, Princeton University, 1966.

On February 7, 1965, I was devastated to learn that, on the preceding day, Kaspar Naegele had committed suicide. In a state of shock and denial, I began to make telephone calls to find out what had happened. I discovered that on February 5, 1965, Kaspar Naegele had been admitted to the Vancouver General Hospital, suffering from a serious episode of depression. Apparently, this was not the first time he had experienced such episodes, but this one was particularly severe. In a decision that defies understanding, he was placed on the 11th floor of the building. On February 6, he wrapped himself in a blanket, ran at a window—breaking through—and fell to his death.

Later on February 7, I received a telephone call from Greig Paul in Montreal. He was in a very bad way. I decided to travel to Montreal immediately. The city was in the grip of a brutal cold spell and the mounds of grimy snow and leaden skies simply magnified my sense of loss and gloom. Greig and I talked for hours and all I can say, even 39 years later, is that it helped.

* * *

Kaspar Naegele's death drove me even more deeply into my work at Princeton. Succeeding at what he had enabled me to do seemed by far the best way of honouring the memory of this remarkable man. For me, his steadfast encouragement and vibrant intellectual example will never die.

The second term of my first year at Princeton continued to unfold, marked by various events. I was contacted by Grant Reuber, chair of the Economics Department at the University of Western Ontario (U.W.O.) and later a Bank of Montreal C.E.O. He told me about the expansion and development plans for sociology at U.W.O. and invited me to come that summer and teach a course in sociological theory. I agreed.

Continued discussions with people at U.B.C. resulted in my being asked to come to Vancouver during the summer of 1965 to organize and develop a bibliography of the many papers and documents Kaspar Naegele had left behind. I agreed, arranging to do the work after my summer teaching obligations at U.W.O. were complete.

Finally, in April 1965, Greig Paul learned that he had been accepted to the sociology doctoral program at Princeton.

* * *

In the summer of 1965, Lorna and I drove to London, Ontario, and assumed occupancy of a pleasantly furnished apartment near the university. The sociological theory course was small and had its interesting moments. I was self-consciously aware that I was learning the junior faculty role and frankly preferred it to being a graduate student. As for London, it was a clean and manageable community but very bland. We went to Toronto almost every weekend, going to jazz clubs like the Colonial and the Park Plaza Roof, visiting Wayson Choy (his book-writing fame still some distance down the road), and generally keeping the company of people in the arts community. Both Lorna and I felt that Toronto was developing in very dynamic directions.

After the summer course was complete, Lorna returned to Princeton and I flew to Vancouver to work on Kaspar Naegele's papers. I had the extremely disquieting experience of working in Naegele's former office—the one in which we had so often sat having conversations that shaped both my outlook on life and intellectual perspective. I also found it difficult to recapture the sense of enthusiasm I once had for U.B.C. and Vancouver generally. I told myself to get over it, but it wasn't easy. I saw Martin Meissner and other friends, and they were very kind. The west coast mountains and ocean—a fundamental part of who and what I am—also had a restorative effect.

Dealing with Naegele's papers was not happy work, but it did contribute to a sort of catharsis. To me, Naegele had seemed invincible. A first-class mind. A man who enjoyed the affection and respect of a great many others. A man who led a gracious and graceful life.

Going through the materials, I learned many things I previously did not know. He had mentioned that his father was an artist and a Protestant, his mother a physician and a Jew. Clearly, his parents' decision to leave Germany for England in 1937 was motivated by the virulent spread of anti-Semitism in German society, fostered by Nazi ideology. I did not know that, after their arrival in England, Naegele's parents were interned as "enemy aliens." In 1940, Kaspar—just 16 at the time—was shipped to Canada for internment.

Shortly after Naegele's death, two respected Canadian sociologists—Theodore Mills and Frank Jones—wrote a piece in which they observed: "Kaspar Naegele's childhood was torn by the aftermath of World War I, by the rise of Hitler, emigration, transmigration, internment, discrimination and rejection. He neither talked about, or wrote directly on, that part of his life."[24] At points, the materials I was working through showed with tragic clarity the horrible price historical and familial disruption had exacted of Kaspar Naegele.

* * *

Back at Princeton, the first term of my second year commenced in September 1965. With the general examinations looming in May, I had largely defined the four fields in which I would present myself. Thanks to the work I had done, and continued to do, with Wilbert Moore and Richard Hamilton, my doctoral dissertation was moving forward.

I took two courses during this term. One was Special Problems in Sociology with Wilbert Moore. Essentially, this course provided a context to continue working closely with my dissertation leader and refining the theoretical and empirical dimensions of the work.

The second course was Comparative Social Institutions with Marion J. Levy, Jr., who received his doctorate in sociology from Harvard in 1947 and joined the Princeton faculty in the same year. Early on, major books marked him as a brilliant mind. These included *The Family Revolution in Modern China*[25] and *The Structure of Society*.[26] Levy had private means, a fact reflected in his striking Frank Lloyd Wright house and the kind of imaginative and creative nonconformity that sometimes accompanies financial independence. Levy was broadly regarded as "a character." He would walk about the campus with one of his handsome dogs, whittling a stick. Some thought him arrogant and abrasive. Many students feared him. I enjoyed every minute in his company. He had a wonderfully sardonic wit and a genuine warm-heartedness that was not really that difficult to discover. But far more important was the incisive rigour of his mind. He was an unwavering advocate of logic and the scientific method, two perspectives I totally shared. Working with him was a challenging but amazingly rewarding experience. I felt truly honoured when he asked me if I would consider doing my dissertation with him. I was too far along the other path and, with some regret, declined. We remained friends.

During that term, I also served as preceptor (Princeton's elevated term for teaching assistant) in an undergraduate social stratification class taught by Mel Tumin. A graduate student colleague had warned me that the Princeton undergraduates were "unbearably arrogant." I found them bright, well-prepared, and genial.

It wasn't until I read Charles Page's 1982 book, *Fifty Years in the Sociological Enterprise*, that I learned of the long-standing enmity between Levy and Tumin. I had never observed any of this at Princeton (I was probably too busy!) and enjoyed working with them both.

* * *

Apart from the constant, ongoing work, two other events stand out in my recollections of my second-year first term.

Greig Paul had been accepted at Princeton and duly arrived. Our financial situation was pretty satisfactory, and Lorna and I had decided to buy a new car. Greig needed a car and wanted my old M.G., so a deal was rapidly consummated. I ended up buying a new M.G. with "all mod cons," as the British put it.

Greig was very happy with his car, but other aspects of his life did not go so well. He soon became involved with a woman in New York City, who (to favour understatement) was somewhat neurotic. She came to Princeton to live and hated it. Their battles soon assumed legendary proportions. My efforts to be helpful were totally useless and I soon retired from the field. Greig's studies suffered irrevocable damage; he soon dropped out. Apart from having dinner with him in Vancouver in the summer of 1969, I have never seen him since and have no idea of where or how he is.

About halfway through that term, I received a notification from the Selective Service Agency requiring me to report to my local draft board. The situation in Vietnam was steadily worsening and "college deferments," although still possible to get, were in increasingly short supply.

The draft board was located in Trenton, a grimy New Jersey industrial city. As one drives over the bridge into Trenton, a large sign—at least in those days—proclaimed "Trenton Makes. The World Takes." That particular morning, driving over the bridge, I was not in the best possible frame of mind.

The registration process involved filling out a great many forms. Then I waited to have an interview with an official of the board. The official turned out to be a pleasant, middle-aged man who went through my forms to check a few facts. Then he asked me some questions about my work at Princeton, which I was happy to discuss. The discussion drifted on to a conversation about Canada. I recall talking about the long history of cordial relations between our two nations and what a great experience I felt it was to be able to live and study in both countries. Then, completely out of the blue, he asked me how I felt about private property. It was an easy question to answer: I said I was very much in favour of it and hoped to have considerably more as time progressed. He stood up, shook my hand and said, "I don't think we'll draft you but, if we did, we'd put you in intelligence work." I drove back to Princeton in a considerably cheered-up frame of mind.

*   *   *

The second term of my second year at Princeton began January 1966. My language, methodology, and statistics requirements were now behind me. My fields had been defined for some time, and I had done the reading. I felt ready to do the general examinations, which was a technical possibility, but I decided to wait until May 1966.

I used the second term to broaden my intellectual base, attending individual lectures and auditing courses, mainly in economics and industrial relations. I also continued working on my dissertation.

Two other consequential events preceded my general examinations. Some months earlier, I had pulled together my pharmacy research and written a paper I submitted to *The Canadian Review of Sociology and Anthropology*.[27] The paper was published in February 1966. It examined how the kinds of occupational values people had, as measured by various scales, influenced the sorts of occupational specializations they entered; the analysis was focused on pharmacists. At this point in time, publishing in refereed journals while still a graduate student was uncommon. Bringing the paper out proved to be beneficial in a number of ways. I decided I would direct immediate effort to other publication opportunities in any time I had remaining after attending to my first priorities: passing the general examinations and completing my dissertation.

A little later in the term, I received a telephone call from Professor John F. "Jack" Kantner, who had recently assumed the chairmanship of the new department of sociology at the University of Western Ontario. He was going to be in New York City in a week's time and hoped that we might meet to discuss "future possibilities." We arranged a Saturday morning meeting.

New York was about a 40-minute drive from Princeton on the New Jersey Turnpike. The most difficult part was finding a parking place once you were in the city. On this particular Saturday morning, I was lucky. I made my way to the skyscraper where the offices of the Population Council were located and proceeded to the 37th floor as directed. The building was deserted, and when I arrived at my floor, I found all the lights were off. The only illumination was some greyish light filtering through the windows from what was an overcast day outside. I found Kantner sitting behind a desk in an office off the long, central corridor. He apologized for the lack of illumination, indicating he had not been able to find the switchbox. I simply said I was delighted to meet him and was looking forward to our discussion.

Kantner was a well-established demographer, a man in his late forties with a pleasant, low-key manner. As we talked, it became clear that he had a strong and sincere commitment to building an effective and competitive sociology department at U.W.O. Coming to the point of the meeting, he asked me if I would teach another summer course—this time in statistics and research methods—and then, in September 1966, come on board as a full-time, tenure-stream assistant professor.

I had been expecting the offer of another summer course, but the proposal of a full-time job came as a complete surprise. I demurred, pointing out that by September 1966 I expected to have passed my general examinations, but that my dissertation would most certainly not yet be complete. I added that completing my dissertation was my number one priority after the general examinations. Kantner countered that my teaching load would be light (two courses), classes would be small, and that "everything possible" would be done to facilitate my completing my dissertation. "It's in our interest, too," he pointed out, "that you have a Ph.D." I asked for a week to think it over.

Lorna and I discussed the matter at great length. I also talked with Wilbert Moore, and he was positive about Kantner's proposal. I decided to accept the offer—for two main reasons. First, Lorna had put her education on hold while I was at Princeton. My going to U.W.O. would mean that she could enrol in third year and be that much closer to completing her B.A. Second, I felt personally confident—and reassured by Wilbert Moore's supportive attitude—that I could do a full-time academic job and complete my dissertation within the timeline I had set for myself.

I telephoned Kantner to clarify a few final details and the deal was done.

* * *

In May 1966, I presented myself for the general examinations. I wrote papers in four fields: (1) Work and Organizations, (2) Economic Development and Social Change, (3) Sociological Theory, (4) the Sociology of Knowledge. It was a pass/fail undertaking. I passed.

About two days later, I got on a bus for Mexico. By this time, Lorna had a very interesting job at Princeton's Office of Population Research and was fully engaged assisting—in various ways—Charles Westoff and Ray Potvin on a major demographic research and publication project.

I travelled by bus quite deliberately. I wanted to visit the southern U.S. states in a way that would give me an opportunity for a close-up look. The bus ticket I had was very flexible, allowing me to break the journey at various points.

After white, rich, and physically beautiful Princeton, the trip through the southern United States was indeed an eye-opener. It is one thing to develop a theoretical or statistical view of the impoverishment and suppression of Black Americans; it is quite another thing to see it first-hand. The bus passed an abundance of shanty towns, the housing stock comprised of decaying fire-traps with no indoor plumbing. In the restaurants, hotels, and other establishments in the prosperous parts of southern towns, there were plenty of "whites only" and "colored entrance" signs. It was, directly put, social and economic apartheid.

I eventually arrived in Mexico City and proceeded to my destination—Villa Jones. This establishment, which I had learned about through friends at Princeton, was run by Roberto Cuba Jones and his wife Inez. Jones was a Quaker, an intellectual, and an internationalist. At Villa Jones, one could rent a comfortable room and bath at a tariff congenial to graduate students and junior professors who, in fact, were the sort of people attracted to the place. Every evening at dinner, hosted by Jones and his spouse, visitors to the Villa sat down at a large, oval table to eat and discuss a wide range of issues from an intriguing variety of perspectives. Never intrusive, Jones had a remarkable ability to draw out and sustain serious conversation. I learned a great deal from him about Mexican culture and literature. Over the following years, I made many return visits to Mexico and developed, among other things, a strong interest in the writings of Carlos Fuentes and Octavio Paz.

After Mexico City, I went on to the charming provincial city of Oaxaca and points south. But time was running out and, after a few days, I returned to Mexico City and caught a plane to Vancouver. The flight involved a change of aircraft in Seattle. I was sitting in the waiting area when an obviously deeply disturbed man (I later learned he was a Vietnam veteran) produced a pistol and started to shoot. I hit the deck very fast. The events seemed to evolve with a kind of surreal slow motion. The weapon made a dull, thudding sound—like a popgun. Then there were the agonized cries of people who had been hit (there were two but it seemed like more). Armed police arrived almost instantaneously and the assailant was subdued without any apparent struggle. I was very glad to get back to Vancouver.

I did a few things in Vancouver and then flew to Princeton via New York. Back on the campus, I learned to my dismay that Richard Hamilton had left Princeton, accepting a job at the University of Wisconsin. For reasons still not clear to me, he had told practically no one about this, including me. My concern, of course, was my dissertation committee, and I telephoned Wilbert Moore without delay. In his usual unflappable style, he told me not to worry; he was committed to leading the thesis to successful completion and would quickly find a replacement for Hamilton.

Reassured, I got into my car to drive to London, Ontario, where I would teach the U.W.O. summer course in statistics and research methods. One of the inducements Jack Kantner had offered me was free accommodation on the campus. This consisted of a modern, well-equipped apartment on the top floor of a three-story residence for male students (this was long before coeducational living arrangements!). In regular session, the apartment was occupied by the "dorm dean." I was expected to help any "troubled students" in the residence but, since it was summer, there were only about five students around, and all of them had better things to do than seek out my sage counsel.

Lorna visited me at various points over the six-week course and we invariably went to Toronto. We also used one of her visits to find an apartment for the upcoming academic year. We located a great building with views only a five-minute walk away from the campus. Then it was back to Princeton to arrange "in absentia" status and organize our move to London for what was going to be an extraordinarily busy year.

* * *

In this chapter, I have emphasized the work-intensive nature of my two years in residence at Princeton. However, apart from its academic excellence, Princeton had another important asset: close proximity to New York. Since no one works all the time, Lorna and I made many visits to that great metropolis, discovering new horizons in art, music, and much else. It remains one of our favourite places.

CHAPTER 5

Becoming a University Professor

In September 1966, I started teaching in the sociology department of the University of Western Ontario. At the same time, Lorna entered the third year of her bachelor's degree program.

Even though I did not yet have my doctorate, I was given an assistant professorship in the tenure stream. The teaching load, as promised by Jack Kantner, was light: one year-long course in sociological theory and a second year-long course in complex organizations. Although not as good as the Princeton undergraduates, the students were pleasant and, by and large, reasonably hard working. The classes were small and, fortunately from my point of view, the preparation time I required was not all that great, given the extensive notes and materials I had brought with me from Princeton. In effect, I had already started to accumulate some intellectual capital.

As I mentioned before, Jack Kantner had a low-key, pleasant personality, and this reflected in the non-confrontational but effective way in which he led the periodic meetings of the department's faculty. Doubtless, his work was made easier by the fact that it was a very small department and we all got on well with one another. Apart from Kantner and myself, there were four other academics: T.R. "Bala" Balakrishnan, a highly capable demographer still at U.W.O.; Dick Osborne, who eventually went to the University of Toronto; Peter Morrison, who returned to the United States fairly soon; and George Jarvis, who remained at U.W.O. for a number of years.

Apart from his administrative leadership responsibilities, Kantner and his spouse arranged a number of social events that helped to build bonds among the new colleagues and their respective family members. On a personal level, Kantner more than honoured his commitment to facilitate my goal of early doctoral dissertation completion. The dissertation was going quite well for two main reasons: first, I started thinking about it early in my

Ph.D. program; second, it built on work I had done in my master's dissertation and work I did with Martin Meissner at U.B.C. All this helped to routinize data gathering and analysis. Also, my contacts were very good about referring me to other contacts. I have to confess that with my short hair, dark suits, and striped ties, I looked more like a "business type" (at least in the prevailing stereotypes of the era) than an academic!

Shortly after my arrival at U.W.O.—October 1966—my paper "Psychological Rigidity and Muscle Tension" appeared in the refereed journal *Psychophysiology*.[28] The paper, which had no connection to my current interests, emanated from earlier activities, including a study of gestures Martin Meissner had involved me in and my small groups laboratory work at U.B.C. Bringing the paper out was part of my overall strategy of trying to build my publications base. I was also continuing to work on my jazz musician research, which had inspired my first paper for Kaspar Naegele. My plan was to develop this into an article for a major U.S. sociology journal.

Later in October, Jack Kantner approached me with a most interesting proposal. He had been talking with Andrew Hunter, U.W.O.'s assistant dean of medicine, who was concerned about an increasing shortfall in the number of medical students who had no interest in entering primary or general practice. Knowing of my interest in occupations generally, and health care occupations in particular, Kantner wondered if I might be interested in meeting and talking with Andrew Hunter. I was very interested. The meeting, involving Hunter, Kantner, and myself, took place on November 3, 1966.

Andrew Hunter was probably about fifty years of age and was a trim, athletic-looking man with closely cropped, greying hair. He set out, in very clear terms, his perception of the magnitude and seriousness of "the general practitioner shortfall." In turn, I outlined my research and publication activities on pharmacy, in particular on the important role that occupational values—which were measurable—played in the occupational sub-specializations people chose. Hunter grasped the idea immediately and showed considerable interest.

Next day, I visited Hunter's office to drop off a copy of my *Canadian Review of Sociology and Anthropology* paper, "Some

Implications of Value Differentiation in Pharmacy," and a "two-pager" outlining my views as to how the approach could work with the medical profession. Then I left for New York City, where I was meeting with Wilbert Moore on Monday morning, November 7, 1966, in his office at the Russell Sage Foundation on Park Avenue.

I gave Moore a draft of the dissertation and a briefing on what I felt remained to be done. I also revisited my concerns about who would replace Richard Hamilton on my committee. Moore was in an avuncular and supportive frame of mind. He agreed to read the dissertation in a week—spectacular turnaround time for someone with his commitments—and then pass it on to Charles F. Wheatley, a new junior faculty member at Princeton. I had never met Wheatley, but Moore assured me that he was a "most able" person. He certainly proved to be that, and more.

Back at U.W.O., I had a further meeting with Andrew Hunter. He came to the point directly. He liked the paper and the two-pager and thought we should proceed immediately with the development of a research program. He told me that he had various contacts in Ontario's Ministry of Health and that he would follow up with them at once to ascertain what we needed to know about proposal development and funding procedures.

Wilbert Moore telephoned me about a week and a half after I had seen him. He had a few relatively minor suggestions for changes in the dissertation and advised me that Charles Wheatley had agreed to join the committee. It was arranged that I would meet Charles Wheatley in Princeton on December 12, 1966—when first-term classes at U.W.O. would be over—and remain until December 20 to work on the draft and have further regular meetings with my new committee member.

Meanwhile, Hunter had been in touch with his Ministry of Health contacts and they were enthusiastic, wanting a proposal by January 16, 1967. Andy—we were now on a first-name basis—and I blocked the document out and I got started on the detailed writing.

On Sunday, December 11, I drove to Princeton for my first meeting with Charles Wheatley. Wheatley turned out to be young, energetic, intellectually excellent, and possessed of a pleasantly informal manner. We got on well from the start. At a time when the Princeton department was virtually deserted because of the fast-approaching holiday period, Wheatley made himself regularly available. I had a much improved draft by December 20, the day I drove back to London, Ontario, for Christmas with Lorna. The respite was brief. On December 26, I was back on the New York Thruway heading for Princeton. Once again, Wheatley made himself readily and frequently available. I expressed my very real thanks for all he was doing, but he simply said that he was glad to do it and that it was part of his job. I think the ideas in the dissertation were of some interest to him but, even so, his level of commitment during the holiday break time was truly exceptional.

I returned to London in time for the start of second-term classes. I brought with me a draft of the dissertation that was almost complete. My plan was to submit the final draft by January 30, 1967, which would mean an April defence would be possible.

* * *

The second term got off to a fast start. I had a number of meetings with students to discuss end-of-first-term assignments. In addition, I was working flat out on two major projects. The first was finalization of the dissertation. Fortunately, this had reached the point where I could use the telephone to work out final details with Moore and Wheatley. The second matter was completing the Ontario Ministry of Health proposal in time for the January 16 deadline. This was important work. Andy Hunter and I envisioned a multi-year study with substantial funding. Extensive data were to be gathered in Ontario from over 1000 general practitioner physicians, specialist physicians, physician educators at medical schools, and medical students. A substantial part of the data was to be obtained through in-depth personal interviews.

Two weeks after we handed in the proposal, Andy Hunter received a telephone call from Dr. Stan Lang, a senior person with the Ministry of Health. Dr. Lang wanted to arrange a meeting in his Queen's Park office. A few days later, Andy and I were on Highway 401, headed for Toronto.

**Edward B. Harvey, as co-director of the Ontario
Medical Manpower Commission, 1967.**

Dr. Stan Lang was an accomplished physician with a passion
for public service, which manifested itself in his work for the
ministry and countless voluntary activities. The silver-haired
doctor was tall, thin, and handsome in a patrician sort of way. He
was modest, was a patient and interested listener, and possessed
a self-deprecating, slightly wry sense of humour. Over the next
few years, I came to know him well and respect him highly. It
soon became clear to me that he and Andy knew one another
quite well—probably from medical school. (Stan Lang wrote
a letter of reference for me in connection with my promotion
to full professor in 1974. It was typical of his total openness of
character that he copied the letter to me!)

Stan Lang told us that he and his colleagues felt this was "the
right study at the right time." The ministry, he advised, had some
funds that would not be expended by the March 31, 1967, budget
year-end. The plan was that these resources would be awarded to

Andy Hunter and myself on the understanding (contractually secured, of course) that we would—over the next two months—develop an overall work, staffing, budget, and deliverables plan for a multi-year program of activity. This, then, was the beginning of the Ontario Medical Manpower Project, an undertaking that was to last six years, produce a great many reports and publications (including Lorna Marsden's Princeton doctoral dissertation, *Doctors Who Teach* [1972]),[29] and make a real contribution to policy and program thinking in the area of family medicine.

The February winter break (officially called "reading week") was imminent at U.W.O. I received a call from Wilbert Moore. He wanted me to come to Princeton for a meeting with Charles Wheatley and himself to discuss the final composition of my dissertation examination committee and also address my dissertation defence strategy. Lorna and I had been thinking of taking the break week off, but at that stage of your career, you don't argue. Anyway, Wheatley had to work with me throughout his holiday break. It seemed fair enough. I hit the New York Thruway again.

* * *

While all this was happening, the job market was heating up enormously. I was having serious discussions with the University of Pennsylvania, New York University, the University of California at Berkeley, and the University of Toronto. A number of other places had also made overtures, but I had ruled them out for various reasons.

It must be remembered that this was an extraordinary—indeed, quite atypical—period in the academic job market. Institutions were expanding rapidly, partly because of increasing government spending and also because of mounting demographic pressures. The number of new graduates—particularly with doctorates—was still lagging. In short, demand was running significantly ahead of supply. Simply put, it was a seller's market.

Despite Jack Kantner's many kindnesses, I knew I could not remain in his department. The University of Western Ontario was a fine place, but the city of London, Ontario, was too far removed from the private and public sector "nerve centres" that I knew would be of strategic importance to my career plan.

I felt myself in the middle of a difficult juggling act. I had to be ready for my impending dissertation defence. The Ontario Medical Manpower Project was in launch mode. And I was dealing with a number of different job opportunities. With regard to that last, I had been buying time because of my looming dissertation defence—but the viability of that position wasn't going to last much longer.

It didn't. I successfully defended my dissertation on April 27, 1967. Now I had to make a job decision.

Lorna and I talked until the small hours of the mornings. We made lists. Central to the "decision dilemma" was the Canada/U.S. trade-off. Our time at Princeton had led us to appreciate the many fine features of the United States: scale, energy, excellence. But we also recognized that we were Canadians at heart. We understood the Canadian system. We felt confident about our ability to negotiate our way in Canadian society and institutions. There was also the Ontario Medical Manpower Project to consider. My being in Toronto would be no impediment to my continued central involvement—in fact, it would be an advantage. Although Princeton had generously supported my studies, so had Canada. I was lucky enough not to be in debt, but I did *feel* a sense of debt—to my country. Finally, we had both come to know Toronto quite well and, apart from liking the city a great deal, we felt it had a great future.

As I look back on the decision to return to Canada—specifically, Toronto—I have no doubt that it was the best thing to do. Our subsequent lives evolved in ways that we could not have even imagined when we were having those discussions and making those lists in our London apartment. Those future significant opportunities presented themselves for multi-faceted reasons, but being Canadians in Canada was a vitally important part of the equation. Being human, of course, I sometimes speculate on what a career in the United States might have been like.

* * *

May 1967 was a remarkable month. After a harsh winter and seemingly endless work and pressure, the arrival of spring was doubly welcome. Early in the month, I learned that the Ontario

Medical Manpower Project had received long-term funding. I accepted a tenure-stream cross-appointment at the University of Toronto and the Ontario Institute for Studies in Education (I will discuss the details of this in the next chapter) and Lorna made arrangements to complete the last year of her bachelor's degree at the University of Toronto.

On May 17, 1967, I went to Europe while Lorna remained in London, steering the Ontario Medical Manpower Project forward. In that era, one could buy a European rail pass that provided unlimited first-class travel. I bought the two-month version and travelled widely in many countries, including Britain, France, Germany, Austria, Denmark, Norway, and Sweden. In Sweden, I met Gosta Rehn and other policy thinkers and was greatly impressed at how far advanced the Swedes were in many areas of policy and practice, including health, education, and labour market management. Although many Swedish policy models were not directly transferable, as such, to the Canadian context, there was a wealth of innovative thinking to draw upon. The initial visit provided a foundation for many subsequent trips to that country.

I returned to Canada on July 11, 1967, arriving in Montreal. It was the year of the Expo, and there was energy, enthusiasm, and optimism in abundance. Lorna and I linked up in Toronto and soon leased a 21st floor apartment in Sutton Place, at the corner of Bay and Wellesley Streets. It was a short walk to the University of Toronto campus and had spectacular views of Toronto's fast-developing downtown skyline. It also had plenty of wall space to support our growing interest in collecting Canadian works of art.

* * *

My transition from graduate student to university professor was now complete. I had emerged from the process with a strong interest in interdisciplinary approaches and bringing the insights and tools of social science to bear on practical, policy-oriented issues. I already knew I would never be content to define and pursue my future work solely within the context of the university.

Part II

A Career

This part of the book contains five chapters that deal with aspects of the career experience in which I combined university teaching and research and operated an incorporated consultancy practice specializing in applied social research and policy-oriented assignments. The section covers a long period of time: from 1967 to the present day (2004).

Chapter 6, "Establishing the Path: Tenure, Promotion, and Consulting," deals with a seven-year period from 1967 to 1974. It begins with my taking up a joint appointment as an assistant professor of sociology with the University of Toronto and the Ontario Institute for Studies in Education (OISE). It ends with my being promoted to full professorship, preparing to enter the fourth year of my chairing the department of sociology at OISE, and having just incorporated my consulting practice. The chapter deals with a period of intense activity. On the university side was teaching, participating in research programs and writing associated publications, and receiving tenure and promotion. There was also the intensely politicized interlude that surrounded the process of my becoming a department chair—events that were a reflection of the highly radicalized context of the times. On the consulting side, the practice continued to grow. A number of projects were brought to a successful conclusion while many new initiatives came on stream. By the end of this period, my career direction as a professor and consultant was clearly established.

Chapter 7, "Travelling the Path: Managing the Journey," sets out an overview of how I went about managing my two career paths of professor and consultant from 1974 onward. In addition to formative experiences before 1974 and supportive personal circumstances, I examine three broad dimensions that kept everything on track. One was my continued development of methodological and technical expertise. Another was the continual upgrading of my project management and client relations skills in the applied setting. A third was creation and the following of a management model that enabled the consulting practice to be successful but not a source of conflict or competition with my university work. In short, Chapter 7 is about how I was able to do it all.

The type of consulting work I have done and currently do falls into three broad categories: royal commissions and task forces, assignments for governments and the broader public sector, and projects for the private sector. Each of these areas has important differences in terms of institutional and organizational culture, needs, and ways of working. Chapters 8, 9, and 10 examine each sector in turn from the perspective of selected projects that my consulting practice has carried out.

CHAPTER 6

Establishing the Path:
Tenure, Promotion, and Consulting

By the time I was interviewed for a position at the University of Toronto, I had already gone through the process with the U.S. universities. In fact, when I drove to Toronto early in May 1967 for my interview, I was leaning toward the University of Pennsylvania. I met with Del Clark, chairman of the University of Toronto's Sociology Department from 1963 to 1969. I had read several of his works at U.B.C. and Princeton and viewed him as a one of the founders of Canadian sociology.

Clark was a somewhat formal man with a manner that combined integrity and directness. He came to the point very quickly, saying that he had "heard about my work at Princeton and the University of Western Ontario" and had "made enquiries" and that it was his intention to offer me a position in the department. Compared to my experience with the U.S. universities, this was indeed quick. We talked for 20 minutes or so, at which point Clark informed me that he had arranged a lunch at the Faculty Club.

The meal was taken in the main dining room, a somewhat cavernous space decorated in a pale blue-and-white style reminiscent of a Wedgewood dinner plate. One of the people present was Oswald Hall, a full professor in the department. Kaspar Naegele had introduced me to Hall's work on occupations and professions in 1963. Not surprisingly, we found a good deal to talk about. Also present was Jan Loubser, an associate professor who was serving as deputy chairman of the department. Loubser was a tall, large man, originally from South Africa. He had a gruff manner and little to say but did liven up considerably when I mentioned Talcott Parsons's *The Social System*.[30] I had not been aware that Loubser had studied at Harvard, where Parsons was sociology's driving intellectual force.

S.D. Clark, University of Toronto, c. 1960s.

After lunch, I returned with Clark to his office. Clark told me that the Ontario Institute for Studies in Education, of which I had never heard, was planning to open a department of sociology in a year's time. He indicated that Cicely Watson, chair of the Department of Educational Planning at the Institute, wanted to meet with me that afternoon. I was agreeable to this and the arrangement was quickly finalized.

Cicely Watson was a short, energetic woman who spoke in a rapid-fire manner. I soon learned that the Ontario Institute for Studies in Education, or OISE as it was commonly called, had been founded just two years earlier, in 1965. A major driving force behind the creation of the Institute was William Davis, who was the minister of education during the 1960s in John Robarts's Conservative government. Davis, who subsequently served as premier of Ontario from 1971 to 1985, had a clear vision of the importance of investment in education as a key to building Ontario's—and, indeed, Canada's—economy. Cicely Watson confirmed Del Clark's observation that OISE planned to open a department of sociology in one year's time. At present, Watson explained, the very small number of sociologists already with the Institute were housed in the department of educational planning. One of these was William "Bill" Michelson, who had been a junior faculty member at Princeton during my residency, although I had neither known nor worked with him at that time. Michelson had come to Toronto one year earlier to take up a cross-appointment involving the University of Toronto sociology department and OISE. Watson arranged for me to speak with Michelson.

As a result of my recent experiences with various U.S. universities, by this time I had become a reasonably sophisticated job candidate. Among other things, I had a list of questions that I asked in a systematic fashion. At the end of the meetings with Watson and Michelson, I had learned several things. OISE produced only graduate degree holders (masters and doctors), and therefore course sizes and teaching loads were typically smaller than those in institutions with a significant undergraduate component. The lighter teaching load was accompanied by an expectation that professors would be extensively committed to research. To facilitate such a commitment, each incoming faculty member was given a full-time research assistant and 50 percent of a secretary's time. Given the Institute's mandate, there was also an expectation that research activities would attempt to maximize their relevance to practical or policy-oriented issues. In terms of working conditions, the Institute was located in a relatively new building on Bloor Street West and professorial entering salaries were 25 percent higher than the norm, a not inconsequential consideration.

I stayed overnight in Toronto and had a long telephone conversation with Lorna. The next morning I saw Del Clark again. I set out for him my fundamental dilemma: I was interested in both places. In an unconcerned fashion, he told me there was a simple solution. A cross-appointment would be arranged. I would work in both organizations and, in turn, they would each make a contribution to my compensation. In addition, I would have two offices. After resolution of a few remaining details, I accepted the arrangement that was to continue throughout my 36-year-long career at the University of Toronto. Some years later, in the 1980s, I divided myself even further by becoming involved—for several years—in graduate teaching and research activities based at the University of Toronto's Centre for Industrial Relations.

Looking back, I cannot say that I ever regretted—in any fundamental way—the cross-appointment arrangement. It certainly made academic life more interesting, especially when the two departments of sociology (OISE and U of T) were at war with one another. Even after the 1996 official merger of OISE and the University of Toronto, the two departments continued to co-exist—in a manner of speaking.

More seriously, the cross-appointment—the terms of which were never renegotiated—gave me more time for large-scale research and publication activities that proved beneficial at each stage of my career.

* * *

Although I had now officially left the University of Western Ontario, I soon discovered that my relationship with its department of sociology was not at an end. Jack Kantner contacted me and asked if I would be prepared to teach—on a consulting basis—a year-long course in theory and social change. The commitment would entail travelling to London and back to Toronto every Wednesday evening. In that era, Air Canada had regular Toronto–London–Toronto flights that meant one could turn the whole thing around between 6 p.m. and midnight. As a bonus, the aircraft were the relatively large and comfortable Viscounts and Vanguards, which were also exceptionally airworthy. Even when winter dealt its worse, these flying workhorses were almost always on time and had a stellar safety record.

* * *

September 1967, my first term at the University of Toronto and OISE, got off to a good start. I enjoyed the mix of senior undergraduate and graduate student teaching and encountered some very capable students. The numbers of my publications continued to grow. In September, my paper titled "Social Change and the Jazz Musician" appeared in a major U.S. journal, *Social Forces*.[31] In addition, a publication entitled "Decision Makers in Conflict"—derived from my Princeton doctoral dissertation—appeared in the fall issue of *The Business Quarterly*.[32] With the latter publication, I was quite deliberately trying to reach an audience broader than the academic world. Because of my publications, I had been immediately appointed to the graduate faculty of the University of Toronto, which meant I could supervise masters and doctoral dissertations, something I started to do in this first term. I also worked intensively with Nigel Boland, the research assistant I had been allocated, developing a research study of the educational and occupational expectations of young people. This led to considerable further work and publication in this area of enquiry. While all this was going on, the Ontario Medical Manpower Project was in full swing, demanding considerable time.

Lorna, meanwhile, was completing her B.A. degree at the University of Toronto and was also deeply engaged in the process of sending off applications to a number of universities to pursue doctoral-level studies in sociology.

* * *

Early in the second term, John Crispo—dean of the University of Toronto Business School—invited me to have lunch with him. Like many other departments or divisions of the university, his was growing rapidly and he had recruitment on his mind. Crispo's ideas for expansion of the Business School were interesting, and I pursued the discussions with him and certain of his colleagues. At the end of the process, I decided to remain in sociology. After all, it was only nine months earlier that I had defended my doctoral dissertation, and I suspect that it is understandable that I would still have a considerable identification with the field. Crispo accepted my decision with equanimity and generously remarked that I "would have a fine career no matter where I was." His judgement proved correct. Ironically, however, I should note that as my career progressed, I became substantially more involved in business-oriented activities, including the development of business strategic alliances and serving as senior author of various business-oriented books with titles like *Information Systems for Managing Workplace Diversity*,[33] *Re-Thinking HR Management: Strategies for Success in an Era of Change*,[34] and *Internet Solutions for HR Managers*.[35]

During the second term, I also met Bruce McCaffrey, who subsequently became a cabinet minister in the Ontario Conservative government of Premier William G. Davis, holding a number of different portfolios with success. At that time, however, he was a broker with Dominion Securities. I had a long-standing interest in both the theory and practice of investment and now had something of an asset base to work with. McCaffrey proved to be a most capable adviser. He was prudent, firmly believed in diversification, and was always prepared to take the time to explain his reasoning and approach as well as technical, market-related matters.

My research and publication activities continued unabated. In addition to the Ontario Medical Manpower project and the new program of educational research I was developing at OISE, I had decided to publish a paper on my doctoral dissertation results in the U.S.A.'s most high-profile sociological journal, the *American Sociological Review*. At one level, I resented that the path to recognition in Canada was through publishing in prestigious U.S. journals. However, if nothing else, I was a realist. I read a considerable number of *American Sociological Review* papers, took careful note of the way they were organized and written, and then got down to work. The paper was published in April 1968.[36]

Also in April 1968, Lorna was accepted at all the graduate schools to which she had applied for doctoral study in sociology. She chose Princeton. The place was becoming a family tradition.

That summer, Lorna and I travelled throughout Ontario, supervising the research team we had assembled and trained for the Ontario Medical Manpower Project. Apart from the interest and importance of the work, it was a wonderful opportunity to obtain a broad view of the dynamic province that was our new Canadian home. (She, like me, had been born and raised on Canada's beautiful Pacific coast.)

In late August, we attended the meetings of the American Sociological Association in Boston. It was a chance to see a number of people from Princeton and others as well. We also found out how effectively professional networks operate. Virtually everyone we saw knew Lorna would be starting doctoral work at Princeton in September. After Boston, we went to Princeton and quickly found and equipped a good apartment in a pleasant neighbourhood near the university. It was the first—but not the last—time we would maintain more than one residence for career purposes.

* * *

For my first year at OISE, I had been located in the department of educational planning. In September 1968, I moved to the Institute's new department of sociology while, of course, maintaining my cross-appointment at the University of Toronto department. The chair of the new OISE department was to be Jan Loubser, one of the people I had met at the recruitment lunch with Del Clark and Oswald Hall.

Early in the term, Loubser invited Lorna and me to a social event at his house. I accepted with thanks for myself but told him Lorna was away from Toronto, pursuing doctoral studies at Princeton. He looked like a man who has just been told an esteemed relative had died. He shook his head in apparent disbelief and gloomily muttered, "It's a big undertaking ... it's a big undertaking ..." Needless to say, the values implicit in such a statement did not endear him to me. I came to realize that there was a huge—indeed, unbridgeable—cultural and generational gap between the two of us. To be fair, I must also say that Loubser showed consistently strong support for my early tenure and promotion to associate professor.

During the first few months of the new sociology department's existence, one of Jan Loubser's major concerns was the drafting of a "departmental constitution." It was during this era that the student-power movement was on the rise in the United States (it was already of pandemic proportions in California) and the rallying cry of "participatory democracy" was in the air. These values were reflected in full measure in the document Loubser was drafting. I was given one version to read and expressed concerns that there were more committees than faculty members and that the complexity of the decision-making arrangements proposed would make it very difficult to get anything done. Loubser was not receptive to these views. I will return to the constitution saga later.

* * *

On October 22, 1968, I was contacted by Dr. Ross Baxter, a senior faculty member and professor of pharmacognosy at the

University of Toronto's Faculty of Pharmacy. He told me that the terms of reference for a major, Canada-wide Commission on Pharmaceutical Services had been established in 1967 and the initiative was now reaching the stage where a wide range of research would have to be undertaken. Dr. Baxter was a member of the commission, and its chairman was Dr. John B. Macdonald, a dentist and bacteriologist who had served as president of the University of British Columbia between 1962 and 1967. (I had been at U.B.C. between 1962 and 1964.)

It turned out that both Baxter and Macdonald were familiar with my work for the British Columbia Pharmaceutical Association, my publications on the subject, and my current activities as co-director of the Ontario Medical Manpower Project. A lunch meeting, which would involve Macdonald, Baxter, and myself, was quickly set up. The meeting proved to be both pleasant and productive. Macdonald and I chatted about U.B.C. and my current work. He briefed me on the goals and activities of his commission and concluded by asking me if I would have any interest in becoming "significantly involved" with the required research. My answer was yes. I found myself thinking about all the work on health professions that Kaspar Naegele had me do and my great debt to him and his exceptional insight into the widespread changes that would transform Canadian health care in the 1960s.

* * *

The rest of the first term and the second term passed in a blur of activity. My university teaching and research were developing in a positive direction. On the consulting side, the Ontario Medical Manpower Project now had a significant amount of data to analyse and even more to still gather. And now I was deeply engaged with a national study of pharmaceutical services. Fortunately, Lorna and I had developed an excellent research team for the Ontario Medical Manpower Project, and some of them were able to assist with the pharmacy-related work while additional staff were located. As for May 1969, it was a very good month. I was granted tenure and simultaneously promoted to associate professor. About a week after this news, I was contacted by the Dorsey Press, a major U.S. publisher, and invited to Chicago to discuss the possibility of preparing a new book on industrial sociology, designed for adoption in undergraduate courses in that subject. Apart from the professional honour, I was under no illusions about the size of the U.S. market.

The meeting at the Dorsey Press resulted in a book contract. Early in the discussions, I learned that my great professor and supporter, Wilbert Moore, had recommended me for the job. I dedicated the book to him.[37]

* * *

During the summer of 1969, I was in Vancouver for six weeks. My presence was required to establish the western component of the research program of the Commission on Pharmaceutical Services. In addition, I had agreed to teach a summer session course at U.B.C. In part, I think I wanted to explore the difference between being a student at U.B.C. and being a professor. In addition, I found myself making comparisons between life in Vancouver and life in Toronto, with a resulting stronger-than-ever commitment to Toronto.

I rented a house from Walter Young—a senior U.B.C. professor away on a research trip—in the 3000 block of West 15th Avenue. It was a fine neighbourhood, close to the U.B.C. campus, and the house had an elevated deck with good views over the city. I entertained a number of old friends and made some new ones. In this connection, I was fortunate enough to meet Jack Shadbolt, one of Canada's great painters and a west coast icon. I acquired some of his work on the Vancouver trip and much more over the ensuing years. His vibrant abstract expressionism drew heavily—and to great effect—on Aboriginal and naturalistic imagery of the west coast. I also invited Greig Paul to dinner. He was now working as a laboratory assistant and had given up all ideas of further study. He seemed terribly morose and, desperate to cheer him up, I suggested driving down to Seattle to attend a rock concert. I have to confess that I knew next to nothing about the rock movement, being almost exclusively interested in classical music and modern jazz. But as a piece of "hippie theatre," the concert was quite amazing—behaviourally and visually. It was the last time I saw Greig. Lorna and I passed the rest of the summer in Toronto, working.

* * *

The term beginning in September 1969 seemed much the same the preceding year, except now I was even busier. Lorna was hunkered down at Princeton, working flat out. With no time for recreational travel, we ran up astronomical telephone bills instead. "Deep discount dialling" was not an option in those days. By the beginning of December 1969, Lorna felt ready to write her general examinations but, like me, had decided to wait until May of the next year. Further reading was always useful and she decided that this could be done in Toronto. Our living apart had lasted 18 months and, despite the gloomy and unsolicited prognostications, we were still married. I should point out that, even in the so-called swinging sixties, it was definitely not the norm for married couples to live apart—any more than it was for young women not to take their husband's last name. In any event, we decided to celebrate our reunion by getting on a plane and going to London (England, not Ontario!). We stayed at The Strand Palace, with its seven-foot-long bathtubs and heated towel rails. We went to restaurants, art galleries, movies, concerts, and more restaurants. One of the concerts was at Ronnie Scott's world-famous Jazz Club. Bill Evans—the brilliant pianist who had often worked with Miles Davis—was playing. It was an electric evening.

We then flew on to Vienna, which had been rendered almost magical by a light fall of winter snow. We stayed at the Inter-Continental Hotel, and our accommodation looked down upon an illuminated skating rink that provided a wonderful winter ballet from early in the morning to very late at night. It was my second trip to Vienna and Lorna's first. The historical and cultural richness of the city left no deficit of things to do and see. There were many high points, but a particularly memorable one was an evening visit to Vienna's magnificent Opera House for an inspired performance of *La Bohème*. To sustain us in these efforts, there was an endless supply of fine restaurants and cafés, the latter particularly redolent of a city where coffee and the intellectual life went hand in hand.

We went on to Copenhagen, a city we both knew, revisited Tivoli, toured many galleries, and saw the latest manifestations of

Scandinavian genius in the design and production of contemporary furniture and other housewares. Then we returned to London, where The Strand Palace again served as our base. There were more concerts and galleries, including a visit to the Tate to see an exhibition of the paintings of William Blake—a stunning visual essay on the intersection between genius and madness.

We arrived back in Toronto on January 5, 1970, the first few days of a new decade. After a trip like that, we felt we could take on anything—which was just as well, given the work agenda that lay ahead. Among other things, we had to bid farewell to the apartment in Princeton and repatriate Lorna's possessions to Toronto. Then it was down to work with a vengeance. However, all this effort was not the product of unthinking compulsiveness. We both had very clear goals. Mine was to achieve full professorship in as timely a fashion as possible and to solidify my position as a person bringing the tools and insights of social science to bear on practical and policy-oriented issues. Lorna's goals were to pass the general examinations, move forward without delay on an already well thought-out dissertation, enter university life, and pursue her various political and advocacy interests vigorously.

* * *

In April of the second term, I was contacted by an official of the recently established Commission on Post-Secondary Education in Ontario. Ontario had experienced rapid post-secondary educational change in the 1960s. The province had gone from none to 21 community colleges. Several new universities had been created. Existing universities were expanding rapidly to accommodate baby boom enrolment pressures and, more generally, the fact that a larger proportion of high school graduates were proceeding to higher education. The commission had a broad mandate to examine what had taken place, assess the current situation, and recommend appropriate policies and programs for the future. Like every such commission, it had a great need for related research.

The commission was under the direction of Douglas Wright, a deputy minister in the Ontario government with responsibilities for university financing and social policy. (An engineer by training, Wright subsequently served as president of the University of Waterloo between 1981 and 1993.) I was asked if I would meet with him in a week's time.

The meeting took place in a small Queen's Park conference room. Apart from Wright and myself, there was a secretary who took minutes. Wright was a short, energetic man who radiated quickness of mind. He asked not a single question about my background or work. I now realize that he had doubtless already been fully briefed. He said he needed two major studies carried out, both with deadlines of slightly less than one year. The first was to address the growing perception (which I shared) that university graduates were beginning to experience somewhat more difficulty obtaining jobs consistent with their level of training. Put another way, supply was beginning to exceed demand. The second was an omnibus study, addressing a wide range of policy issues, including these questions: (1) How do key groups in Canadian society view higher education? (2) What are the costs and benefits of higher education? (3) How effective is the university as an agent of attitude change? (4) How does the university address equality of opportunity in society? (5) Is the university "in crisis"?

When he finished outlining his needs, he leaned back and offered a one-word question: "Interested?"

Of course I was. The policy issues seemed to me not only fundamental but fascinating. I realized that I was already heavily committed, but I also firmly believed that there was always a way of getting the work done. One could organize for optimum efficiency, one could delegate certain tasks, one could develop effective work partnerships, and one could simply work longer hours. I answered Wright in the affirmative. "Good," he responded. "You have a week in which to develop the two proposals. They don't have to be long. They have to be specific and clear."

"Educational Systems and the Labour Market Study" was the name I gave to the investigation of the changing employment situation for university graduates. I was confident I could direct this project on my own, given that it would be based on two of my key areas of specialization: institutional-level policy analysis and broadly based survey research. The omnibus study was more daunting, simply because of the range of issues involved. Jos

Lennards had been a member of my entering cohort at Princeton. He had, among other things, specialized in the sociology of education. And he was now a colleague in the University of Toronto sociology department. I approached Jos immediately and gave him the full background. He was enthusiastically interested and started work directly on the proposal for the omnibus study. Douglas Wright had his documents in a week and made his decision to accept and proceed within four days' time. Compared with today's fiscally constrained and highly competitive situation, research opportunities in that era were numerous and fast-breaking.

In the educational systems and labour market study, the commission timelines made it utterly impossible to establish a baseline and then track how university graduate employment patterns were changing. I had to retroactively determine what was going on.

My starting point was to judgementally select four Ontario universities that I felt were reasonably representative of the range of universities in the province. I focused on people who had received arts or science bachelor's degrees (the bulk of degrees granted) during the years 1960, 1964, and 1968. Lists of graduates and mailing addresses were obtained from the universities included in the study, and I proceeded to create probability samples. At the end of the day, an 11-page, 52-question survey was mailed to 6316 graduates. A total of 3817 surveys (60.4 percent) were returned. This represented over 42 percent of the total population of bachelor's level arts and science graduates for the three cohorts (1960, 1964, 1968) in question. The numerical size of the sample, the magnitude of the response rate, and a careful analysis of the characteristics of non-respondents left me with no doubt that the data were highly representative and deserving of a very high level of statistical confidence. I joked with Lorna that I had enough data to keep busy for 20 years. This wasn't totally accurate, but close.

Using a carefully devised framework of statistical controls—to make sure I wasn't comparing apples and oranges—I examined the occupational situation for the 1960, 1964, and 1968 graduates. There was clear evidence of a decline in occupational outcomes. This result, and many associated findings, had a number of policy implications for issues such as the rate of return on the investment of public funds in higher education, the ramifications of unemployment and underemployment among the relatively highly educated, and questions about aspects of the university curriculum relative to the changing labour market.

In immediate terms, the project produced a research report published by the commission,[38] my book *Educational Systems and the Labour Market*,[39] and a large number of papers in refereed journals and other professional publications. It also led to other research studies—I subsequently surveyed 1972 and 1976 graduates—and further government commission and task force work.

The technique I used—synthetic cohort analysis—had previously been used in demography. I had stumbled across it while studying with Charles Westoff at Princeton's Office of Population Research. For me, it was another instance of how research methods could be used in a boundary-spanning way.

As for the omnibus study, it was submitted as a report to the commission entitled *The Changing Nature of Post-secondary Education: Attitudes, Costs and Benefits*.[40] It became the basis for the 1973 book, *Key Issues in Higher Education*,[41] which Jos Lennards and I co-authored.

While this was going on, all the other projects were moving forward. Two major reports had been prepared for the Commission on Pharmaceutical Services, and two more were completed for the Ontario Medical Manpower Project. I believe they call it multi-tasking nowadays.

* * *

In May 1970, Lorna went to Princeton and successfully wrote her general examinations. After appropriate celebrations with the many new friends she had made there—notably Mike Soroka (now a leading sociology professor in San Diego, California) and Tom Corl (now a senior executive with the American Red Cross and someone I had once recruited to the OISE sociology department during my term as chair)—she returned to Toronto to start writing her doctoral dissertation. It was a study of medical educators based on some of the results from the still-ongoing Ontario Medical Manpower Project.

* * *

In the summer of 1970, I was contacted by Robert "Rob" Mills about becoming a member of the board of directors of Pollution Probe, an organization with which he was much involved. Rob had been one of my undergraduate students in the preceding academic year and had distinguished himself with his first-class intellect and considerable personal charm. During his bachelor's degree program, Rob had studied in such areas as literature, philosophy, history, and sociology. Despite this distinctly non-vocational approach, he had a great flair for business: specifically, housing renovation and property development. Indeed, he had already created his own company. As it turned out, Rob and I ended up doing considerable business together.

I found Pollution Probe to be an interesting organization with an important mandate. Other board members included Donald Chant, then-chairman of the University of Toronto's Zoology Department; Monte Hummell, still a leader in Canadian environmental affairs; and Peter Middleton, who went on to form his own environmental consulting firm and then moved on to serve as a senior federal public servant.

Rob and I both felt that population-related issues were of vital importance, both in an environmentally connected sense and by themselves. We formulated a concept for a not-for-profit, charitable-status foundation that would foster research and informed debate on population-related policy issues. We consulted with a number of senior-level people we had access to, including H. Ian Macdonald, the deputy treasurer of Ontario; Omand Solandt, vice-chairman of Canadian National Railways and a former head of the Science Council of Canada; and Robert Andras, a federal political figure who had served as minister of manpower and immigration. We received encouragement and good advice. The next step was to hold discussions with Clayton "Clay" Hudson, a talented young lawyer and a friend of Rob Mills. The Population Research Foundation came into being in 1972, and I had the privilege of serving as its founding president.

The foundation successfully organized conferences, conducted research, and fostered publication activities, which included Lorna Marsden's 1972 book for Copp Clark, *Population Probe: Canada*,[42] and *Canadian Population Concerns*,[43] a 1977 collection of symposium papers edited by myself and Lorna.

The summer 1970 annual meeting of the International Sociological Association was held in Varna, Bulgaria, and Lorna and I had decided, several months earlier, that we would attend. This advance planning was essential. Bulgaria was still very much a police state at that time, and security checks and visas were required.

Another part of the advance planning involved my contacting the Lotus Car Works in England. Lotus automobiles were produced under the direction of Colin Chapman, a famous racing car driver and enthusiast. Each car was in large part built by hand and, if you wanted one, you had to order months in advance. I wanted one.

On a bright late-July morning, Lorna and I arrived at the Lotus Works. The car was ready. It was a lemon yellow Lotus Elan 2+2. The "2+2" meant there was room for two people in the front bucket seats and theoretical room for two more suitcase-sized individuals prepared to sustain the rigours of a virtually unpadded and very narrow leather-covered bench. The car's aerodynamic body was crafted from light but very strong fibreglass. This lightness, combined with a sophisticated and powerful engine, made for a seriously fast vehicle, which, of course, is what Colin Chapman had in mind. We drove the car in England, France, Italy, and Yugoslavia. We did not take it into Bulgaria. Somehow, that didn't seem wise.

I shipped the Lotus back to Toronto and eventually sold it for more than I paid. If it still exists today, it would be worth some unspeakable sum.

* * *

The 1970–71 academic year witnessed continued progress and production. My OISE-based educational research program was producing publications on the educational and occupational expectations of young people and changing patterns of accessibility to post-secondary education. Three more research reports were prepared for the Ontario Medical Manpower Project and one for the Commission on Pharmaceutical Services. I also published another paper based on my doctoral dissertation. In June 1971, *Pharmacy in a New Age*[44]—the report of the Commission on Pharmaceutical Services—was published, marking the conclusion, at least for me, of what had been an extremely interesting project. The report of the commission contained a great many far-sighted recommendations that helped to shape the profession and its practice for years to come.

Lorna was completely preoccupied with finishing her dissertation; however, we found time to change our residence in July 1971. We had learned of an apartment at the corner of Spadina and Lowther. The apartment was located in an architecturally interesting building with high ceilings and had an amount of space not easy to find in Toronto, including two studies, two bathrooms, and a large living room with a fireplace. The elevator, with its polished brass sliding door, would have been at home in the Victorian era. We leased it immediately.

Our move complete, I left for Europe, a trip that this time included my first excursion to Morocco, including such interesting destinations as Casablanca, Marrakech, Fez, and Tangier. I even managed to travel on the Marrakech Express, memorialized by Crosby, Stills and Nash.

* * *

The 1971–72 academic year got off to a very rocky start. Jan Loubser announced that he was resigning from OISE and would be leaving directly to take up an academic administrative position in South Africa. He observed that it would be necessary to strike a committee for a new department chair but, since it would take a year to perform the search and select a successor, it would be necessary to appoint an interim chair at once. He concluded by saying that he had consulted with Andy Effrat and that Effrat was prepared to take on the responsibility.

Effrat had come to the department one year after my arrival. Although I did not know him well, our collegial relationship had always been perfectly cordial.

What offended me in the situation was Loubser's spectacular arrogance. He talked endlessly about "participatory democracy," had developed a department constitution enshrining his perception of what participatory democracy was, and was now seeking to slide Effrat into his position without even a hint of participatory process.

I soon discovered that I was not alone in having these feelings, although there were other members of the department who strongly supported Effrat and his immediate ascension. In short, the place was deeply divided. All this surfaced in a matter of a few days. Meanwhile, Loubser had packed his bags and left.

The department constitution ensured that everyone (faculty, research assistants, secretarial staff, and students) could be involved in every departmental decision that was made, including staffing. I soon found myself being approached by members of each and every constituency enquiring if I would consider standing for interim chair of the department. Quite frankly, I had never had the slightest interest in being a department chair, interim or otherwise. However, the department was in a state of administrative paralysis and something had to be done. In the spirit of participatory democracy, what was done was to hold meetings, followed by more meetings, followed by even more meetings. The level of campaigning and political manoeuvring was intense, much of it with no direct input from either Effrat or myself. Students who had not been seen in aeons reappeared in the department. It was as if the circus had come to town and, in a sense, it had.

The whole matter finally came to a head at a meeting of the department's "general assembly" on November 19, 1971. A vote was held. Effrat received 23 votes. I received 23 votes. Some bright soul suggested a coin be flipped. It was. I won.

I commenced my new responsibilities immediately with one overriding priority—to get the department back on track. I was greatly helped in this by my administrative assistant, Barbara Justason, who was highly supportive. Barbara was calm, efficient, and immediately gave me a crash course in the department's administrative process.

* * *

With the department restored to some semblance of order, I boarded a plane to Cairo, via London, on the evening of December 18, 1971. Some time earlier, Lorna had completed a draft of her doctoral dissertation, submitted it to her principal adviser, and left for Ethiopia—a country in which she had a long-standing intellectual and cultural interest. I was now going to join her.

In Cairo, I stayed at the historic Shepherd's Hotel, toured the sprawling, chaotic city extensively, and visited several major archaeological sites—including the Great Pyramids. I then flew on to Addis Ababa, Ethiopia's capital, to link up with Lorna. She had arranged long-term accommodation at a pleasant ho-tel—with a very friendly and caring staff—and had used this as her base of operations for various trips to other parts of the country. I would have to write a different book to capture what travelling in Ethiopia was like. Simply put, it was an extraordi-nary experience. Lorna already knew her way around, a great advantage, and we travelled to many places, including remote areas where malaria was endemic. Thanks to mosquito repellent, netting, and the foul-tasting pills I started to swallow 10 days before my journey, nothing ever happened.

We then went on to Kenya, where (against no doubt sound advice) we rented a car and proceeded to drive around, includ-ing taking a visually spectacular trip from Nairobi to Mombassa, where our accommodation was on the Indian Ocean. The beach had the whitest sand I have ever seen and was almost deserted. We also stayed at a game protectorate where the elephants am-bled within a few yards of one's cottage. It was all quite wonder-ful and neither of us was ecstatic about the prospect of returning to Toronto in January.

However, return we did. Lorna received positive feedback on her dissertation draft. Some further modifications were neces-sary, but her final defence was not far away. Back at the OISE sociology department, a Department Chair Search Committee was struck early in the term. It comprised two faculty, two mem-bers of the support staff, and two students. One of the faculty members was Andy Effrat and, over the next three months, he worked diligently to do everything he could to prevent my eleva-tion from interim chair to chair of the department. Candidate after candidate was brought in, none proving acceptable to a deeply divided department. The last candidate was John "Jack" Seeley. Seeley had been at Toronto's York University some years earlier and had become involved in a bitter dispute with York's founding president, Murray Ross, after which Seeley departed for the United States. As a candidate for chair of the OISE sociology department, Seeley faced a very serious problem: he was totally unacceptable to OISE's central administration and board of governors. In May 1972, Robert W.B. Jackson, OISE's founding director, telephoned me to ask if I would be willing to take a full term as chair of the department of sociology. After some negotiations, I agreed.

* * *

The sociology department at the University of Toronto was also going through a turbulent period at this time. The chairman who had hired me, Del Clark, was deposed, and a new regime made its appearance. In keeping with the spirit of the times, it was based on an elaborate constitution that called for student–faculty parity in all matters of departmental governance. Jim Giffen was asked to serve as acting chair while a search was conducted for Clark's successor. Giffen's task evolved into a three-year term. In writing about that period much later, Giffen observed: "The task of constitution-making was unbelievably time consuming .... If we had deliberately set out to do so we couldn't have devised a system better suited to wasting time and fostering discord."[45]

Giffen's term ended in 1972, when Irving Zeitlin was recruited—from Washington University in St. Louis—to serve as chairman of the department. No internal candidate had proven acceptable to a sufficient number of people. Zeitlin later wrote that he seriously considered resigning after one year in the job. The central principle of the departmental constitution required student parity on all committees. Zeitlin observed that "the parity system carried with it considerable intra-departmental strife, as well as unfavourable publicity throughout the university's media."[46] It seems that, as a scholarly person, Zeitlin had little enthusiasm for the administrative and political battles that would have to be fought to change the situation. His successor actively engaged with these issues and the parity system came to an end, returning the department to a more peaceful and stable condition.

* * *

Despite the seemingly endless turmoil of academic politics, the year witnessed a number of important accomplishments. Lorna successfully defended her doctoral dissertation at Princeton in June 1972 and proceeded to deal with various job offers, ultimately deciding to go to the sociology department at the University of Toronto. A research report on the attitudes of medical students toward their training and career plans was produced for the Ontario Medical Manpower Project. My OISE-based contract research for the Ministry of Education and the Ministry of Colleges and Universities produced the first monograph in what was to develop into a series of ministry publications I authored. The year 1972 also saw the publication of a book I edited, and contributed to, for the University of Toronto Press: *Perspectives on Modernization: Essays in Memory of Ian Weinberg.*[47] Ian, a brilliant doctoral student in sociology at Princeton and a valued colleague in the department of sociology at the University of Toronto, tragically died of cancer at the age of thirty. My goal was to shape the book so that it would be wide-ranging and intellectually provocative—like the work of the man it was written to honour.

My work on educational systems and the labour market was proving to have significance beyond the boundaries of Canada. Discussions I had with officials of organizations like the United Nations and the Canadian International Development Agency made it clear that many developing nations—notably, a number of countries in South America—were experiencing serious disjunctions between their human capital preparation systems and emerging employment and economic needs. During the summer of 1972, I travelled to Peru, Chile, Argentina, Uruguay, Brazil, and Venezuela and met a number of people in education, government circles, and the private sector. This was the beginning of a program of work that would involve several further trips to South America.

* * *

Shortly after the academic year began in September 1972, Jan Loubser returned to Canada. He had evidently fallen into grave conflict with various government and university officials, which made remaining in South Africa an impossibility. There was an abortive "Bring Back Loubser" movement—spearheaded by a handful of individuals—in the OISE sociology department I now chaired. It went nowhere. I am told that there were similar discussions at the University of Toronto sociology department, but these were soon dropped. In short, Loubser had burned his academic bridges.

As for chairing the OISE sociology department, I was beginning to find this quite interesting. I had been dealing with large-scale research budgets for a few years and I now had a departmental budget to manage as well. Fortunately, I had always been interested in finance and did not view this sort of work as an unwelcome imposition but rather as an exceptional learning opportunity. There was also the challenge of working with a disparate group of people, forging coalitions, and moving people—at least some of the time—toward agreement and collective action. I often found myself quietly thankful that my doctoral dissertation had dealt with the politics of organizational decision making.

I enjoyed the opportunity to have more direct contact with Robert W.B. Jackson, OISE's director. Bob Jackson was a quiet and modest man with a first-rate mind. He understood the significance of demographics for the education sector long before most others and had been successful in attracting the attention of key figures like William G. Davis, a highly successful minister of education in Ontario and later premier of the province.

Relationships with other department chairs were complicated by competition over budgets and other resource allocation decisions. One delightful exception, however, was Alan Thomas, chairman of the Department of Adult Education. A bright and genial person, Alan had served as an assistant to Robert Stanbury, a one-time federal cabinet minister. Alan had a fine grasp of the policy and political process and we found ourselves with much to talk about.

Department chairing took time but, for a number of reasons, did not interfere with my various projects and publication activities. In recognition of my administrative duties, my OISE teaching load had been reduced to one half course a year. I was fortunate to have a number of technically excellent and motivated research assistants working with me thanks to the funding I had been able to obtain. As for my administrative assistant and secretary, both shared my highly organized approach to work and so we all got on well and, even more important, got the job done.

The industrial sociology book for the Dorsey Press was nearing completion. Also, Andy Hunter and I organized and co-chaired a crucial two-day conference of the Ontario Medical Manpower Project, which brought together medical decision makers from across the province. Increasingly, we were beginning to "go public" with the policy and program implications of our extensive research. To keep up the momentum, I wrote an article entitled "The Vanishing Practitioner" for the prestigious *Journal of Medical Education*.[48]

At the beginning of May 1973, I left for Brazil on a five-week mission supported by the United Nations. My mandate had two main components. The first was working with education and government officials to develop educational system/labour market research strategies that would produce policy and program-relevant results. The second was to teach an intensive course in policy research methods to a small group of government research officials and advanced students. The venue for the course was the Federal University of Bahia; accordingly, my main base of operations was Salvador, where I lived on a high floor of the Plaza Hotel. One set of windows overlooked the charming colonial architecture of the town. Another set provided a discouraging vista of shanties with roofs made from flattened-out tin cans.

I also made business trips to other Brazilian cities, including Rio de Janeiro, São Paulo, and Brasilia. My overall impression of Brazil was that of a place of great energy and promise but a nation beset by massive problems of socioeconomic inequality.

Only a few weeks after my return to Toronto, I was once again on a plane to Brazil. There were several follow-up matters, related to my preceding trip, that had to be dealt with. It had been arranged that I would then go on to Santiago, Chile, to meet with education and government officials for discussions pertaining to the education/employment/economic development agenda. I was put up at the Crillon Hotel, a charming Paris-style establishment located on the same square as the Presidential Palace. My mission in Chile was to last four weeks and I got down to work immediately. However, it soon became clear to me that the country was in more perilous condition than the pre-briefings had suggested. Hyperinflation was ravaging the economy. A huge black market had taken hold as people desperately sought to exchange the increasingly worthless Chilean currency for U.S. dollars or, indeed, anything of value. Supply lines had broken down. In stores, the shelves were mainly empty. When some supplies did come through, they were snapped up in a panic of frenzied buying.

The international media periodically converged on the city, making the Crillon Hotel their headquarters. The stately grand piano that graced the elegantly appointed main dining room became a parking place for television cameras, portable lights, and other media paraphernalia. Santiago was besieged with demonstrations—at least one a day and more often two. Strangely enough, I didn't fear for my personal safety. I was a Canadian; I was working for the U.N. These seemed like pretty good credentials. I'm not sure I would be so sanguine now.

Despite the chaos—which made sociology departments look like a piece of cake—I arranged meetings, talked with people, and developed research plans. But I had a bad feeling that people were simply going through the motions and that a terrible paralysis had set in. What made it even more dispiriting was that although political destabilization was an endemic feature of many Latin American states, Chile had for many years been a stable exception, with a civic culture reflected in the grace and charm of its people. I had read books on economic disintegration and institutional collapse. Reading about it was one thing; living it quite another. I refused to surrender to despondency. I had the use of a car and, on available weekends, explored some of the country, including such visually amazing places as the steeply ascending seaside city of Valparaiso.

On the morning of September 11, 1973, I received a 4 a.m. telephone call at the Crillon Hotel. It was from a Canadian official in Santiago whom I knew well. It was rapidly followed by a call from my U.N. contact. The message was very clear: "It's time to go." I was to pack immediately. A car would take me to the airport. I would be assisted through customs and immigration.

I caught an early-morning Iberia flight to Bogotá, Colombia. It turned out to be the last flight leaving Santiago for some little while. I learned the full story when I arrived at the U.N. offices in Bogotá a few hours later. Shortly after my departure, Chilean military forces had launched a coup against President Salvador Allende. The Chilean airforce bombed the Presidential Palace. Evidently, the Crillon Hotel, a stone's throw away, avoided collateral damage. Allende, and most of his praetorian guard, died in a hail of bullets. The Pinochet regime was launched. I was back in Toronto three days later.

* * *

The 1973–74 academic year was a year of large personal and professional developments.

The Ontario Medical Manpower Project was in its final stages. It had produced important research and publications. Of special importance was the fact that it had made a substantive contribution to policy and program discussions related to primary care medicine. The results had underscored the importance of initiatives to further strengthen family medicine, both educationally and in practice terms. The research provided a clearer understanding of the declining interest in general practice and pointed to strategies that would ensure a continued strong presence for primary care medicine. Among other things, we learned how exposure to the behavioural sciences could help family practitioners in fulfilling their mission. We also worked diligently to disseminate these understandings to the world of practice. Andy Hunter and I stayed in contact and remained committed to the values that had initiated the project in the first place.

For a number of months, I had been in regular contact with Rob Mills, dealing with various issues related to the Population Research Foundation. Among other things, we were jointly in-volved in fundraising activities. I was also becoming increasingly interested in the Toronto real estate market, particularly since it was now clear that Lorna and I would be pursuing a significant part of our careers in the city. Rob proved to be an invaluable guide in this area. We looked at various properties together and exchanged ideas on renovation and development strategies. We saw an interesting three-storey brick house in the Annex—a neighbourhood close to the University of Toronto. After consultations with Lorna, I bought it. Working with Rob and his team of skilled craftsmen, we virtually gutted the place and set about recapturing its original charm.

During the preceding year, I had been doing some consulting work with the Ministry of State for Urban Affairs and the Canada Mortgage and Housing Corporation. The Ministry of State for Urban Affairs was part of Prime Minister Trudeau's agenda to create departments of government that would not be weighed down by day-to-day operational concerns and could instead dedicate time and thought to innovative approaches to public policy. Canada's experience with "urban renewal" (the razing of whole areas and putting up of new structures) had not been a happy one. Such interventions into the urban landscape were enormously destructive of neighbourhood cohesion and people's lives. A new emphasis was emerging on rehabilitation and improvement combined with a large component of preservation—not only of historical infrastructure but also of social coherence. I was strongly attracted to this view and was pleased to be commissioned to prepare two position papers.

By the time September 1973 came around, two national-level programs were in place. The first was the Neighbourhood Improvement Program (NIP), which was dedicated to preserving, improving, and developing neighbourhoods in a context of extensive consultation with and involvement of neighbourhood members. The second program was the Residential Rehabilitation Assistance Program (RRAP), an initiative designed to assist individual citizens and neighbourhood groups in the preservation and rehabilitation of existing housing stock. I was asked to take on a large program of consulting work that would involve—while the programs were in actual operation—an extensive assessment of program design, delivery, and results. This type of in-process work is particularly valuable because it facilitates policy and program "course corrections" in an ongoing way.

It was a lot of work, and I was going to need help. Fortunately, I had become reasonably experienced at putting together teams and project management strategies. One of the first people I contacted was Rob Mills. It seemed to me that there was a perfect fit between his interests and capabilities and the work to be done. Happily, he saw it the same way and we spent the next two years working in close conjunction on the NIP/RRAP files.

In April 1974, I learned that I had been promoted to full professor. I had managed to realize my goal of achieving senior rank within seven years of having joined OISE and the University of Toronto.

In the same month, I incorporated my consulting practice. In connection with the Population Research Foundation, I had regular dealings with Clay Hudson, the lawyer who had incorporated that entity. Clay was well aware of my business activities and interests, and we had many lengthy and informative discussions. The fact that Clay was my contemporary in terms of age was a great benefit. As they say nowadays, we both liked thinking "outside the box." My involvement with the Population Research Foundation had given me a clearer vision of the benefits of incorporation, which included an orderly framework for management and proper fiscal accountability and the creation of a business identity, which is such an important part of marketing and delivering services. Incorporation proved to be a very sound decision.

* * *

Despite my experiences in Chile, I remained committed to the international work I was doing. In June 1974, I returned to Brazil to continue work on the education, employment, and economic development initiatives. As I sat in the climbing plane looking at the receding lights of Toronto, I felt I had established the path I knew I would continue to follow in my life. Fifteen years had passed since I first arrived at Victoria College. It didn't seem nearly that long ago.

CHAPTER 7

Travelling the Path: Managing the Journey

Although universities attract a certain amount of criticism (elitist, impractical, hotbeds of ideology), and anti-intellectualism is not an unknown commodity in Canadian society, they are important institutions for various reasons. Universities generate knowledge, a not insignificant amount of which contributes to our social, cultural, and economic well-being. They are also an important mechanism for passing on information and understandings from one generation to the next. In addition, universities operate, at least in part, as meritocracies. In this sense, they provide a vehicle for talented people to be upwardly mobile in the society and, in so doing, contribute to the renewal and revitalization of elites.

In order to achieve their mission, universities are collegial, not line authority, organizations. This relative absence of rigid hierarchy provides the professoriate with considerable freedom in how their work is defined and carried out. This was probably even more true in the 1960s, 1970s, and 1980s than it is today.

Although, given the nature of my work, it was necessary for me to cross boundaries and work with jurisdictions outside the university, this did not mean that I did not value university work or the university as an institution. Quite the contrary. I enjoyed teaching, dissertation advising, and university-based research. The challenge was to find an effective way of meshing university work with outside activities.

Fortunately, during the seven years it took me to achieve the senior rank of full professor, I was able to shape my university work in this direction. The content of my teaching (which involved senior undergraduates and graduate students) was increasingly focused on issues related to applied social research and policy studies. My dissertation advising work tended to be with students interested in problem solving or applied issues rather than students with mainly theoretical and/or ideological agendas. As for my university-based research, I had developed contacts with officials of the Ministry of Education and Ministry of Colleges and Universities. These contacts led to large-scale contract research in various areas, including studies of the Student Guidance/Information Service, the Career Development Course, the Occupational Program in Ontario Schools, the changing employment situation for post-secondary graduates, and employer-sponsored training programs in Ontario. All of these studies were distinctly policy-oriented and were focused on the changing education–employment linkage. The work also produced a series of monographs.

In addition to these activities, I was engaged in a number of consulting missions, including work for the Ontario Medical Manpower Project, the Commission on Pharmaceutical Services, the Commission on Post-Secondary Education in Ontario, and assorted international missions in Latin America.

An increasing amount of the work—both university-based and consulting—was finding its way into an expanding stream of publications and improved course offerings. But even more important, from my point of view, was the growing evidence that the projects were helping to shape policy and program thinking. As an engineer friend at the University of Toronto said, "It's hard to teach students how to construct a bridge if you've never built one." I shared this view entirely. I could see how work within the university and work outside the university cross-fertilized one another with fruitful consequences.

In the Marxist 1970s, such a view was anathema to many colleagues in sociology. To work for a government commission was to be "an instrument of the state oppressors." To have dealings with people in the private sector was to be "a lackey of the corrupt capitalist system."

In an era when Marxism as political practice has imploded, all this may seem almost funny. At the time, it was not. Overall, however, I was more saddened than angered by these views. They reflected such a fundamental lack of understanding of how progressive change is realized in Canada—incrementally and within a framework of institutions.

I felt self-confident in my value system and approach and would have continued even if I had been alone. But I was not. There were some like-minded colleagues, students, and research assistants. Also, I was discovering a constantly increasing number of people in the public service and private sector who had insights and intellectual capabilities equal to those of the best that the university offered. This is not said to denigrate the university but to celebrate the fact that there are talented people in all sectors and that much is to be gained from boundary-spanning activities.

* * *

The path I was on involved a work-intensive way of life. However, I have never regarded an abundance of interesting work as an imposition but rather as a privilege. Also, my family circumstances helped. My spouse joined the University of Toronto sociology department in 1972 and, five years later, was its chair. This position was quickly followed by her appointment, in 1979, as associate dean (Social Sciences) in the university's School of Graduate Studies. This lasted to 1983, at which time she became vice-provost (Arts and Sciences) of the university. She reverted to being a part-time professor when Prime Minister Pierre Trudeau summoned her to the Senate of Canada in 1984. She returned to university life full-time in 1992, first as president and vice-chancellor of Wilfrid Laurier University and, since 1997, as president and vice-chancellor of York University—which, with over 55,000 people, is Canada's second-largest English-speaking university. This brief account leaves out her many political activities, continued activism for the women's emancipation movement, and many other initiatives. The point is simply that we both found high levels of activity congenial. The conflict that can sometimes arise from asymmetrical arrangements was not part of the picture.

What was very much part of the picture was juggling difficult schedules. There was also the issue of managing more than one residence, given major obligations outside Toronto. For work reasons, we travelled a great deal—occasionally even managing to do it together. Of central importance was learning to "protect some time" for holidays and other opportunities for recuperation.

Lorna R. Marsden, president and vice-chancellor, York University.

In late 1975, I abandoned all pretense of not being bourgeois at heart by buying a house in Toronto's Rosedale neighbourhood. It seemed a bit large at the time, but we filled it up anyway. It has been our main base for nearly 30 years—large enough to bring many different projects home and located on a quiet, heavily treed ravine.

* * *

By April 1974, I had a clear sense of what my future career path would be. On the university side, I intended to maintain the level of productivity that had led to early promotion to full professor. As for department chairing, I would complete my term (in June 1976) and do whatever I could to leave the department in better circumstances than when I originally took the job. But as far as further administrative jobs were concerned, I had no interest in pursuing that type of career. For one thing, I found department chairing very time-consuming—both in terms of administration-related meetings and social events.

By this point, I had been or was currently involved in a number of policy-oriented consulting projects. I was certain that doing this type of work, given the nature of my training and experience, was the best way I could make a difference in various areas of social, institutional, and organizational change. In short, I was going to continue to have a career as a consultant as well as a career as a professor.

Effectively managing this career trajectory required a number of resources. First, I needed to continue developing my methodological and technical expertise in applied policy-oriented social research. Second, I needed to keep building my project management and client relations abilities. Although applied research and academic (or basic) research often draw upon the same intellectual resources, the circumstances of the applied setting mean that the research—compared with academic research—is typically carried out under very different constraints and pressures. Third, I needed a management model that would enable me to run the consulting practice effectively and also ensure that consulting and university work would mesh productively rather than producing situations of conflict and competition.

* * *

Sociology, particularly in combination with other disciplines like demography and economics, offers perspectives and methods directly useful to work with an applied or policy-driven agenda. To successfully conduct my university-based work and consulting activities, I found it necessary to assemble and use an ever-expanding "skill set" or "tool kit." Many different approaches were used: sometimes by themselves; sometimes in combination with one another.

My involvement with the board of directors of Pollution Probe led me, early in my career, to work on various environment-related issues. In 1972–73, I carried out a major study of air pollution for the York-Toronto Tuberculosis and Respiratory

Disease Association. As an advocacy organization, the association was seeking hard data on which it could base its ongoing lobbying activity for improved public protection standards and more effective legislation to ensure observance of such standards. A short while later (1974–75)—with Lorna Marsden as my co-investigator—I conducted a study funded by the Atkinson Foundation on public attitudes toward and prospects for greater use of recycling. Around the same time, I was engaged in studies for the City of Toronto of transportation-related noise pollution. The latter work involved collaboration with engineers who were trained and equipped to take the actual noise level measurements. No single method was appropriate to these studies. One had to draw upon a variety of perspectives and techniques, including broad-based surveys, in-depth interviews, and analysis of existing (often statistical) data. In addition, there was a frequent element of collaboration with non-social science disciplines.

In the environmental area, this multi-method, interdisciplinary work is often referred to as impact assessment. These early experiences led me to develop a particular approach to social impact assessment that I deployed in a wide variety of consulting missions. These missions included a long-term examination of oil sands development in northern Alberta, the impacts of ultra-high voltage transmission corridors on television transmission systems and reception quality, and the effects of using landfills as a solid waste-disposal strategy. In northern Alberta, I directly witnessed the social and cultural disruptions (even destructions) that accompanied rapid resource-based economic development. (Those Princeton readings on modernization assigned to me by Wilbert E. Moore came to life!) In the work on ultra-high voltage transmission corridors, I collaborated with Wasyl Janischewsky, a brilliant University of Toronto engineering professor and someone I was delighted to count among my friends.

Still on the subject of the tool kit, demographic projections became a staple of my consulting practice. A large number of clients—both in the private and public sectors—wanted to know what was happening to the population in terms of key factors like age, gender, education, income, and occupation. The ability to add detailed regional breakdowns—which I had—simply made the information more useful. The work I did with Charles

Westoff at Princeton had given me an early insight into the power of demographics, particularly when combined with computer-based analysis and large-scale data—such as the census. The fact is that whether you are seeking to market a private sector product and/or service or deliver a public sector program, information about target populations is strategic intelligence.

Economic projections and forecasts of future labour market requirements are related to demographic forecasts, given the significance that population factors have as drivers in economic and labour force processes. My interest in this line of activity dates back to economics courses I audited in the final term of my residency at Princeton. When I returned to Canada, I found an expanding interest in this area—not surprising, given the economic and employment changes the country was going through. As my work in this field evolved, I found it necessary to learn more about the complexities of econometric modelling. I developed a collaboration with K.S.R. "Ram" Murthy, a professor of economics at Trent University in Peterborough, Ontario. Ram and I worked together for many years, and he brought a high level of sophistication to the consulting missions we performed for the Technical Service Council and other organizations.

The 1960s witnessed a huge growth in the public service and a corresponding expansion in the number and types of programs delivered or available to Canadians. These developments made evaluation research an increasingly important part of the consultant's tool kit. In its most classic form, evaluation research involves one group receiving "the treatment" while another group—a control group—does not. This method is often associated with drug trials and other kinds of health care interventions. In the case of evaluating the efficacy of government programs, achieving such control is difficult at best and often impossible. But, as government programs proliferated, there were increasing demands that they be subject to evaluation in order to answer questions such as: Are they achieving their stated objectives? Do the benefits justify the costs? How lasting are the benefits? Do the programs require modification or replacement with more effective initiatives? As with social impact assessment, program evaluation is a multi-method approach and often crosses disciplinary boundaries.

Over the years, I have engaged in a wide range of program evaluations, including assessments of job creation programs, quality of working life programs, and specifically targeted initiatives designed to advance certain groups (e.g., women, racial minorities, persons with disabilities) in terms of educational and employment opportunity. Evaluation research has many complexities, but the two aspects I found most challenging were: (1) achieving some sort of "control" effect, so one can determine if it really is the program (rather than something else) that is making the difference; (2) enlisting the genuine co-operation of program officials (whose future career trajectories sometimes depended on evaluation outcomes).

Another crucial method for any applied social researcher is secondary analysis or data mining. Although Statistics Canada is the most notable example, there are many government agencies across Canada engaged in regular data gathering activity. A significant amount of these data is available for legitimate purposes—either free or at some cost. Indeed, over the more than 35 years I have used the agency as a resource, Statistics Canada has changed from being a place where there was typically no charge for information to an organization that actively markets and sells data products.

The essence of data mining is accessing existing data and then subjecting them to new or different forms of analysis to investigate the issues or questions with which one is concerned. The census of Canada is a veritable goldmine as data sources go, but there are many other resources as well. The key is to keep oneself highly informed about what kinds of data products are coming on stream and how they can be accessed. In connection with the latter point, it is important to develop working relationships with the relevant agency personnel so as to avoid wasting large amounts of time searching for the data one requires. These efforts are highly worthwhile because success means access to data of a quality and scope that no individual consultant or researcher, or even a group of consultants or researchers, could hope to gather themselves. Over the years, I have conducted many studies based on data mining. The richness of the technique is reflected in the range of program and policy issues addressed, including studies of labour market and educational trends and emerging requirements, immigration patterns and related policy issues, health care and income distribution concerns, and tracking over time the social and economic progress (or lack of progress) of certain traditionally disadvantaged groups in Canadian society. With the direct costs of primary research constantly rising, data mining presents a cost-effective and high-quality alternative. I believe it has a great future.

With each passing year, all organizations—in both the private and public sectors—face an increasingly complex operating environment. Apart from competitive pressures and regulatory obligations, organizations are bombarded (as, indeed, are all of us) with vast amounts of information on practically every conceivable topic. The challenge can be summed up by two admittedly oversimplified questions: What's important and what isn't? What needs to be acted upon and what doesn't? Enter environmental scanning, another crucial resource for organizational operations and the consultant's tool kit.

Figure 1 presents a basic schematic for an environmental scanning system. The approach begins with the eminently reasonable assumption that all organizations face change in their operating environments—competition, regulation, market shifts, and so on. A key first step is for the consultants to meet with organizational management to identify and conceptualize for the organization the key issues generated by environmental change. It then becomes possible to design and operationalize a systematic procedure for defining what the key information needs (or data elements) are and put in place regularized procedures to ensure they are captured. Such data must, of course, be analysed in terms of the organization's mission and operating environment challenges. The zones of interpretation represent a menu of issue areas in which such analysis takes place while recognizing that the zones may change over time. The inclusion of the geographical aggregates component is simply a recognition that many organizations operate in many different locations and that analysis and interpretation must be attuned to such locational differences. The analysis must then be interfaced with existing organizational policies and practices to assess if modifications or whole new approaches are required. The results of this process

Figure 1: An Environmental Trends Information System (ETIS)

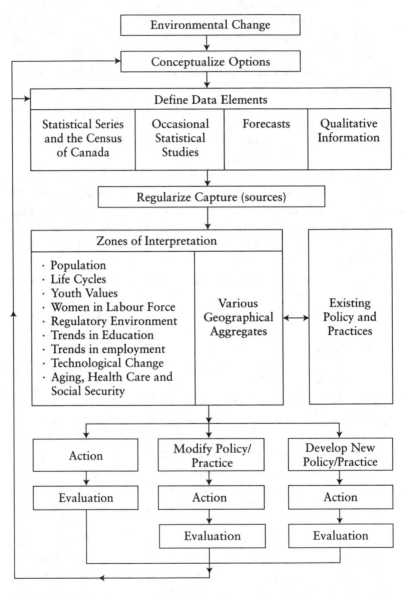

Source: Edward B. Harvey, *Information Systems for Employment Equity:
An Employer Guide* (Toronto: CCH Canadian Publishers, 1988), p. 103.
Copyright CCH Canadian Limited, Toronto, Ontario. Reproduced with
permission.

feed back to the earlier stages of issue identification and defining critical informational/data needs.

In a 1986 study for IBM Canada, I developed this model in collaboration with Lorne Tepperman, a long-time colleague in the University of Toronto sociology department. Lorne and I have collaborated on various projects, to which he has always brought a first-rate analytical intelligence and lively appreciation of reality factors. The environmental scanning model has continued to evolve over the past 14 years but remains an important part of my consultant's tool kit.

Whether the work was university-based or consulting, I have found survey research to be the single most useful method for addressing practical problems and policy-oriented issues. Surveys can be conducted in a number of ways, including by mail (both conventional and electronic), by telephone, and by bringing people together in a group setting for the purposes of survey administration. Surveys can also be based on personal face-to-face interviews, but this technique is seldom used in large-scale initiatives because of the very large cost involved. I have found personal face-to-face interviews of great help in two specific applications. First, they can be used in relatively small-scale exploratory studies designed to help develop a large-scale, broadly based survey. Second, such interviews can also be used very effectively after a large-scale survey has been done to "get behind the numbers" and provide interpretive insights into the statistical results of the broadly based survey.

Surveys, of course, can be combined with a variety of other methods, and this is often done in applied or policy-oriented work. The bottom-line appeal of surveys is the way in which they enable a researcher to gather a large amount of information in a relatively cost-effective way. Of the more than 150 surveys I have directed, some have been wide-ranging national initiatives involving considerable staff and extensive coordination; others have been targeted on specific applied and/or policy issues. Regardless of the scale or focus involved, survey research methods are a fundamental part of the applied/policy researcher's tool kit.

In applied or policy-oriented social research, I have often found it useful to use the various methods I have been describing in conjunction with certain analytical techniques from other disciplines. These include demographic forecasts or projections, economic forecasts or projections, cost-benefit analysis, labour market flows analysis, and return on investment analysis. The particular mix of methods being used will vary greatly with the nature of the problems or issues being dealt with. Fundamentally, the most important consideration is to have a flexible outlook. One simply cannot afford to be methodologically doctrinaire in applied and/or policy-oriented work.

* * *

The preceding, then, are some of the approaches I have found particularly useful for the performance of work oriented toward practical problems and policy issues. As noted, many of them are multi-method and interdisciplinary in nature—essential features given the nature of the issues they are used to address. However, there are many other important components of the consultant's tool kit, and these are not typically dealt with in the methodology textbooks. In my case, I learned them from experience. I describe these other components below.

There are several considerations that must be taken into account when defining a problem to be investigated in the applied setting. It is essential that the problem or issue be investigated in such a way that the results will be of practical use to the sponsoring organization or client. In addition, the problem or issue must be defined in such a way that the research will actually be feasible in terms of such reality factors as the availability of information, time pressures, and costs. Academics engaged in basic research can afford to go on "fishing expeditions" and, indeed, such an approach can produce important results. Clients facing serious problems or issues, however, are simply not prepared to accept uncertainty about outcomes.

In such circumstances, it is important to recognize that compromises will be inevitable. The successful applied social researcher will have the skill and insight to achieve the optimal match between strong, effective research methods and the realities of practical constraints and pressures. Achieving this outcome is complicated by the fact that the problems or issues being addressed are almost invariably interdisciplinary in nature. A further complication arises from the fact that many of the people one works with in the client organization have little knowledge of social science methods. Accordingly, the effective applied social researcher will quickly banish jargon from his or her vocabulary and develop a large inventory of plain-language explanations and examples that can be used to communicate effectively with diverse groups. Even so, the applied social researcher is likely to encounter different interpretations of how the problems or issues should be defined. In part, this is because of the different training and experiences people bring to the table. In addition, it may also arise from differences between people's private versus their "official" agendas. The applied social researcher needs to be a good communicator and negotiator to help forge broadly acceptable but fundamentally accurate problem definitions.

Unlike the academic researcher in the social sciences, the applied social researcher has a more limited range of factors or variables to work with. This is because in the applied or policy setting only certain factors are legitimate or effective levers of change, given the realities of legal regulations and organizational culture. Simply here is no point in wasting time and resources gathering information on factors outside the realm of feasible action. It is also of central importance that the original definition of the problem or issue be explicitly linked to an overall coherent work plan for the accomplishment of the research and its implementation.

In applied social research, one does not have the option of making it up as one goes along or retracing flawed steps. Milestones must be clear, feasible, and achieved on time and within budget. It is of the greatest importance that the process of defining the problems or issues establish for the client a set of realistic expectations of what the program of work will accomplish. It is a sure path to failure to enter into a definition of the problem that leads the client to expect outcomes that are not achievable in terms of the timetable and budget or, even worse, not achievable at all. This is sometimes called "managing client expectations." It is important to recognize that it is a process that goes on for the life of the project, given the fluidity and frequent change that typically characterizes the applied setting.

Assuming that problem definition and data gathering have been successfully achieved, the applied social researcher then faces the challenge of analysing the results and translating them into a practical, feasible framework for action. For every practical problem a client faces, there is a related realm of probable/feasible action. There is no point in carrying out analyses and making recommendations for courses of action that cannot—or will not—be acted upon.

By their very nature, data vary in quality. The higher the data quality, the greater the confidence one can typically have in the results. But higher levels of data quality (with associated higher levels of confidence) come with a cost. It is important that the applied social researcher help the client understand this cost/efficiency trade-off. If the actions to be based on the results are highly critical, then it is only prudent to invest more resources in the scope and quality of the data gathered.

I have already noted that in many client organizations, the applied social researcher will work with people who do not have a social science background. This reality needs to be taken into account when presenting results in reports or briefings. Overall, there is great merit in keeping it simple without being simplistic. One example of this is using plain language rather than jargon. Put, the

There is also the issue of how the applied social researcher handles statistical data. People vary widely in their numeracy skills and their understanding of—or even interest in—statistical analysis. In this connection, I have found graphics invaluable. Straightforward and clear presentations of data—such as bar charts and pie diagrams—are readily understood by most people and help the applied social researcher get the message across. Of course, one also gives the client the full statistical background material but, in my experience, this is usually only of interest to a small handful of technicians who typically do not make policy decisions. Also, the more user-friendly one can make reports and presentations, the better. By this I mean such things as readable type, good formatting, and the creative use of graphics and colour.

In fact, the applied social researcher's reports and presentations are directed to three distinctly different audiences in the client organization: top management, middle management, and technical staff. Top management is interested in the big picture and brevity. Lengthy and complicated presentations are not a good idea at this level. Middle management is interested in operational substance.

What does it all mean for such issues as the day-to-day running of the organization and program structure? Technicians are, not surprisingly, interested in techniques. They will have questions about the robustness of the data and the appropriateness of the methods used. A well-organized report will serve all three audiences by including a brief, clear executive summary for top management, a substantively strong main body of the report for middle management, and detailed appendices for the technicians.

Typically, the applied social researcher's work does not end with the analysis of the information gathered and the presentation of results. The applied social researcher also has an important task to perform in translating the results into forward action recommendations for the client organization. Doing this requires a solid understanding of the organization's structure *and* process, as well as knowing where the organization is endeavouring to go in the future. The best way for the consultant or consultants to acquire this type of understanding is to work with a project steering committee whose members come from various key areas of the client organization.

In their operations, such steering committees provide a two-way learning mechanism that leads the consultants and the organizational members to shared definitions and understandings of the situation. The existence of such a steering committee also contributes to organizational "buy-in" of the consultant's report and recommendations. The committee also provides a broader base of organizational legitimacy for the implementation of recommendations and related actions.

Finally, it is important that both consultants and clients understand the reality of "weak effects" in the realm of social and organizational change. In some fields (certain areas of medicine, for example), interventions can produce rapid positive change. Generally, human society does not work that way. Change is typically slow and incremental. This is particularly true when one is working at the institutional level. Quite deliberately, social institutions incorporate various mechanisms to foster stability and continuity. While these are clearly important, they can also impede or slow the introduction and acceptance of needed adaptations.

* * *

Sometimes the consultant's mission ends when the final report and its recommendations are handed in and the final briefings given. But in other instances the consultant carries on, becoming involved in the implementation of recommendations for action.

The effective implementation of organizational change is affected by a number of factors. First, I have never encountered an organization where there is a single agent of change. Even powerful C.E.O.s rule through a process of consultation and consent. In short, effective change (the kind that takes hold) is almost always negotiated, not ordered.

In my consulting missions, I have found an applied social research and policy background very helpful in understanding the sociopolitical dynamics of a given organizational or institutional change situation. Developing such an analysis is of great help in identifying the forces for, and the impediments against, the implementation of change. It is of direct practical use in putting together the kinds of coalitions that are needed to drive change forward. Doing this is complicated by the realities of personnel turnover and change in fluid situations and by the fact that much human behaviour is inherently conservative—most people do not eagerly embrace change.

The consultant with an understanding of such social dynamics can make a positive contribution to the change implementation process. For example, when recommendations are set forward in the consultant report, care should be taken to ensure that some of the recommendations are of the type that can be implemented relatively quickly with a high probability of success. This contributes to "a climate of achievement," which provides a solid foundation and positive incentives for tackling the more complex and difficult-to-implement recommendations. To paraphrase an old cliché, even organizations have to walk before they can run.

* * *

What, then, are the attributes of an effective applied social researcher/policy consultant? First, such a person needs a practical tool kit of flexible, multi-method, interdisciplinary strategies for problem definition, data gathering, and analysis. He or she has to be good at communicating, negotiating, and working with diverse groups of people. In addition, he or she has to understand how organizations and institutions work—both formally *and* informally—and how to connect research results to practical agendas for change and innovation.

How does one prepare to do such work? In my case, I feel fortunate that the doctoral program at Princeton encouraged a flexible and interdisciplinary outlook. I obtained a solid foundation in sociology but also had important exposure to ideas from economics and demography. Most important, the nature of the experience was such that it encouraged continued learning in all these areas—and others—long after I had earned my doctorate.

As for the type of sociological work I pursued during my preparatory years, it was heavily focused on how organizations and institutions worked, on the nature of policy (including its development and change), and the acquisition of strong technical skills in a variety of research methods and statistical analysis. I was, and continue to be, interested in the practical, hard-nosed side of the discipline.

I have heard some colleagues dismiss applied social research as "anti-theory." This, simply put, is nonsense. Applied social research and policy work is typically a rapid-response business. The "I need it yesterday" syndrome is widespread. When attempting to devise research strategies—on which important decisions will be based—and get the work done in a timely fashion, it is vitally important to have some well-established prior ideas about what is likely to work (and what isn't). That is where theory comes in. It provides an intellectual foundation for determining the most promising research directions. It provides a means for developing a coherent conceptual framework for tying together the many disparate elements of the applied research process. Princeton placed strong emphasis on the acquisition of theoretical and logical capabilities. Put another way, it taught me how to build frames of reference. It continues to be useful on a daily basis.

Good writing and computer skills are vital in a wide range of fields today, and applied social research and policy work is no exception. But beyond these matters of technique, the successful consultant must have well-developed skills in the "presentation of self" department. It is essential to make a connection with the culture of the client organization. Being a detached technician never works. Even worse is the "I'm a learned professor and I'm here to help you" syndrome. It isn't that clients don't appreciate learning—they do. But you have to let them appreciate it in their own way, on their own terms.

* * *

The decision to incorporate my consulting practice, which came to fruition in April 1974, was driven by several factors. The practice was now well established, had grown considerably, and was showing prospects of solid future growth. I needed a proper legal framework for managing the practice and dealing in a systematic way with various matters relating to taxes, payroll, subcontractors, and the like. Having a corporate identity was likely to be useful in terms of marketing consulting services and building up a business reputation for performance and reliability. As a result of my involvement with Population Research Foundation—the foundation Rob Mills and I had conceived of—I now had two years of direct experience with corporate structure and process. Also, chairing a university department was providing me with useful additional experiences in such areas as personnel, budgets, and project management. I discussed all of this with my lawyer, Clay Hudson, and he agreed that incorporation was a sound move.

Of course, a corporation is just a legal framework until it has been energized by a business model. I was fortunate in not having to deal with start-up challenges such as extensive marketing or promotion. When I had returned to Canada in 1966, the country was undergoing rapid change. Sustained economic growth was enabling governments—both provincial and federal—to make huge investments in physical and social infrastructure. New initiatives and programs were emerging with great regularity, spawning new research needs and consulting opportunities. As for my particular corner of the market, there were very few people around with doctorates from top institutions, considerable training in practical research techniques and policy analysis, and several years of research and consulting experience. I was also fortunate to be in Toronto, which was expanding very rapidly and was only a short flight away from Ottawa, an increasingly frequent destination for me.

In this environment, most of my consulting work came from referrals. Some of it came from people reading something I had written or hearing me speak at a conference or similar event. I realized that there were three keys to getting referrals: doing good work for the client whether the job was small or large, not missing deadlines, and keeping within budget. I continued to write academically oriented books and papers but also began to write much more for broader audiences. The freedom to do the latter was one of the benefits of full professorship. In addition, I believed—as I do today—that it is in the best interests of universities to build bridges to other parts of the larger community. I could see the importance of building, maintaining, and extending networks of contact. I became increasingly involved in public speaking and attended a greater number of non-academic conferences.

Finding a niche and building a network are important parts of the business model, but there are others as well. In my experience, I have found seven additional guiding principles very helpful.

First, the time to market or develop new projects is when the practice is busy. Waiting until the work on hand is done before developing new opportunities will inevitably lead to a period of having no work to do. Among other things, this creates serious problems for cash flow planning and maintaining the motivation and activity levels of the people with whom one is working.

Second, it is important to keep the overheads of the consulting practice low and flexible. It is true, for example, that travel and face-to-face meetings are an important part of the consulting business. However, in some instances, certain cost- and time-saving alternatives may work just as well. These include the use of conference calls and, particularly during the last decade, electronic mail, with its speed and convenience. Cost savings and flexibility can also be realized by avoiding fixed overheads—such as payroll obligations. A better way is to arrange subcontracts with the individuals or organizations whose help will be needed on a given project. This approach allows the practice to quickly "scale up" or "scale down" in response to workload variations and the effects of the business cycle.

Third, it is important that the owner/manager of the consulting practice have direct involvement in the financial operations of the enterprise. There is no better way of getting a handle on where the business is and where it is going. When Rob Mills and I created the Population Research Foundation, the fine old Toronto firm of Clarkson Gordon agreed to serve as our auditors. At the end of the foundation's first fiscal year, I assembled the financial records and took them to a meeting with Geoff Clarkson at the firm's downtown Toronto offices. At that time, I had a number of things on my mind and my financial record keeping for the foundation had been less than perfect. Geoff Clarkson looked at the material, shaking his head almost imperceptibly. He didn't become upset. He took an hour to calmly and carefully take me through the steps of establishing a rational system of accounts. I took notes. I have never forgotten that meeting and the blueprint it gave me for proper financial management of all my subsequent business activities. Two years later, the low-key and gentlemanly Clarkson paid me the ultimate compliment: "You keep good records." He could have quite properly ended his sentence with the word "now."

Fourth, it is of great importance that the owner/manager of the consulting operation practise good labour relations. By this, I mean such things as recognizing that the people with whom one is working have lives and responsibilities of their own. It also means paying people fairly and on time. And it includes sharing the credit for the work done by such mechanisms as co-authorship recognition in consultant reports and related publications.

In 1981, my company won a contract from the Department of National Defence for a large national study of how young people felt about educational opportunities sponsored by the Canadian Forces. I needed a national research coordinator who could travel all over the country. John Blakely became that person. I had the good fortune to meet him through my involvement with the University of Toronto's Centre for Industrial Relations, where John had just completed a master's degree in industrial relations. Twenty-four years later, John and I continue to work together, having collaborated over the years on countless projects and co-authored five books and many articles. Although John is the record holder, there have been a number of other people who have worked with me for many years. Such stability is a definite business advantage. In addition, when people work together over a longer term, they have more opportunity to learn from one

John H. Blakely, c. 2002.

another, something that invariably results in the consulting practice producing better quality work for its clients.

Fifth, it is of central importance to maintain good client relations and communications. It is a very ill-advised strategy to get the contract, disappear, and then show up with the final report. By paying for the project, clients have earned the right to regular briefings, particularly at critical points. They have also earned the right to raise questions and make suggestions—things the consultant is well advised to take very seriously. Regular, effective communication is beneficial to both the client and the consultant. Its consequences include a much greater probability of a shared understanding of what is being done and enhancing the prospect that the work performed will be viewed as successful and worthy of implementation into organizational practice.

Sixth, I have found that one of the most effective ways a consulting practice can expand its business base and range of services—without incurring additional fixed overheads—is to enter into strategic alliances with other consultants or consulting firms. Over a period of 10 years, I became significantly involved in various studies of the public library sector. The purpose of the projects was to gather and analyse data that would improve library service delivery systems and make libraries more relevant and more interesting to their surrounding communities. Associated questions included how libraries should be organized and how staff should be trained to realize these objectives.

I was comfortable with the organizational design and data gathering/analysis components of the work, but was not overly familiar with the intricacies of the public library system and the training of library staff. Fortunately, I knew Dr. Anne Woodsworth, a person who had held senior positions in the library sector and had her own consulting firm. We formed a strategic alliance that proved highly successful. Indeed, when the Canadian Library Association put out tenders for a large-scale national study of the current status of and future directions for the Canadian public library service, our alliance—despite stiff competition from some very large consulting firms—won the contract. The alliance ended only when Anne received an offer she couldn't refuse from a prestigious U.S. university to serve as its dean of library science.

Another strategic alliance, which lasted seven years, was with Stephen Gibson, an Osgoode Hall graduate who specialized in labour and employment law. Instead of practising law, Stephen turned his considerable talents to creating publishing companies, initially focused on law-related materials. We met, in late 1989, when he became interested in diversifying his activities to include publications dealing with the implications for employers of employment equity legislation and regulation. My work for Judge Rosalie Abella's Royal Commission on Equality in Employment (1983–84) had given me a large strategic advantage, and my consulting firm was now deeply involved in all aspects of employment equity implementation in both private and public sector settings. The alliance with Stephen resulted in further expansion and growth. We created the *Employment Equity Review*,[49] a monthly publication containing expert opinion and information related to employment equity and its implementation. We also developed a program of regular two-day-long conferences on employment equity. These conferences attracted a wide range of human resources professionals from both the private and public sectors. In many cases, their organizations became clients for specific employment equity implementation projects. The alliance eventually came to an amiable conclusion when Stephen moved to the U.S. to pursue expanded opportunities, which he has realized in the dynamic Boston-centred marketplace. Apart from the obvious business benefits, strategic alliances are, in the most positive sense, mind-expanding experiences.

Seventh, operating a successful consulting practice is greatly helped by four kinds of mental outlook. An enthusiasm for continued learning, upgrading, and adaptation is highly important. So is an entrepreneurial attitude. Specifically, it is important to view new developments as opportunities, not problems. It is extremely helpful to have a flexible style, in both intellectual and personal terms. Such an outlook makes boundary-crossing activities easier and facilitates working effectively with people from a wide variety of backgrounds. Finally, it is important to cultivate a capacity for working on several tasks simultaneously. Unlike a sustained basic research project, consulting typically involves moving back and forth among projects, often within very tight time frames.

* * *

My consulting practice is now in its thirty-first year as an incorporated entity. It is not my intention here to even attempt to summarize the experiences of such a long period of time. However, there are a few broad themes that capture important elements of the experience.

One of the things that made the consulting practice interesting in a sustained way was the great variety—and constant change over time—in the missions it undertook to perform. Consulting is a bit like being on a perpetual learning curve, and sometimes the new assignments can be very challenging. However, if one prevails in the business, one does learn how to routinize some tasks and also how to identify "adaptation and transfer" opportunities; in plain language, this simply means being able to see how strategies that worked in earlier projects can be adapted to the needs of new missions. One of the very best features of consulting work is the variety. It is difficult to become bored.

Over the years, governments have come and gone and policy-making strategies have changed. I have to say that none of this ever made much difference to my consulting practice, although, of course, the practice adapted quickly to the new areas of opportunity. It would appear that there is always a market for technically sound work, delivered on time, and within budget.

Throughout my university career, my focus has been on applied social research and policy studies. Most of my university research falls into this category. As for my teaching, it is focused on giving students the skills to do applied social research and policy analysis and, more specifically, on preparing practitioners in such areas as equity and diversity management in organizations. Much of my consulting work found its way into my teaching and publishing activities. In a reciprocal way, the intellectual discipline involved in teaching senior undergraduates and graduate students and publishing books and articles made important contributions to the conceptual capital of the consulting practice.

What are my personal feelings about a career that combines professing and consulting? First, the two kinds of work energized one another. Second, I found a real sense of personal efficacy on those occasions when the tools and understandings of applied social research made a difference to institutional policy or organization practice. Third, as I have suggested earlier, the sheer range of problems to be addressed was endlessly interesting. Finally, consulting missions provided expanded opportunities to meet and work with many gifted people: great legal intellects like Judge Rosalie Abella, international policy thinkers like Senator Jack Austin, visionary medical educators like Dr. Andrew Hunter, and many others.

* * *

As I noted in my introduction to Part II of this book, my consulting work falls into three broad categories: royal commissions and task forces, assignments for governments and the broader public sector, and projects for the private sector. In the following three chapters, I will look at each of these areas in turn, examine some of their cultural and institutional differences, and discuss certain of the works for which I was the sole consultant or on which I took the lead.

CHAPTER 8

Consulting to Royal Commissions and Task Forces

In Canada, when large-scale policy change or innovation is contemplated, royal commissions (or, more simply, just "commissions") are frequently created by governments to help guide the process. Commissions can vary from undertakings involving several commissioners to initiatives under the direction of a single commissioner. Commissions do not make policy. They make recommendations about policy directions to elected officials in government. Typically, task forces—compared to commissions—are smaller, shorter-term, and more flexible mechanisms for the investigation of policy issues and the making of recommendations to elected officials in government.

Commissions have a long history in Canada and, over time, have addressed a wide range of issues fundamental to our society, including the development of a national health care system, bilingualism and biculturalism, economic growth and its management, and equality in employment. Task forces are more likely to be used after broad new policy directions have been established and further fine-tuning or evaluation is required.

Commissions typically involve extensive and carefully designed supportive research. They also typically involve a broadly based public consultation process. In the case of commissions involving several commissioners, the commissioners are selected to ensure effective representation of different groups and sectors having an interest in the policy area under examination. These steps are taken to maximize the prospects for broad-based acceptance of commission recommendations rather than creation of protracted conflict. This is consistent with the Canadian approach to managing social change. As Lorna Marsden and I observed in our 1979 book titled *Fragile Federation*, the Fathers of the Canadian Confederation wanted to achieve for Canada the "sense of continuity, the capacity for slow and secure change, and the protection of minority rights and social diversities" which characterized the British parliamentary system. "Slow and secure change" has consistently characterized Canadian society.[50]

Governments establish commissions in response to various factors that may include, for example, economic change, demographic factors, technological developments, and the impact of international trends. In some cases, commissions represent a response to changing public expectations as expressed through the operation of interest groups. In other instances, the impetus for commissions is elite-driven, emanating from government circles or, in some cases, initiated by an individual minister of the Crown.

In my experience, commissions and task forces typically draw heavily on applied, policy-oriented social research. If that capability is augmented by an understanding of policy-oriented economics and demography, so much the better. Much of this work is contracted out to expert consultants, partly for reasons of external, objective credibility and partly because commissions and task forces are seldom self-sufficient in terms of such research needs. I have invariably found commission and task force work to be of the greatest interest. One reason for this is the social and/or institutional importance of the work. Another reason is that such work frequently provides a direct path for bringing applied research to bear on matters of national importance. What follows illustrates the types of task forces and commissions in operation in Canada from the mid-1960s to the present day, and in doing so shows how, as an applied researcher, I was able to contribute to the building of policy in Canada.

* * *

The Ontario Medical Manpower Project, 1967–72, which I co-directed with Dr. Andrew Hunter, was essentially a task force, although one slightly irate faculty of medicine dean once characterized it as a "two-person Royal Commission of Inquiry into the Medical Profession." The idea for the six-year long initiative was first championed by Andy Hunter but soon found a highly receptive audience at the Ontario Ministry of Health. We certainly behaved like a task force or commission—conducting research, consulting various constituencies, writing and publishing reports, making public presentations, and—of central importance—putting forward recommendations for action. As the project evolved, the Ontario Ministry of Health made greater use of it as a source of information on various policy issues and questions.

The Ontario Medical Manpower Project was my initiation into commission and task force work, and it proved to be an excellent foundation for what was to follow. For one thing, I learned how to deal with a disparate group of people, including general practitioners, specialists, medical educators, and government health officials. Because of Andy Hunter's reputation in medicine, I also learned how important it is to work with specialists respected by their colleagues. The project also provided an opportunity to discover and develop ways of convincing a sometimes skeptical, hard-science–oriented audience that applied, policy-oriented social research could also be rigorous and relevant.

The 1968–71 Commission on Pharmaceutical Services came along while I was still deeply engaged with the Ontario Medical Manpower Project. Fortunately, the latter had been in operation long enough to provide something of an experiential base for the new assignment. In addition, I had the added advantage of having done consulting work on related issues for the British Columbia Pharmaceutical Association while still a graduate student at the University of British Columbia. Like the Ontario Medical Manpower Project, the Commission on Pharmaceutical Services also involved a great deal of research, but this time on a national—rather than provincial—scale. The Pharmaceutical Services Commission was my introduction to managing a Canada-wide project and it produced a number of new challenges, including cross-country coordination and training of research staff and establishment of a French-language research operation in Quebec. Many of my subsequent assignments were national in scale, and the Quebec contacts and operational knowledge I acquired through the Pharmaceutical Services Commission proved invaluable in later work.

The commission itself was large and complex, and I was able to work with a team of researchers in different fields. On the social science side, the commission had attracted the involvement of Oswald Hall, one of my colleagues at the University of Toronto's department of sociology, and also Bruce McFarlane, a professor of sociology at Carleton University. The commission had also hired a full-time research assistant, George Torrance, who some years later went on to complete a doctorate in sociology at the University of Toronto. In addition, the commission was fortunate to have the participation of Dr. John Bachynsky of the Research and Statistics Directorate of the federal Department of Health and Welfare. John had the ability to work effectively with pharmaceutical, social science, and public policy perspectives and contributed significantly to the development of the commission's synthesis of the issues. As well, the commission involved a wide range of talent from the profession of pharmacy. Harold Segal, now a professor of pharmacy at the University of Toronto, served as a full-time research assistant working closely with George Torrance. Ross Baxter, a senior professor at the University of Toronto's Faculty of Pharmacy, brought a wide-ranging and in-depth view of pharmacy and was always available for consultation. In the field work part of the commission, the varied group of people involved included retail pharmacy owners, pharmacist employees, pharmacy educators, and students.

Both the Ontario Medical Manpower Project and the Commission on Pharmaceutical Services grew out of the highly significant 1964 Royal Commission on Health Services, led by Mr. Justice Emmett M. Hall. This commission provided the foundation for sweeping changes in Canada's health care system. Despite rising costs and other policy challenges, our national health care system is a central pillar of Canadian society, a society that has thus far avoided the excesses of being driven mostly by market forces. Medicare is now so much a part of the national landscape that many Canadians nowadays have neither experience nor recollection of the unjust system it replaced—a system where the health of many ordinary working Canadians suffered because a visit to the doctor cost money they didn't have.

Similarly, many Canadians have no knowledge of the struggle to implement national health care in the face of scare-tactic campaigns by the private insurance industry and some physicians who preferred to look back rather than forward. But medicare was implemented, and initiatives such as the Ontario Medical Manpower Project and the Commission on Pharmaceutical Services were simply examples of the post-Royal Commission on Health Services activities designed to fine-tune aspects of the new Canadian health care system. It was a privilege to be a part of that process.

* * *

Driven by baby boom demographics and a growing demand for more highly educated workers, the 1960s in Canada witnessed a huge expansion of enrolments and expenditures in the education sector. Over the decade of the 1960s, education spending practically doubled—rising from 4.5 percent of Gross National Product (GNP) in 1960 to 8.8 percent of GNP by the end of 1969. University enrolments alone increased by 213 percent between 1961 and 1971, an average annual growth rate of 11 percent. In the province of Ontario, 21 community colleges were created and several new universities opened.[51]

After such a period of dramatic expansion, it is not unusual for the policy area in question to enter a period of consolidation and assessment. The Commission on Post-Secondary Education in Ontario (COPSE), which I served between 1970 and 1971, clearly fitted this model. When I had my first discussion with the commission's leader, Dr. Douglas Wright, we agreed that the rapid expansion had produced much that was good but that some post-expansion concerns appeared to be emerging, such as changes in the employment patterns of undergraduate degree holders. The problem was that none of us had any hard data. Hence the need for rigorous, data-intensive projects that would have to be completed on very tight timetables. As I have indicated elsewhere in this book, the Commission on Post-Secondary Education led to large-scale research, policy insights, substantial publications, and considerable subsequent work—both national and international in scope. The results of this work have been described elsewhere in my publications and those of many colleagues and have led to a much more sophisticated approach to the study of higher education and its relationship to the economy. The same concerns prevail today, and researchers will build on that earlier work.

One of the downstream activities the Commission on Post-Secondary Education led to was a 1975 invitation from the Honourable J.S.G. "Bud" Cullen, the then-minister of employment and immigration, to join a ministerial working party on youth unemployment. Because of the number of people and jurisdictions involved, it was substantially more complex than a task force. However, the minister had stopped short of establishing the full paraphernalia of a formal commission. I believe this decision had been taken to maximize policy flexibility in dealing with a problem of national consequence that was highly variable in regional terms. For this reason, great care was taken to ensure regional representation on the working party. Diverse sectors were also involved, including employers, universities, colleges, secondary education institutions, trade unions, and student organizations.

My role was to represent the university sector and provide input as a person much involved with research on the changing linkage between educational systems and the labour market. A great many meetings were held and, as the process unfolded, it was clear the working party had a major challenge in shaping a diverse—and often competing—set of interests into a viable compromise that could provide a basis for policy and program action. Bud Cullen, who was trained as a lawyer, was skilful at making this happen. He had a low-key, pleasant manner and listened carefully. When he intervened, it was usually to draw people out or identify points of commonality.

Depending on a given meeting's agenda, different members of the minister's senior political staff and senior civil servants would be involved. The primary role of the public servants was to describe and discuss existing program initiatives targeted on youth employment issues. We members of the working party reacted to these presentations in different ways, and out of this dialogue there emerged many proposals for policy and program change. I could see and hear the process by which the minister and his political staff evaluated the political feasibility of these proposals and considered complex issues of maintaining regional and sectoral balance. It was fascinating to observe this interplay of interest groups, the minister, political staff, and public servants in the forging of new approaches to public policy and programming in an area of critical importance.

One of the things the working party asked me to do was carry out a national study of 1976 university graduates. Among other things, the study was designed to assess the efficacy of existing federal job-creation programs for university-educated young people and suggest possible improvements. By now, I had data on graduates from 1960, 1964, 1968 (the COPSE research), and 1972 (a post-COPSE study commissioned by the province of Ontario). The addition of data for 1976 provided detailed information on the education, employment, and unemployment (including underemployment) experiences of thousands of graduates representing five cohorts over a critically important 16-year period. The data proved a significant asset for policy thinking and program development.

As for the working party, it wound down after two years, having provided the minister, his political and public service staff, and Canadian society generally with a better set of tools and understandings to manage a major problem of the times.

* * *

In 1980, the then-minister of employment and immigration, Lloyd Axworthy, asked me to take a lead role in the Task Force on Immigration Practices and Procedures. As a nation, Canada has always been significantly dependent on immigrants to help meet its labour market needs. In addition to this kind of "economic" immigration, Canada also has well-established programs in the immigration area for such purposes as family reunification, opening its doors to refugees from political oppression, and encouraging the immigration of entrepreneurs who will create businesses and jobs.

Over the years, Canada has benefited both economically and socially from immigration. The nature of this immigration has changed over time. After World War II, immigration from western Europe was common. The pattern then shifted to

Lloyd Axworthy and Edward B. Harvey, 2002.

immigration from southern Europe. Over the past two decades, an increasing number of immigrants to Canada have come from the developing countries of the world. In addition, the nation's immigrant needs (particularly in the economic area) have varied over time, depending on the state of the economy, the labour market, and other factors.

In establishing the task force in question, Minister Axworthy felt the time had come for a detailed, data-based look at immigration practices and procedures and the formulation of specific recommendations for future directions. I took responsibility for designing and carrying out two major surveys: one of a cross-section of organizations that were significant employers of immigrants; the other, a broadly based survey of immigrant and visa workers. In addition to the survey initiatives, interviews were conducted with people in sectors having immigration-related interests. These included educators, representatives of provincial governments, and persons associated with immigrant advocacy organizations. I was also provided with considerable data on entrepreneur-class immigrants that had been gathered by officials of Employment and Immigration Canada.

The analysis of these various types of data resulted in the development of an overall framework that could then be used to analyse and assess existing immigration practices and procedures. These processes resulted in a number of recommendations for change that fell into several broad areas. There was clearly a need to introduce changes that would make immigration a more effective tool for meeting the skilled labour requirements of a wide range of employers across Canada.

Various new measures were introduced, including reducing the paperwork burden for employers, speeding up the process by which employers could get the skilled immigrant workers they needed, generally improving communication between employers and Employment and Immigration Canada, and providing better information to overseas consulates to improve staff awareness of skilled workers needs in Canada. A number of improvements were also introduced to provide immigrants with more effective settlement services that would facilitate their social and economic integration.

As for the entrepreneurial immigration program, the review and analysis indicated that it was generally successful in meeting the objective of creating viable businesses and associated employment opportunities. Procedural improvements included tightening up communication between federal and provincial authorities so that the latter could respond more quickly and effectively to the settlement needs of entrepreneur immigrants. Steps were also taken to ensure that overseas consulates pursued consistent practices in the granting of temporary admissions to Canada for entrepreneur-class immigrants, a practice that contributed to the success of the program.

The employment and immigration ministry has always been a difficult one partly because of the truly complex nature of the work. Provinces, cities, employers, social service agencies, foreign governments, and many branches of the federal government all interact with immigrants and refugees who are often frightened, exhausted, confused, and desperate to get a foothold in Canadian society. Lloyd Axworthy is a people person. He was committed to ensuring that good opportunities existed and that fairness prevailed in the system. He visited immigration offices all over the developing countries from which we were receiving immigrants and spoke passionately about the issues. He reached out to individuals and fervently wanted those of us working on the task force to "get it right." One of the key differences between these assignments for task forces and commissions and other work in the public sector and for private companies is the leadership of a minister or a commissioner, that is, someone with a personal interest in the pursuit of an idea. The personality and interests of the minister matter, and the goal is better policy or practice rather than greater profit or regulatory compliance.

The Task Force on Immigration Practices and Procedures produced three reports and many briefings, and it provided an important foundation for subsequent work I did on immigration issues.

* * *

My work on labour markets, which began in 1970, led me to an early interest in gender differences in employment opportunity, and part of my academic research and writing was focused on this area of enquiry. In 1977, the Ontario Ministry of Labour opened discussions with me about a consulting project that would evaluate the effectiveness of an affirmative action initiative in the Ontario Public Service that was designed to increase the numbers of women in senior management positions. At this point in history, women were very seriously underrepresented in such types of employment. It is to the credit of those senior officials in Ontario's government that this was a concern. Since the end of World War II, the federal and provincial governments had a senior person watching the situation of women in government employment, and clearly those officials—distinguished women as they were—had caught the ear of the minister.

My company was awarded the contract. In 1977, there was no affirmative action (or employment equity) legislation in Canada. In order to develop an effective analytical/evaluation model, it was first necessary to formulate a solid understanding of well-established affirmative action programs. Given the situation in Canada, that meant looking to other jurisdictions—particularly the United States, where affirmative action legislation and regulation had been in place since 1964. A detailed review of U.S. Equal Employment Opportunity documentation and discussions with senior program officials in Washington, D.C., led me to develop an approach that would use Ontario Public

Service personnel data in conjunction with advanced statistical techniques to chart over time the distribution and movement of women employed in the system. Although this project, which produced various reports and senior-level policy briefings, was neither a commission nor a task force, it provided the foundation for changes in Ontario's public service that opened up the channels to promotion for women. In addition, it provided the basis for the work my company did for the Royal Commission on Equality in Employment, led by Judge Rosalie S. Abella.

*   *   *

My work on the Ontario Public Service affirmative action program reinforced my view that Canada was long overdue for some form of affirmative action or equal employment opportunity legislation. Some argued that equality of employment opportunity could be realized by voluntary means. My experience suggested that, in the absence of statutory or regulatory measures, relatively little was likely to happen. Although I strongly believed that the labour market barriers facing women needed to be addressed, my work on immigration issues had also made it clear to me that Canada's increasing population of racial or visible minorities faced serious obstacles to equal employment opportunity. The Ontario Public Service affirmative action program work had also sharpened my view that, to be successful, Canadian equal employment opportunity policy should require employers to maintain data on their workforce demographics and periodically file reports with a regulatory agency of government. I found myself discussing these ideas with an increasingly wide range of people, particularly in government circles. These discussions left me in no doubt that pressure was building for a Canadian equal employment opportunity policy.

On June 27, 1983, a press conference was held in Ottawa at which the Honourable Lloyd Axworthy announced the formation by the federal government of the Royal Commission on Equality in Employment under the leadership of a single commissioner, Judge Rosalie Silberman Abella. The terms of reference for the commission set an October 31, 1984, reporting date.

Madam Justice Rosalie S. Abella, Supreme Court of Canada, 2004.

Judge Abella was a leading personality in the Toronto social scene and a legal intellectual of the first rank. We had an acquaintance already, and it was clear we shared many of the same values. We met on August 4, 1983, at the offices of her commission. We had a wide-ranging discussion about equal employment opportunity issues, and I emphasized my strong belief that, among other things, equal opportunity goals should be based on hard data to ensure that they were realistic, achievable, and measurable. My thinking in this connection had been influenced by an argument put forward in 1974 by E. Earl Wright and Rodger Lawson with respect to the U.S. affirmative action program. Wright and Lawson contended that:

> In the absence of any theoretical foundation, hiring quotas have been formulated on purely subjective grounds, and herein lies the difficulty. The establish-ment of purely subjective job quotas tends to restrict

employment or advancement opportunities to members of particular groups in an artificial and unjustifiable manner. The development of employment goals based upon the availability of workers, however, tends to establish realistic and measurable objectives which institutions endeavour in good faith to achieve on a timely basis within the framework of the institutions' system of employment.[52]

Judge Abella saw merit in this line of reasoning, and by the time the meeting concluded, we had an agreement that my company would carry out for her commission a study of affirmative action goals and timetables.

John Blakely and I immediately commenced work on the assignment. Fortunately, the earlier work on the Ontario Public Service affirmative action program and many subsequent discussions with other policy thinkers provided an excellent foundation for the work required.

Our study succeeded in establishing the appropriateness and feasibility of certain general principles that have become a central part of the employment equity implementation and compliance process in Canada. These principles are: (1) that employers survey their workforce to determine the representation of the employment equity target or designated groups in terms of such factors as occupational level, income, and employment status (e.g., permanent/temporary, full-time/part-time); (2) that employers analyse their workforce data in various ways, including the identification of employment equity designated group under-representation problems, by making comparisons between their workforce data and data on the larger labour market (or markets) from which they recruit; (3) that employers address problems of underrepresentation of employment equity-designated groups by setting goals and timetables to rectify such situations.

The federal Liberal government was defeated before Judge Abella's royal commission report was translated into legislation. At the time, this was a source of concern among many equal employment opportunity advocates because of the possibility that the new Progressive Conservative government would simply shelve the commission's report. Fortunately, this did not happen. For one thing, Judge Abella's report presented a clear and strongly argued case that was hard to dismiss. In addition, the Honourable Flora MacDonald, minister of employment and immigration in the newly formed government, had a long-standing commitment to women's rights and human rights in general. To use the Ottawa expression, she was a red Tory. Minister MacDonald put her personal prestige and the power of her office behind Judge Abella's report.

Bill C-62, an act respecting employment equity, was passed in the House of Commons on April 23, 1986. Royal assent followed on June 27, 1986 (three years after the announcement of the commission), with proclamation taking place on August 13, 1986. The Employment Equity Act of 1986 regulated those Canadian employers who employed 100 or more people in connection with a federal work, undertaking, or business as defined by section 2 of the Canada Labour Code, and included any corporation established to perform any function or duty on behalf of the government of Canada that employed 100 or more people. Thus, all Crown corporations were regulated, and so were federally regulated employers such as banks, radio and television stations, and transportation companies.

At the same time as the Employment Equity Act came into force in 1986, Minister MacDonald announced the creation of the Federal Contractors Program for Employment Equity. The program requires employment equity implementation by employers with 100 or more employees and bidding on federal goods and services contracts worth $200,000 or more.

Both the Employment Equity Act and the Federal Contractors Program for Employment Equity identified four employment equity designated groups: women, racial or visible minorities, persons with disabilities, and persons of Aboriginal origin.

The Abella Commission was a highly successful royal commission. The main report, written by Judge Abella and published October 1984, is a model of rigorous and compelling analysis and recommendations that clearly follow from the data and analysis presented. In addition, the work of the commission was completed in a relatively short period of time, and its translation into legislative and regulatory initiatives was quick by the usual standards. The second report of the commission—the research studies—was published April 1985 and added additional weight to an already strong argument for policy change.

Judge Abella did all that a commission requires: she formed a strong and focused staff; she held public hearings and accepted briefs from advocacy groups; she used her wide-ranging networks to hear critiques and best practices; and she kept to her timetable. Her leadership was remarkable and fascinating to observe.

Starting in 1985, my consulting practice became more and more involved in the design, implementation, and maintenance of employment equity programs for a wide range of employers in the public sector, the broader public sector, and the private sector. I will discuss some of these projects in Chapters 9 and 10. The increasing consulting activity fuelled a growing stream of employment equity-oriented publications, both academic and business-directed. It also led to a considerable amount of public speaking and conference activity. At the university, I began to teach courses on equity-related issues. These offerings attracted students—often outside sociology—who were interested in becoming employment equity practitioners in a wide variety of organizational and institutional settings.

When it was passed into law in 1986, the Employment Equity Act made provision for a parliamentary review of the legislation every five years. My consulting practice has been involved in all of these reviews, performing a number of policy-oriented studies. One of the studies used census data from various periods to assess, over time, the socioeconomic circumstances of visible minorities at the level of specific ethnocultural subgroups. The policy mission in this connection was to develop an actionable understanding of why some subgroups appeared to benefit more from employment equity initiatives than others.

Another study focused on persons with disabilities and developed improved definitions and estimates of the population of persons with disabilities realistically available for employment. A subsequent project engaged the question of what constitutes success in employment equity and used various types of hard data and advanced multivariate statistical techniques to develop performance indicators.

Most recently (2001–02), John Blakely and I used econometric modelling techniques to estimate losses to the Canadian economy arising from the labour force underutilization of women, visible minorities, persons with disabilities, and persons of Aboriginal origin over the period 1996–2021. In terms of Gross Domestic Product (GDP), the projected loss over the period is $1863 billion in respect of women, $1327 billion in respect of visible minorities, $62 billion in respect of persons with disabilities, and $20.5 billion in respect of persons of Aboriginal origin. In short, labour market discrimination and underutilization are accompanied by a hefty price tag.

* * *

In 1985, the government of Ontario created a task force to examine challenges to and opportunities for Ontario's service sector. The task force was under the direction of George Radwanski, who had formerly served as an editor of *The Toronto Star* newspaper and had authored a well-received biography of Pierre Elliott Trudeau.

The Canadian economy entered a period of rapid economic development and income growth for some 25 years after the end of World War II. These events gave rise to many consequences, including significant expansion of the service sector. By the time the Ontario service sector task force came along in 1985, six out of seven new jobs being created in the province were in the service sector.

The data also showed that increasingly these jobs were being created in small firms—establishments with 20 or fewer employees. Fallout from the severe economic recession at the beginning of the 1980s had already established the trend toward downsizing in larger enterprises. Part of the problem was that, typically, small employers were not well represented in the development of public policies and programs. If the full job creation potential of such smaller firms was to be realized, new policy mechanisms needed to be developed to ensure that they were "brought into the loop" and supported in their initiatives.

A growing body of research also made clear that many of the service sector jobs being created would be at the low end of the service sector spectrum. This trend was at the core of increasing concerns that many such workers would require educational upgrading and retraining in the years to come and that meeting such needs would be costly.

In addition to these considerations, there was escalating concern in policy circles that the export potential of higher-end services was not being realized. As more and more newly industrialized countries proved able to produce and export goods on highly competitive terms, it became clear that developing and exporting high value-added services had to be an increasingly important part of the economic strategy pursued by developed countries wanting to maintain their standards of living.

Finally, the situation was complicated by the fact that many educators and the general public did not have a good understanding of the developments taking place in the service sector and the broader implications of such changes.

The consulting mission I was asked to head up for the Ontario Service Sector Task Force was focused on identifying and/or developing educational strategies to maximize service sector opportunities in the province. Apart from analysing a great deal of relevant trend data, the approach my team and I took to the task involved in-depth interviews with knowledgeable persons in the education, government, and private sectors. In the search for models that might be imported to Canada, a certain amount of this interview activity took place in the highly developed parts of the northeastern United States.

The study produced various recommendations, a number of which have been taken up—to varying degrees—in the education sector. As is well known, co-operative programs are a particularly useful vehicle for building bridges between educational institutions and private sector employers. They also play an important role in providing students with practical, work-related experience. My group's report to the service sector task force recommended that such programs—particularly in community colleges and universities—be expanded and increasingly oriented toward service sector opportunities. Over the years since the task force, this direction has been pursued more effectively.

The report also proposed strategies for increasing student awareness, in secondary education, of the institutional characteristics and nature of Canada's major trading partners. The Ontario secondary curriculum now includes this type of material. As for post-secondary education, the report recommended continuing efforts to internationalize the curriculum. This has been achieved with greater success in some areas than in others. In particular, certain business schools have done well.

The in-depth interview phase of the project revealed a clear need for improved mechanisms to identify the sorts of service sector skills that employers were looking for, so that educational institutions could respond more effectively and government program initiatives could be better targeted. In specific terms, my group's report recommended greater use of employer surveys, a proposal that appears to have received some response judging from the number of such projects my consulting practice carried out in the years following the service sector task force. A further proposal, closely linked to this recommendation, was that private sector employers become more involved in service sector educational and training initiatives either through their own programs or by financially supporting such initiatives in educational institutions. Considerable progress has been made on this front in the years following the task force.

The report also recommended the creation of local area networks that would bring private sector, government, and educational institution stakeholders together in partnership arrangements designed to foster service sector economic growth. A good example of how successful this approach can be is to be found in the Kitchener-Waterloo-Cambridge area of Ontario. When the Canada–U.S. Free Trade Agreement (FTA) came into effect at the beginning of 1989, many traditional industries found themselves adversely affected as tariff protections were phased out and new competitive dynamics came into place. The revenue base of the region suffered and unemployment escalated. Fortunately, the region had access to four top-ranked post-secondary education institutions (Conestoga College, University of Waterloo, Wilfrid Laurier University, and the University of Guelph), with established strengths in such enterprise-relevant fields as business education, information technology, and engineering.

Today, thanks to creative partnership building among educators, government officials, and businesspeople, the region is known as Canada's Technology Triangle, an area that encompasses a wide range of high-technology manufacturing and service industries and accounts for $8.9 billion in exports to 104 countries worldwide (2003 data). In summary terms, the work my group performed for the services task force was to identify strategies by which the Ontario education sector could make significant contributions to realizing the substantial value-added potential of high-end services in a rapidly evolving knowledge economy. The strategies and models identified were by no means limited to Ontario in their relevance, as I discovered in subsequent assignments.

* * *

For several reasons, I have found commission and task force work of particular interest. First, there is the closeness to the overall policy process. Second, and closely related to the preceding point, is the breadth of the engagement. Such work provides an opportunity to participate in the big picture of policy change. Third, working with both elected officials and public servants is an education in how institutional change takes place in this country. Commissions incorporate important checks and balances, serve the public interest, and maximize the probability that the results of the work will find their way into viable public policy. Fourth—and this applies to multi-constituency commissions—engagement in this type of activity is an education in the reality that virtually all institutional change in Canada is the consequence of constructive compromise. Ideological proposals for change are appealing because of their simplicity; their central flaw is that they don't work. Fifth, the commissions and task forces with which I have been involved were addressing leading-edge issues. The opportunity to participate and gain knowledge in new policy areas proved to be a large strategic advantage in the development of subsequent consulting assignments.

In carrying out the work of the various commissions and task forces I have participated in to date, I have relied on the highly skilled assistance of many people who have worked with me over the years. These assignments gave us an opportunity to contribute to progressive policy and program change in such areas as health care, education, employment, immigration, and socioeconomic equality. The perspective we brought to the work has its foundation in applied social research, but it is also a perspective that keeps an open mind about what other disciplines can contribute. Having said that, I believe that sociological modes of thinking can add significant value to the policy process. This is particularly evident in the case of commissions and task forces, since they are so close to the policy-shaping process. However, as the next two chapters describe, there are also other important ways in which applied, policy-oriented social research can make a contribution of value.

CHAPTER 9

Consulting to Governments and the Broader Public Sector

Over the years, my consulting practice has carried out a great many assignments for all levels of government—federal, provincial, and municipal—and also for organizations in the broader public sector. The latter category includes school boards, colleges, universities, libraries, associations, foundations, and other non-governmental public sector organizations.

Just as with commissions and task forces, this work is also about public policy. There is, however, an important difference. In the case of commissions and task forces, the consultant is working with a commissioner or minister—and his or her staff—on the development or shaping of the policy process. In general consulting to governments and the broader public sector, the consultant works with public servants or officials who are operating within given policy parameters.

In this area of activity, the work of my consulting practice falls into nine broad areas: (1) urban preservation and development; (2) assessment of the social impacts of development or other causes; (3) environmental studies; (4) arts and culture, recreation, and libraries; (5) tracking socioeconomic patterns over time for disadvantaged groups; (6) human resources management and employment studies; (7) immigration; (8) implementing and maintaining employment equity; (9) North American relations.

* * *

The Trudeau era brought large changes to public policy thinking and implementation in Canada. I was a consultant in several of the areas undergoing transformation, including the field of urban preservation and development. This area of policy underwent much change in the 1970s. Prior experience with "urban renewal" had been less than satisfactory. The physical razing of neighbour-hoods and the construction of impersonal high-rise buildings had dealt a serious blow to social coherence. At its worst, urban re-newal was a prime example of a policy totally unencumbered by any sense of sociological realities. The new approach was focused on rehabilitating, not razing, existing buildings and energizing, not eviscerating, neighbourhoods. Consultation with and direct involvement of neighbourhood residents was central to the new strategy. It was, in effect, a productive form of participatory de-mocracy.

Two new programs captured and institutionalized these values. One was the Neighbourhood Improvement Program (NIP) and the other was the Residential Rehabilitation Assistance Program (RRAP). Working closely with officials of the Ministry of State for Urban Affairs and the Canada Mortgage and Housing Corporation, my company—over a two-year period—carried out 11 separate studies of the new programs. I was ably assisted in this work by Rob Mills, whom I wrote about in Chapter 6. The core objective of the consulting mission was to engage with the program process while it was still ongoing and carry out a dynamic evaluation of how NIP and RRAP were performing and where program improvements might be made. In order to do this properly, it was necessary to look at a great many projects from coast to coast.

Perhaps I am a frustrated architect, but I derive great satis-faction from seeing buildings preserved and renewed, whether they are grand edifices or the simple houses of ordinary working people. In the NIP/RRAP cross-country study, I had a remark-able opportunity to see how creative Canadians have been—at varying points in their history—in shaping the built environment to widely different regional conditions. The project was also an education in how preserving neighbourhoods is bedrock for the creation of a civil and cohesive society. As for the evaluation results, these showed that NIP and RRAP were fundamentally good approaches that, with some fine-tuning, could be made even better.

* * *

The development of our natural resources has always been a critical engine of growth for the Canadian economy. By their very nature and scale, natural resource developments typically have large impacts in both environmental and social terms. The distinguished Canadian economist Harold A. Innis described the process as "cyclonic development." As Lorna Marsden and I observed in our 1979 book, *Fragile Federation*,

> Suddenly, almost overnight, a fantastic change would take place in the area where the resources were found. Workers were attracted for the sake of jobs, they brought the demand for the necessary services of a community, and the area exploded in terms of money, people, goods and services.[53]

Such a place is Fort McMurray in northern Alberta.

Early in 1977, I was contacted by Barbara Kasinska, then working for the Alberta Oil Sands Environmental Research Program (AOSERP). I knew Barbara from her earlier life as a Torontonian and she was familiar with various of my applied, policy-oriented social research projects. The AOSERP initiative had a wide mandate to examine the impacts of oil sands development on both the physical environment and societal patterns. Barbara had been given major responsibilities in the social impact area.

The area around Fort McMurray, and smaller communities such as Anzac, Fort MacKay, and Fort Chipewyan, is rich in oil sands deposits. The elevated price of oil—a result of the energy crisis that began in 1973—made exploitation of the resource even more attractive. That exploitation process was, to favour understatement, massively intrusive in both physical environment and social terms. Simply described, oil sands exploitation involves the use of huge machines to dig up the deposits, which are then subjected to various complex processes to derive the oil and other usable byproducts. Such an enterprise requires an abundant supply of all three factors of production: technology, capital, and labour. Fort McMurray is a classic example of Innis's theory of cyclonic development. As a result of ongoing oil sands exploitation, the population of the community increased twenty-one-fold between 1961 and 1979.

Edward B. Harvey and Barbara Kasinska, Alberta Oil Sands, 1979.

In the mid-1970s, increasingly concerned about these impacts, the Alberta government put in place a strictly enforced requirement that all corporations wishing to engage in oil sands development would have to first prepare detailed studies of the physical and social impacts of what they were proposing to do. Only when such impact studies had been fully accepted by the relevant governmental officials would a licence to proceed be granted.

The problem was that the AOSERP lacked the kinds of informational and technical resources that would be required to properly vet the corporate impact studies and identify shortcomings.

I was invited to Edmonton to discuss the development of a multi-year program of work to support AOSERP's function with highly specialized consulting services. Since this was February, my first action was to visit the Eddie Bauer store on Toronto's Bloor Street and buy the warmest parka I could find. Then I flew to Edmonton.

I was impressed by the professionalism of the Alberta government officials with whom I met. For my part, I had come well prepared with examples of the approach my group took to social impact assessment. It became clear early in the discussions that we would be contracted to do the work, subject to submission of an acceptable proposal. I drafted most of the proposal on the flight back to Toronto and it was accepted two weeks later.

The program of work was ambitious and involved three main objectives. The first was to develop an overall planning and policy information framework that would identify and conceptually interrelate all the variables and indicators AOSERP would need to properly assess corporate impact studies. The second objective was to assemble and analyse all the relevant data relating to the variables and indicators that had been identified. The third objective was to create an information network of the relevant Alberta governmental agencies to provide a mechanism that would ensure a timely flow of information and data to AOSERP.

Given the nature of the work, much of it could be done from my base in Toronto. However, I did make periodic trips to Edmonton to brief government officials, and I also made field trips to Fort McMurray and the surrounding area. The latter travel provided a direct and at times shocking view of the socially disruptive consequences of rapid development. Fragile Aboriginal cultures were, in particular, negatively affected.

During the project, I was ably assisted at points by Steven McShane, a highly capable graduate of the University of Toronto's master of industrial relations program. Steve is now a professor and the director of graduate programs at Simon Fraser University's Faculty of Business Administration. Our work produced several reports, created a large social impact assessment database, and enabled AOSERP to effectively review and critique the social impact assessment studies submitted by corporate developers. My consulting practice carried out a number of other social impact studies related to resources development, noise pollution, ultra-high voltage electric power transmission lines, and solid waste-disposal strategies. In the nature of social impact assessment, this work involved using a multiplicity of methods and frequent interdisciplinary collaboration.

* * *

Throughout my adult life, I have been interested in environmental issues. My activist involvement started in 1970, when (with Rob Mills's encouragement) I became a member of the board of directors of Pollution Probe. In addition to a wide range of pollution-related issues, Rob Mills, Lorna, and I were particularly interested in the interrelationships between various environmental issues and demographic development patterns. This interest led to the creation of the Population Research Foundation, which I have discussed in greater detail in Chapter 6.

Peter Middleton—who later went on to senior responsibilities in the federal public service—was also a member of the Pollution Probe board. In the early 1970s, Peter created Peter Middleton & Associates, an environmental research consulting firm that was soon engaged in important projects. One of these was a groundbreaking study of recycling funded by the Atkinson Foundation. Peter contracted with my company to take on a major component of the work that involved interviewing 50 key individuals about their attitudes toward municipal solid waste recycling. The individuals represented various sectors, including the federal sector, the provincial sector, the municipal sector, the industrial sector, and disposal-service companies.

Conducting personal interviews takes a lot of time, and they are not easy to arrange—especially when a sensitive topic is involved (which recycling certainly was in those days). Fortunately, Lorna agreed to co-direct the study and her networks of contact proved invaluable. Together, we assembled and trained a research team. One of the members of that team, Cathleen Morrison, now serves with distinction as the C.E.O. of the Cystic Fibrosis Foundation.

Our collective labours produced a detailed report, published in 1975, which identified barriers to the recycling movement and proposed remedial policy directions, a number of which have been adopted into practice.

Throughout the 1970s, I was active in consulting and writing on the subjects of air pollution, noise pollution, and the impacts of ultra-high voltage electric power transmission systems. Much of this work involved collaboration with engineers and technicians. The fact that I had a background in quantitative analysis helped in the formation and management of those relationships.

The work also involved a wide range of organizations, including governments, private companies, and advocacy groups. A side effect of this work was that I became increasingly risk-averse where noise, electromagnetic radiation, and polluted air were concerned!

At the beginning of the 1990s, I was approached by the Ontario Ministry of the Environment about the possibility of conducting studies that would support a growing interest the ministry had in the "social marketing" of various environmental programs. Social marketing is about developing strategies to change public behaviour. Literacy campaigns, family planning, and programs to combat teenage pregnancy, drug abuse, and AIDS are but a few examples.[54]

With respect to achieving behavioural change in the environmental area, the ministry officials recognized that only so much could be done with regulations and economic disincentive/incentive measures. The next level of real gains was to be realized by changing public values and behaviours. In order to do this, much more needed to be known about those values and behaviours and about how they varied by socioeconomic and other factors. Only then could effective social marketing initiatives be designed and targeted.

Initially, the thinking revolved around the conduct of several large-scale surveys. However, the substantial cost of such an approach was a legitimate concern. Further discussion resulted in my discovering that the ministry subscribed to various data and trend analysis services such as Environics and Decima Research. Among other things, these data contained information on environmental attitudes and behaviours and their socioeconomic correlates. I suggested a data mining approach, where existing data would be subjected to further analysis specific to the ministry's objectives. This strategy would require some co-operation and assistance from the data supplying organizations, but since the ministry was a paid-up subscriber and major department of government, I could not imagine that this would prove to be a problem.

It didn't. The supplier organizations co-operated fully, and various special tabulations of data were obtained. In addition, the project database was usefully supplemented with information from Statistics Canada's 1991 Survey of Households and the

Environment. Over the next year and a half, two major reports were produced and many briefings provided to ministry officials. The analysis revealed clear differences in how different segments of the Ontario population felt about a wide range of environmental issues, including conservation, recycling, landfill use, and air quality. The various sources of data also permitted building up a picture of how much different segments of the Ontario population "cared" about the environment and the extent to which they would entertain behavioural change and/or cost increases to produce a better, safer environment. The analysis resulted in the development of a number of different social marketing approaches that could be effectively targeted on different segments of the population.

I was extensively assisted in this project by J.W.P. "Jack" Veugelers. Jack worked with me on various projects during the time he was living in Toronto and completing his doctoral dissertation for the Department of Sociology at Princeton University. He brought exceptional analytical powers and logical rigour to every piece of work he did and working with him was a consistent pleasure. After successfully defending his dissertation, Jack accepted a position with the University of Toronto's sociology department, where he is well launched on what will be a distinguished career.

In 2001, I became involved with the Commission for Environmental Cooperation, headquartered in Montreal. The commission was created as a result of the North American Free Trade Agreement (NAFTA) and has a mandate to address environmental issues and initiatives on a North America-wide scale. My connection with it came about as a result of my increasing involvement with the Alliance for Higher Education and Enterprise in North America, an organization I will get back to later in this chapter.

As part of its concern with the global warming issue, the commission wanted to explore strategies for the reduction of carbon emissions. I was asked to design and conduct a study that would involve gathering interview data from senior spokespeople for the oil and gas, mining, and forest products industries. Although the study was intended to be exploratory, not definitive, 18 people were interviewed in as many organizations and considerable information useful for policy purposes was obtained. As the implications of the Kyoto Accord continue to unfold, and public awareness of the global warming issue escalates, work on this file is very much "in progress." This project also demonstrates the extent to which dealing with environmental challenges is a moving target, even more complex nowadays, given the need to more effectively harmonize Canadian, U.S., and Mexican environmental standards.

Looking back over more than 30 years of environment-related projects, I am encouraged that some demonstrable progress has been made and that the informational and policy tools being used have become increasingly sophisticated. There is still a lot to do.

* * *

Arts and culture, recreation, and public libraries represent another sector where my consulting firm became involved in a number of significant projects. My introduction to this area of work came early—just one year after I had incorporated my consultancy practice.

In late April 1975, I was contacted by Douglas Herman, a senior policy person in the Ontario Ministry of Culture and Recreation. I had previously met Doug at one or two social events of the Ontario Research Council on Leisure, where, among other things, we had chatted casually about a mutual interest in promoting more data-based approaches to policy development. The proximity of Toronto's Sutton Place Hotel to Queen's Park made it a favourite gathering spot for politicians and senior public servants. Doug and I met there for lunch, during which he explained that he had "a pleasant problem." Wintario, the Ontario lottery, was generating large amounts of revenue, significant portions of which were being directed toward development of the province's recreational facilities.

The problem was that the ministry did not have a system for determining recreational needs that would facilitate the development of spending priorities. I soon learned the ministry had in its possession two large sets of survey data. One was the Ontario Recreational Facilities Survey, which provided extensive province-wide detail on the nature and distribution of such facilities. The second set of data was the Ontario Recreational Survey, which provided detailed information on the recreational preferences and participation patterns of a representative sample of over 10,000 Ontarians. Neither of the two datasets had been subjected to detailed analysis.

It seemed to me that some form of supply and demand analysis might be possible. Specifically, I wanted to investigate the feasibility of cross-plotting the supply of facilities against the demand side, which in this case was recreational preferences and participation patterns. This would make it possible to identify areas of unmet need and areas of underutilization and, in so doing, derive a rational set of spending priorities. Doug liked the idea. We returned to his office and immediate arrangements were made for me to access all the relevant data. It didn't take very long to determine that what I had in mind was technically feasible. The next step was to develop a work plan, list of deliverables, and a cost estimate. A contract quickly followed.

Over the next several months, supported by two statistically inclined research assistants, I carried out a multiplicity of analyses. The central challenge was to distill a huge amount of data down to a simple and clear framework that could be used to guide important spending decisions. It worked. We were able to provide quantitatively precise estimates of under-supply, over-supply, and equilibrium. Overall, the project was an excellent example of what Doug and I had casually discussed at an Ontario Research Council on Leisure reception—a data-based approach to public policy development and decision making.

Every completed assignment leaves the consultant with an increased store of intellectual capital. It was clear to me that the thinking behind the recreation supply and demand study was applicable to a wide range of areas where governments were trying to match up public needs and preferences with program design and delivery. Over the ensuing years, the concepts and methods used in the recreation-related work found their way into work for various other government departments, including the arts and culture area, as well as the several projects my company carried out in the public libraries sector.

During the 1970s in Canada, the public library service was being increasingly affected by a wide range of socioeconomic, demographic, and technological changes. Forward-thinking decision makers in the sector recognized that public libraries would have to change if they were to remain relevant and, of course, continue to receive funding adequate to their mission. My company's involvement in this type of work began almost immediately after incorporation. In late 1974, I was approached by the Toronto Public Library Board about the feasibility of a study of the changing needs of the city's east end libraries. I was very much at home with the organizational change part of the agenda but had a less sure grasp on the intricacies of the public library service.

As I mentioned in Chapter 7, I fortunately knew Dr. Anne Woodsworth, a senior librarian with great depth of experience in the profession and a person who had for some years been operating her own consulting business. The strategic alliance we formed resulted in the Toronto Public Library Board study being a great success. Equally important, Anne and I discovered that we were able to add real value to each other's expertise and that our respective consulting styles were highly congenial. Both of us favoured practicality, good client relations, staying within budget, and meeting all timelines without exception.

Over the next 10 years, Anne and I collaborated on a number of library-related projects, the most significant of which was a national study of the public library service that took place between 1979 and 1982. Anne was very well connected in library circles. In late 1978, we learned that the Canadian Library Association had plans to invite competitive bids for a far-reaching national study of the public library service. The fundamental purpose of the proposed initiative was to study all operational aspects of public libraries and librarian training; assess the effects of socioeconomic, demographic, and technological change; and set out recommendations for the future.

Anne and I felt well qualified for the assignment but recognized that there would be strong competition for this important project. We took several steps to maximize our prospects. First, we assembled relevant background material from Canadian and U.S. sources and analysed it to identify key public library issues and effective research approaches. Second, we invited Lorna Marsden to join the team. Her knowledge of demographics, policy, and social change in the professions was central to the project. Third, we developed an exceptionally detailed proposal, which set forward a multi-method, multi-stage strategy that would include interrelated studies of public library organization and characteristics, public library workers, and public library users and non-users.

In addition to submitting a written proposal, all of the short-listed consultants would be interviewed by the 10-person, regionally representative project steering committee. Fortunately, Anne had—at one time or another—met or worked with all of the steering committee members and therefore had a good understanding of their views. Anne, Lorna, and I met well in advance of the interview to work out strategies and generally prepare ourselves. The interview itself was thorough, lasting about an hour and a half, and we left with a feeling it had gone well. Our perception proved correct. We were awarded the contract a few days later.

National studies always present coordination challenges but are exciting assignments because of their scope. We dedicated the first few months of the project to the development of a detailed research operations manual. This document set out everything we were going to do and exactly how we would do it. It included, for example, all survey forms, interview schedules, and sampling strategies. The research operations manual was accepted by the steering committee with a few minor modifications. We now had a solid foundation on which to proceed. A little over a year later, the Canadian Library Association published our report in both official languages and orchestrated its wide dissemination. In addition, the project steering committee engaged us to perform a second assignment, which involved designing and carrying out a series of seminars across Canada that would stimulate debate and understanding relative to the research and the various recommendations. We had crossed over from research to implementation.

* * *

Since returning to Canada in 1966, my well-established interest in data led me to develop professional relationships at Statistics Canada and other data-oriented government agencies. In particular,

I wanted to identify and understand all the datasets that were pertinent to applied, policy-oriented issues and were amenable to secondary or further analysis—a process I have also referred to as data mining.

Although many government datasets have proven of great help to many projects, in my experience the single most useful governmental source of data is the census of Canada. The magnitude of census data—in terms of the number of people and variables covered—is outstanding. Also, given that the census is carried out every five years, it comes along with sufficient frequency to permit the meaningful monitoring of many trends and patterns.

There are different strategies for accessing census data. I have on occasion signed off on the Statistics Act confidentiality requirements and been given access to the master tapes. In other instances, I have obtained special tabulations of census data from Statistics Canada. In particular, I have found the Public Use Microdata Files (PUMF) to be highly useful. Basically, the PUMF are a statistically robust sample of all the census data and permit the user to carry out a wide range of statistical analyses related to particular interests or research questions. Statistics Canada, of course, charges for all these data products and services, but these costs are small when one considers the scope and quality of the data.

I have used census data in many ways for a wide variety of academic and consulting projects. One of the particularly interesting uses of census data is tracking various types of trends over time. In 1985, I had discussions with Glenna Carr, head of the Ontario Women's Directorate, about studies that would track the socioeconomic situation and progress of women in Ontario relative to men. I outlined how census data could be used to make gender comparisons over time for a wide range of variables, including employment, unemployment, occupation, education, age, family situation, and income. I was asked to proceed with a feasibility study, which, after its acceptance, led to various studies for the directorate of gender equality trends over time.

I soon discovered that other jurisdictions, such as the City of Toronto and Human Resources Development Canada, were interested in having the same sort of studies done for the geographical areas with which they were concerned. As the work proceeded over the years, the data resources available to me became more sophisticated, and I was able to go beyond gender differences and examine socioeconomic trends in terms of factors such as visible minority status, Aboriginal origin status, and disability status. Since it was possible to sub-specify these patterns by gender, the analysis became increasingly interesting and useful.

From a policy point of view, the ability to do increasingly fine-grained analysis and make comparisons over time proved a valuable tool in assessing the efficacy of policy and program measures designed to address problems of socioeconomic inequality.

As usual, I received a lot of help in carrying out these projects—including assistance from Lorne Tepperman (an expert on social indicators, among other things), John Blakely, and many staffers at Statistics Canada who were invariably available, interested, and helpful with their technical support and conceptual insights.

* * *

In both my academic and consulting careers, studies of the changing nature of employment and associated issues of human resources management have been an ongoing feature of my work. The roots of this interest are deep, dating back to my early explorations of work and the professions under the guidance of Kaspar Naegele at the University of British Columbia.

In the 1970s in Canada, much policy thinking in the employment and economic growth areas was focused on concerns relating to youth unemployment, job-creation programs, and managing persistently high levels of inflation in the economy. Indeed, those troubled times—triggered by the energy crisis—had led economists to coin a new term, "stagflation," a deadly combination of stagnant economic growth and high inflation.

In the 1980s, with economic recovery taking hold, the employment policy agenda shifted. Emerging issues included concerns over critical skill shortages, the impact of technological change on work, and developing strategies to ensure that education and training initiatives produced a capable and competitive workforce that would contribute to productivity gains and economic growth. I found myself becoming involved with all these areas.

Federal job creation programs for youth had been a frequent topic of discussion at the many meetings of Minister Bud Cullen's working group on youth unemployment. Views were expressed that such initiatives should go beyond being "make work" programs and be designed in such a way that the public funds invested in job creation would also serve to enhance the industrial development capability of the nation. It was felt that, with such an approach, the jobs created would have greater prospects of becoming lasting jobs and could even serve to create additional, spinoff employment opportunities.

On January 21, 1978, the Honourable A.C. Abbott, minister of state responsible for small business, announced the creation of such a program. Called Employment Opportunities in Product Development (EOPD), the initiative was designed to create jobs that would be linked to new product development and enhanced competitiveness for the companies receiving job creation funds. An Ottawa-based consulting firm—Kelly, Gairns & Connolly Ltd.—was contracted to design, implement, communicate, and evaluate the EOPD Program.

I met Charles Kelly, a founding partner of the firm, in 1974, when he was advising the Ontario Institute for Studies in Education on various matters related to government relations and increasing government research funding support for the Institute's programs. Charles and I soon began to work together on various projects. Given the scale of the Employment Opportunities in Product Development Program, Charles realized that his company was going to need help and invited me to join the team. Although I worked on all phases of the program, my primary responsibilities were in the areas of program design and performance evaluation.

In the area of program design, our collective thinking was to create as simple and seamless an application and approval process as possible. It worked, and the rate of program take-up by employers was exceptional. We had originally projected the creation of 1000 new jobs within seven months of program launch. In fact, that number was 1366. Program evaluation results revealed that over 40 percent of the jobs created under EODP became permanent, a high proportion for job creation programs. Many employers attributed this successful outcome to the program's emphasis on linking employment creation with new product development.

Compared to the troubled 1970s, the decade of the 1980s in Canada witnessed stronger economic growth and improved employment numbers. The policy focus shifted. By 1983, I was working on skill-shortage issues for the Ontario Ministry of Labour and IDEA Corporation, the latter being an Ontario Crown corporation with a broad mandate to support and stimulate business and investment in the province. Over a two-year period, I worked closely with Ross Perry, one of IDEA Corporation's most insightful and imaginative policy thinkers. Ross was really quite visionary about the rapid evolution of the technology and knowledge-based economy and clearly recognized the significance to Ontario of an adequate supply of workers in a number of critical skill areas. He wanted my group to survey a broad cross-section of technology-oriented Ontario companies in order to ascertain views about training adequacy and possible future shortages in various critical and emerging occupations.

The survey results were disquieting. A significant majority of our informants saw major future shortages of engineers, technologists, and computer specialists. Concerns were also raised about the adequacy of training in some fields. The survey results provided a foundation for identifying and bringing together a group of senior industry representatives, who explored and debated such key issues as avoiding future critical skill shortages, the responsiveness of the education and training sectors, increased use of employer training schemes, and strategies to promote the development of boundary-spanning skills.

The IDEA Corporation projects illustrate several important features of the policy process. One is the fluidity of policy fields, reflected in this case by a shift from job-creation strategies to critical skills shortages within roughly a five-year period. Another is the importance of having solid, practical data to ascertain the dimensions of the problems and develop appropriate responses. The third feature is the necessity of bringing together key people from various jurisdictions to build issue awareness and promote action.

The Employment Opportunities in Product Development and IDEA Corporation projects were large-scale initiatives with

Canada-wide and Ontario-wide implications respectively. My other public sector work in the employment area has focused on particular human resources management issues in specific organizations.

I first met Major (later Lieutenant-Colonel) Frank Pinch at an international conference in 1979. Frank was serving with the Canadian Forces Personnel Applied Research Unit (CFPARU), a unit of the Department of National Defence. He had a doctorate in sociology and was highly informed about the society-wide changes that were affecting young people's views on education, training, and employment. The Department of National Defence was concerned about these changes and the impact they appeared to be having on recruitment to the Canadian Forces.

After exploratory discussions with Frank and other members of the CFPARU staff, I was asked to prepare a proposal for a national study of the occupational and educational plans of Canadian youth and how these affected their assessment of subsidized educational opportunities in the Regular Officer Training Program (ROTP). Essentially, the ROTP is an arrangement by which young people are subsidized in their post-secondary education in return for service in the regular officer core.

The proposal was accepted and work commenced in October 1981, with John Blakely serving as my national research coordinator. A Canada-wide sample was designed to represent 13- to 19-year-olds in secondary school grades. A total of 1503 questionnaire surveys were obtained, supplemented by 87 in-depth interviews. The study produced a large volume of data on the educational and occupational objectives of Canadian youth, on how they felt about training and employment opportunities related to the Canadian Forces, and on their sources of information about such opportunities. Because of the way the study had been designed, it was possible to sub-specify these patterns by factors such as gender, age, ethnicity, grade at school, and geographical location. The information obtained proved of direct practical use in the design of Canadian Forces recruiting programs, including the design of promotional materials and advertising campaigns.

The project was the beginning of what proved to be a long-term relationship with the Department of National Defence. Between 1984 and 1985, I became involved in the design and implementation of a Quality of Working Life Program at a large Canadian Forces Supply Depot located in Montreal. The project was of particular interest because it afforded an opportunity to use a classic evaluation strategy in which pre-program (or baseline) measurements are taken, followed by periodic monitoring during the program, and a final set of measurements some months after the conclusion of the trial. The evaluation study clearly showed positive results, both in terms of employee satisfaction and productivity gains. Quality of Working Life Programs were subsequently implemented at several National Defence locations.

The Quality of Working Life project was followed, in 1986, by an assignment to build an environmental scanning system for the Department of National Defence. Named The Canadian Forces Social Demographic Trends Information System, the project involved a number of interrelated stages. These included: (1) identifying the policy or program areas that were to be included; (2) identifying the data required to properly support the policy and program areas chosen; (3) setting up routine procedures for capturing the data and integrating them into the system; (4) setting up analytical frameworks and procedures so the data could be interrogated in terms of the policy and program concerns; (5) establishing organizational and operational procedures to link analysis outcomes to organizational decision-making processes.

Subsequent work for the Canadian Forces reflected the growing policy significance of equity and diversity issues in employment, including sexual orientation. Although the Canadian Forces are sometimes characterized as socially conservative, I have found that the organization is capable of implementing large social changes quickly and efficiently. Examples include the integration of French Canadians in the Canadian Forces, expanded opportunities for women serving in the military, and a continuing pursuit of greater ethnocultural diversity.

* * *

As I mentioned in my earlier discussion of the 1980 ministerial Task Force on Immigration Practices and Procedures, immigration makes a highly important contribution to Canada in both social and economic terms. It is in the national interest that immigrants have opportunities to enter the economic mainstream as quickly as possible. However, as the decade of the 1990s unfolded, disturbing evidence began to surface that many immigrants were facing barriers to their full social and economic participation in Canadian society. An increasing number of immigration policy and program issues were being debated. In response to this situation, I found myself—between 1995 and 2002—becoming involved in a number of different but interrelated studies pertaining to immigration policy questions.

The starting point for this series of projects was on the academic side of my work. I received grants from the Centre of Excellence for Research on Immigration and Settlement (CERIS) to investigate changes over time in the socioeconomic adaptation of immigrants to Canada. Using special tabulations of 1991 and 1996 census data, the study made comparisons between visible minority immigrants and immigrants who are not visible minorities. The comparisons involved various indictors, including unemployment rate, average employment income, and average percent below the poverty line. Data were analysed for Canada, Ontario, and the Greater Toronto Area.

The analysis revealed patterns of socioeconomic decline for visible minority immigrants between 1991 and 1996, an important consideration given that close to 80 percent of immigrants to Canada are now members of visible minority groups. Focusing on the Canada-wide data, the analysis showed that the average employment income of visible minority immigrants (measured in constant dollars) had declined from $24,380 in 1991 to $23,298 in 1996. The corresponding figures for immigrants who were not visible minorities were $30,285 in 1991 and $31,194 in 1996. Equally disturbing trends were found in other areas as well. In 1991, 25.1 percent of visible minority immigrants were below the poverty line. By 1996, the figure had risen to 34.3 percent. The corresponding numbers for immigrants who were not visible minorities were 14.4 percent in 1991 and 17.8 percent in 1996.

As the policy debates heated up, my consultancy practice soon found itself involved in immigration-related projects. As a result of discussions with research and policy officials of Citizenship and Immigration Canada, my group took on a two-year study to develop links between longitudinal immigration data and census of Canada data, so that the changing socioeconomic circumstances of immigrants could be evaluated in much greater detail.

At the same time, I became involved as a consultant to a study being conducted by the Access to Professions and Trades Unit of the Ontario Ministry of Training, Colleges and Universities. The study involved gathering and analysing data on a sample of 643 immigrants who were seeking employment in Ontario's regulated professions. Regulated professions are self-governing and have the authority to establish their own standards with respect to training, entry requirements, and assessment of competence. A number of occupations are involved, including accountancy, engineering, law, medicine, nursing, occupational therapy, pharmacy, and teaching. In-depth interviews were conducted with the 643 immigrants sampled in order to learn more about barriers they experienced when seeking employment in the occupational areas for which they were trained.

The Access to Professions and Trades Study provided a foundation for several policy and program actions by the government of Ontario. These included: (1) providing new and prospective immigrants with up-to-date information on licensing requirements and labour market conditions in the regulated occupations and professions; (2) funding community-based immigrant settlement services through the Ministry of Citizenship's Newcomer Settlement Program; (3) creating, in co-operation with World Education Services (Canada), faster and more efficient mechanisms to assess the academic credentials of new immigrants; (4) promoting, in collaboration with various professional and occupational associations, greater use of prior learning assessment strategies with new immigrants to ensure that non-classroom learning and experience is properly taken into account.

In carrying out the research for the Centre of Excellence for Research on Immigration and Settlement, I was extensively assisted by Kathleen Reil and Dr. Bobby Siu. Kathleen had, many years earlier, been a highly capable student in my University of Toronto applied social research and policy studies course. Bobby, a sociologist, served in the first half of the 1990s as a director of compliance for the Ontario Employment Equity Commission, and I met him in the course of consulting work my group performed for that organization. When the government changed in Ontario in 1995, the Employment Equity Commission was disbanded and Bobby proceeded to create his own consulting firm. Our two organizations have collaborated on a number of projects. In addition to assisting with the CERIS research, Kathleen and Bobby joined forces with me in disseminating our research results in various venues, including *Canadian Ethnic Studies*,[55] the CERIS working papers series,[56] and a wide range of conferences.

In 2000, the Maytree Foundation learned of the work John Blakely and I were doing for Human Resources Development Canada on the costs to the Canadian economy of the labour market underutilization of women, racial minorities, persons of Aboriginal origin, and persons with disabilities. The foundation wanted a study that would identify present and future costs to the economy arising from the underutilization of immigrants. Because of the close link to the other immigration-related studies, I asked Kathleen Reil and Bobby Siu to join the team. The study report, which was tabled with the foundation early in 2001, showed significant losses to Gross Domestic Product (GDP) relating to underutilization problems.

Along with much other important work done by colleagues in the immigration field, the various projects just described helped stimulate policy debate on immigration issues and foster new thinking and approaches to the timely and effective socioeconomic integration of new immigrants.

* * *

The work I did for Judge Abella's Royal Commission on Equality in Employment in 1983–84 led my consulting practice to a long-term involvement with the establishment and maintenance of employment equity programs in a wide range of organizations. These activities, which will shortly enter their twentieth year, take place in both the public and private sectors. Below, I look at some of the public sector assignments.

When David Peterson and his Liberal colleagues entered the 1985 Ontario election campaign, their prospects did not look good. The polling numbers were not promising, there was a Canada-wide trend against electing Liberal politicians, and the

David R. Peterson, Premier of Ontario, 1985–1990.

Progressive Conservatives had been in power in Ontario for 42 years. In fact, Peterson came within four seats of defeating Premier Frank Miller's government, producing a minority government that could not survive without the support of the third party in the House—the New Democrats, led by Bob Rae. Rae proposed a coalition government with the Progressive Conservatives but was rejected. He then made the offer to the Liberals and was accepted by David Peterson. Peterson became the twentieth premier of Ontario on June 26, 1985. The coalition agreement expired in 1987, at which time the Peterson Liberals went on to win a majority.

The Peterson government ushered in an important period of widespread reform in Ontario, including reform in the realm of social policy. On this front, several initiatives were involved, including pay equity, environmental protection measures, public service employment equity, changes to the Ontario Human Rights Code to enforce accommodation for persons with disabilities, and the establishment of the Native Affairs Secretariat as a cross-governmental initiative. My group was involved in various social policy areas, but the one that was the most extensive for us was the development of employment equity policy and programs for the Ontario Public Service.

In the mid-1980s in Ontario, there were approximately 90,000 people employed in the province's public service. The former Civil Service Commission had been reinvented as the Human Resources Secretariat, which was under the capable leadership of George R. Podrebarac, a dynamic deputy minister. Overall, ministerial authority rested with the Honourable Elinor Caplan in her capacity as chairman of the Management Board of Cabinet.

In late 1985, I received a telephone call from Linda Mahoney, an official with the Human Resources Secretariat. It turned out she was aware of the work I had done with Judge Abella's Commission and wondered if I could meet with her and her director to discuss employment equity. One week later, I arrived at the Frost Building on Queen's Park Crescent for discussions with Linda and William "Bill" Rooke, a middle-level official of the Human Resources Secretariat. It soon became clear that significant political pressure was building for the development and implementation of an Ontario Public Service-wide employment equity program. I talked about my earlier work for the Ontario Public Service affirmative action initiatives for women and the Abella Commission, as well as some work I had done with federal public service employment equity programs.

I left the meeting having agreed to submit, within a week's time, a two-pager that would set out terms of reference for a feasibility study of developing and implementing an employment equity program in the Ontario Public Service. The proposal was quickly accepted, and John Blakely and I set to work on the feasibility study report. It was a comprehensive document that outlined, among other things, how the entire Ontario Public

Service would be surveyed, how the data would be managed and brought to bear on equity program development, and how the initiative should be administered and communicated to ensure a successful result.

One of the central strengths of the feasibility study report, I think, is that it went beyond technical issues and explored the sorts of employment equity program and policy models that could work best in the context of the Ontario Public Service. The thinking presented owed a great deal to the experience John and I had gained from the Royal Commission on Equality in Employment work and a careful reading of Judge Abella's lucid and powerful final report.

I tabled the feasibility study with Bill Rooke and Linda Mahoney early in February 1986 and gave them a detailed briefing. In rapid succession, I was asked to brief the assistant deputy minister, the deputy minister, the minister, and the cabinet. All of this can best be described as the "advise and consent" process, which is such a fundamental part of policy building. With the support of her cabinet colleagues, Minister Caplan was now in a position to direct her officials in the public service to take the next steps to commence operational development of an employment equity policy for the Ontario Public Service.

In the next short while, officials of the Human Resources Secretariat developed a request for proposal in respect of a project that would survey the entire Ontario Public Service workforce to determine the representation of the four employment equity designated groups: women, visible minorities, persons of Aboriginal origin, and persons with disabilities. My group was one of the organizations invited to bid. I knew that there would be strong competition for a project of such magnitude and importance. John Blakely and I proceeded to develop a very detailed proposal that, at the end of the process, emerged as the winner.

The logistics of surveying approximately 90,000 people defy quick or easy explanation, so I shall not even try. Suffice it to say that the survey produced a 70 percent rate of return, which, by any survey research standard, is phenomenal. On the Ontario Public Service side, Linda Mahoney was, for all practical purposes, assigned full time to the project. She was a great person to work with, and the initiative would not have been possible without the constant support she and many of her public service colleagues provided.

My group's engagement with the Human Resources Secretariat lasted over two years. There were other tasks besides the survey. The results had to be effectively communicated, policy strategies had to be developed, and a long-term data management capability created. During much of the process, I had regular meetings with a 12-person steering committee chaired by George Podrebarac. The committee had been carefully formulated to cover off the various key interests than could make or break the new Ontario Public Service employment equity policy that was emerging. Podrebarac had energy to burn and an intellect to match. He was determined to ensure that the new policy would be a model for public service organizations everywhere. His approach to the committee combined unflappable geniality with total goal directedness. He would describe the most daunting task as "a pleasant problem" and proceed to get everyone on side. It was an education to see him in action. He was also a consistent pleasure to work with.

The Ontario Public Service employment equity initiative was a success thanks to the efforts of many different people. I found the work intensely enjoyable for several reasons. There was no short-age of interesting technical and research challenges to be resolved. There was the excitement of working with a diverse group of people, including researchers, public servants, and outstanding elected officials like Elinor Caplan and the then-attorney general of Ontario, Ian Scott. There was also the permanent satisfaction of seeing an important and progressive policy come into opera-tion—a new way of thinking with its roots in the work of Judge Rosalie Abella's Royal Commission on Equality in Employment.

I had been involved with the Ontario Public Service initiative for only a few months when I was contacted by Mary Bruce, the director of the Equal Opportunity Division of the City of Toronto. Mary, an indefatigable crusader for equality rights, wanted to ensure that the city was doing everything possible to embrace and promote employment equity. For the next five years, my group worked closely with Mary and her staff on a number of different projects.

The starting point was a program of work designed to ensure that heads of the various municipal departments had an accurate understanding of employment equity and appreciated the importance of setting clear goals and timetables for improving the representation of employment equity designated group members in the City of Toronto workforce. Working with Brenda Billingsley, a highly capable member of Mary's staff, my group developed a plain-language set of briefing materials entitled "Goals and Timetables Made Easy." This was produced in booklet form and disseminated to the people who would be involved in the process and their senior managers. Over the next several weeks, Brenda and I followed up with a series of in-depth briefings to all department heads and members of their staff with human resources management responsibilities. This sequence of events established a process by which each department would develop action plans—subject to annual review—setting out goals and timetables for employment equity designated group hiring and promotion.

It soon became clear that if departments were to produce accurate and meaningful action plans, they would require better equity data than what they were currently receiving. This led to a series of projects designed to restructure and otherwise improve the City of Toronto equity database. A significant part of the employment equity process is "numbers driven." The data on which these numbers are based must be up-to-date, detailed, and—above all—correct. In addition to these considerations, several types of data have to be combined in an employment equity database, including equity group characteristics, personnel information (such as job, pay level, and employment status), and external labour market data (for comparison purposes) obtained from the census of Canada. This type of work is complex, but the product it produces cannot be complex. On the contrary, the data have to made as intuitively understandable as possible, or they will never be effectively used by the human resources people who have to implement the front-line mechanics of employment equity programs.

In addition to working with the three levels of government—federal, provincial, and municipal—the employment equity work of my group includes various other types of public sector and broader public sector organizations such as Crown corporations, Crown agencies, community colleges, universities, labour organizations, and school boards. As the number and range of equity clients continued to expand, I made efforts to systematize components of the implementation and maintenance process. This was successful, up to a point, but it could never be done at the expense of not recognizing the cultural differences that exist among organizations—even organizations in the same field of activity. Correctly perceiving and working with these differences is absolutely fundamental to implementation success in employment equity and many other areas of organizational change as well. This is equally true in the private sector, which I deal with in the next chapter.

* * *

With the passage of the North American Free Trade Agreement (NAFTA) on January 1, 1994, North America took another significant step toward becoming a continental system. Increasingly liberalized trade arrangements present Canada with new economic opportunities but also pose institutional and policy challenges. In broad terms, a central question is how to take advantage of greater integration while maintaining important and distinctive features of the Canadian institutional system.

Over the many years since the Employment Opportunities in Product Development project, Charles Kelly and I had kept in touch and our respective companies had collaborated on various projects. Early in 1999, Charles and I met in Toronto, and he briefed me on a new not-for-profit organization called the Alliance for Higher Education and Enterprise in North America. With considerable support from the then-minister of foreign affairs, Lloyd Axworthy, and other influential Canadians, Charles had played a lead role in bringing the new organization into existence.

The Alliance's mission was to foster the creation, on a North American scale, of partnerships involving institutions of higher education and private sector organizations. An Alliance board of directors had been established and included Senator Jack Austin, David J.S. Winfield, Tom Axworthy, Senator J. Trevor Eyton, Roy L. Heehan, David Strangway, the late François Tavenas, Thomas L. Wood, and Charles Kelly.

Jack Austin, whom I had known socially for several years, was the chairman of the board, and Charles Kelly was serving as acting president of the organization. I was also acquainted with two other board members: David Strangway, from his time as acting president of the University of Toronto, and Tom Axworthy, dating back to when he was Prime Minister Trudeau's principal secretary. My reaction was that the Alliance seemed to have a timely and important mission and a highly capable group of people to bring it to fruition.

The challenge the Alliance now faced, Charles explained, was developing a full operational capability with substantive programs. There was also a need for research initiatives that would establish the databases required for partnership-building activities. He wanted to know if I would be prepared to serve as a consultant to the Alliance and develop an initial view of an operational plan that I would bring to a series of meetings in Mexico City on April 8 and 9, 1999. The meetings had been timed to coincide with a state visit of Prime Minister Jean Chrétien to have talks with the president of Mexico, Ernesto Zedillo. In addition to Jack Austin and Charles Kelly, two other members of the Alliance board—David Winfield and Roy Heenan—would also be coming to Mexico City.

My responsibilities in Mexico City were to be threefold. First, I was to meet with Austin, Kelly, Winfield, and Heenan to present the operational plan ideas and generally brainstorm with them over forward strategies for the Alliance. Then we would go on to a meeting with a group of leading Mexican businesspeople and educators, brief them on the operational plan ideas, and seek to enlist them as members of a formal Mexican Advisory Group to the Alliance. The final part of the program involved briefing Prime Minister Chrétien, President Zedillo, and various of their respective officials.

I agreed to take on the assignment. Over the next month, I carried out a thorough review of Alliance-related documentation and relevant North American research and policy literature. I also had discussions with a number of knowledgeable people, including the late Dr. John Wirth, Gildred Professor of History at Stanford and president of the North American Institute (NAMI)—an organization that had played a key role in creating the Alliance.

Members of the Higher Education and Enterprise Board meet with President Ernesto Zedillo of Mexico and Prime Minister Jean Chrétien of Canada, 1999.

The meetings in Mexico City went well. Both the Alliance and the initial operational plan ideas received strong endorsement. After a final meeting involving Jack Austin, Charles Kelly, and myself, I was asked to undertake a full-scale management study that would develop the initial operational plan ideas into a fully articulated platform for action.

The study, which had a six-month time frame, revolved around three central objectives: (1) build the Alliance's networks of contact; (2) develop proposals for fundable projects in all three countries and work with the relevant officials to ensure support would be forthcoming; (3) strengthen the Alliance board and advisory groups to make them larger and increasingly representative of all three countries. The project was labour-intensive, given the number of meetings involved, and also required considerable travel to Mexico City; Washington, D.C.; and Ottawa. However, at the end of the day, a detailed operational plan was in place.

I soon found myself serving as a member (and later as president) of the Alliance board of directors with particular responsibility for the organization's research program. Over the ensuing months, I was able to make a number of projects operational with the support of the Mexican government, the U.S. Department of State, the Canadian Department of Foreign Affairs and International Trade, and Human Resources Development Canada. A significant part of the work involved creating databases on the North American activities and plans of higher education institutions in Mexico, the U.S., and Canada. Other projects examined such issues as the state of North American higher education collaboration and strategies for increasing Canadian community college involvement in North American activities.

At the University of Toronto in 2001–02, Richard Liu was a student in my applied social research and policy studies seminar. Richard, who was completing the final year of his honours B.A., demonstrated exceptionally high levels of skill in both conceptual and quantitative analysis. Over the past two years, Richard has worked with me on a number of projects, several of which relate to Alliance research initiatives. Among other things, he co-authored three major Alliance reports and articles on Alliance research that have appeared in *Policy Options*[57] and *The College Quarterly*.[58] Richard is presently completing an M.A. in sociology at the University of Toronto and will then proceed to the study of law. With that combination of training and his intellectual gifts, he will make a significant contribution to public policy work.

* * *

Working for governments and the broader public sector has accounted for a little over half of my consulting activity. In my experience, a prominent feature of the work has been the diversity of the problems and issues involved. This diversity, plus the intrinsic interest of moving the policy process along, has given the work continuing interest. Several things made it possible to do. The colleagues and research assistants who agreed to join forces with me have been indispensable. The intellectual strength and professional commitment of most public servants has been a sustaining force; they are fine people to work with. Finally, it wouldn't have been possible without the training I received—both in institutions and from working with knowledgeable people who were prepared to share their insights and expertise in an open and enthusiastic way.

CHAPTER 10

Consulting to the Private Sector

Over more than 30 years, I have spent thousands of hours in the offices of private sector firms, ranging from small, struggling enterprises to huge financial institutions. In all cases, I was assisting them either with regulatory compliance concerns or two types of market-related concerns—labour market planning to meet critical skill needs and initiatives to target and expand market share. This is very different from the intrinsic policy work of the public sector.

Particularly over the past 10 years, the Canadian public sector has undergone changes that have resulted in increased emphasis on cost recovery for services provided, the establishment of public sector profit centres, and increased demands for productivity and accountability in the public service. Such changes have softened, but by no means eliminated, differences between the public sector and the private sector.

In the private sector, the bottom line is the bottom line: meeting shareholder expectations, dealing with competition, coping with regulatory pressures. These operational realities have always shaped the corporate mindset. As competition becomes tougher and shareholder expectations higher, they penetrate even more deeply into all aspects of corporate culture. Understanding that culture—and how it differs from university culture or public sector culture—is a central element in private sector consulting success. My early dissertation-related research on corporate decision making and the management of organizational change provided insights into the private sector that proved helpful to my subsequent consulting work.

One of the challenges I experienced fairly frequently was the ambivalence some of my private sector clients had about "university people." My private sector clients (or potential clients) clearly valued knowledge and expertise. They had concerns, however, about the knowledge being delivered on time, in a practically useful way, and at a realistic cost.

Early in my incorporated consultancy career, I met with a vice-president of marketing in a company that was interested in having some demographic profiles and projections prepared. I had a set of colour graphics that showed—in very straightforward terms—various trends that had been taking place in Canadian demographics and where these trends were likely going in the future. I handed these to the V.P., who looked at them carefully, asked a few questions, and then said, "This is interesting information. Have you used it in a marketing context for other clients?" I replied that I had, but couldn't name the clients until I'd cleared it with them. This elicited a positive response from the V.P.: "Yeah, I understand the sensitivities. We don't want our marketing plans broadcast either." Then he added, "I suppose all this will cost an arm and a leg." I had worked up some provisional cost estimates that outlined what I'd have to spend on data, who would be assisting me in the work and how, and what the breakdown of professional fees was. The V.P. looked at the estimates in some detail. "Not as bad as I thought," he commented, still looking pretty sombre. "Are you sure you can do this in two months?" I told him I was. He asked me when I could start. I said, "Tomorrow." The work was done in the form promised, on time, and within budget. I ended up doing a lot of business with that company.

Over the years, I had this type of conversation with many private sector managers interested in contracting consulting services. Although the nature of the assignments being discussed varied widely—many had nothing to do with demographics—there were a number of important common principles that paved the road to a successful outcome. First, the consultant has to do his or her homework and know something about the company and its operating environment. Second, he or she should have a brief but clear presentation of how to approach the kind of problem under discussion, remembering that graphics communicate far more effectively than dense text. Third, if the consultant has been cleared to do so, it's perfectly all right to talk about similar work for other clients, but it should be made plain that confidentiality is not being broken. This is the major point of difference between university culture and the private sector. In university circles, people typically can't wait to publish what they're doing. In the private sector, harsh competitive realities produce a quite different outlook. Fourth, it's important to have on hand some concrete and realistic material on costs and timetables.

I also find it of great help to have a corporate identity by virtue of having incorporated my consulting practice. This helps to telegraph to the client that I, and the people who work with me, have some appreciation of what the private sector is about.

The comments I've made suggest that the private sector has its own culture, and that is certainly true. However, it's important to remember that, within the private sector, there are important variations among industries. For example, I have found that manufacturing organizations are typically more hierarchical in their operating style than high-technology companies. There are many ways the consultant can learn about these differences: read business publications, go to business conferences, have social relations with businesspeople.

* * *

The private sector consulting work performed by my company falls into six broad categories, which emerged for several reasons. Partly, they developed the way they did because of the kind of training I had received. But the direction taken was also extensively shaped by the expertise and influence of many people I worked with, including K.S.R. "Ram" Murthy, John Blakely, Kathleen Reil, and Stephen Gibson. Consulting businesses are not hierarchical—they are fluid, information-sharing entities. My private sector consulting work was also sometimes influenced by academic research that jumped into the realm of practical problem solving. Similarly, work done in other settings—such as commissions, task forces, and the public sector—proved to have important private sector applications. A particularly notable example in this connection is the employment equity work I did with Judge Rosalie Abella's Royal Commission on Equality in Employment.

The six broad areas of my private sector specialization are: (1) demographic forecasts designed to ascertain how the client's marketplace is changing over time; (2) corporate human resources planning studies focused on such issues as turnover, succession planning, and future supply and demand patterns for key occupations; (3) market studies designed to assist the client in finding the best way of positioning existing products in the marketplace or developing and positioning new products; (4) social impact assessment studies of the consequences of new developments; (5) environmental scanning studies designed to identify new challenges and/or opportunities the client organization will face in its operating environment; (6) implementation of employment equity and fair compensation programs and development of human resources systems for managing and valuing diversity.

* * *

As I learned from Charles Westoff at Princeton, demographic forecasts can be made with a high level of accuracy. In a country like Canada, birth and death rates are not subject to wide fluctuations over short periods of time. Immigration is a policy variable, which means that numbers can be estimated with reliability. Neither internal migration (e.g., moving from Ontario to British Columbia) nor emigration (e.g., moving from Canada to the U.S.) is monitored, but reliable estimates are available. Using census of Canada data, one can factor in other variables such as gender, education, occupation, and income. It is also possible to develop such forecasts at different levels of geography: the entire country, the provinces and territories, and metropolitan centres.

I discovered early in my private sector consulting work that many organizations had great interest in such forecasts as a marketing tool. A good example was the major credit card company that wanted to know future growth trends in their target market in different parts of the country. The target market was defined in terms of various factors, including age, gender, education, occupation, and income. I learned this over lunch at the Windsor Arms Wine Cellar Restaurant (alas, long gone) with the company's marketing manager. He confided the nature of the problem: "We're spending a fortune on advertising across the country, and we're not sure how many people are in the target market, where they are, and how fast it's growing. In fact, we're not even sure we've got the target market properly defined, things are changing so much these days." "These days," in this case, happened to be 1975, another reminder that change is a constant in our society.

I developed a proposal that led to a consulting engagement lasting over two years. I created a number of forecasts—two, five, and 10 years out—using different definitions of the target market and examining different regions of the country. I had numerous discussions with corporate management that led to the selection of "the most probable scenario." This was then subjected to final testing and fine-tuning. The scenario showed that there would be faster than expected growth in certain key occupation and income groups. In addition, the number of women entering the target market was growing significantly. A number of unexpected regional differences had also shown up.

The next step was arranging a meeting that would involve two senior members of the client organization's marketing department, two representatives of the company's advertising company, and myself. The advertising people were certainly creatively minded, but I think it would be safe to say that demographic forecasting was not something they were overly familiar with. Fortunately, my tool kit included a number of straightforward explanations of demographic forecasting that I proceeded to offer. However, the advertising company representatives still had a great many questions, such as "How can we be sure?," "How sure can we be?," "What if we're wrong?" and so on. The client organization's marketing department had essentially "bought in" to my forecasts and, as the meeting progressed, they became more vocally supportive of going forward with the responses implied by the forecasts. The meeting ended with a decision that I would work with a representative of the advertising firm to design focus groups that would be demographically representative of the trends indicated by the forecasts. These focus groups would then be formed and discussions held to learn more about what members of the target market were looking for in credit cards and credit card-related services. All of this went forward and, at the end of the day, produced results that led to change in the company's advertising strategy and business planning.

In a subsequent assignment with another organization, I worked with company officials who were concerned about whether or not the firm's market share was growing adequately. The company sold goods that had warranties. The card the purchaser mailed back to activate the warranty had a brief questionnaire that elicited information on customer demographics. Most of the questionnaires were filled out and returned. The company entered the information into a database but looked at it only in a snapshot kind of way. In short, trends were not being examined.

The project I designed had several components. First, I reorganized the database and software in such a way that trend graphics could be produced. Second, using various geographical areas, I compared the demographic profile of purchasers with the demographics of the external potential market. This provided a measure of market penetration. The last part of the work involved producing demographic forecasts for selected geographical areas and comparing the company's customer trend data with external trend data in order to find out if market share was growing, lagging, or staying put. As it turned out, the analysis indicated market share growth was lagging (confirming management's initial perceptions) and also provided geographically disaggregated demographic information that was helpful to more targeted marketing initiatives.

* * *

As Canada's industrial and economic development has proceeded, and technology has continued its forward march, highly trained and skilled human resources have become an increasingly strategic part of achieving productivity gains and maintaining a competitive position in a globalizing marketplace. Skill shortages have a large economic cost.

Early in my consulting career, I came into contact with companies that wanted to develop a better understanding of what was happening with their workforces. The issues included estimating and predicting turnover, developing succession planning systems, and addressing the future availability and cost (in compensation terms) of workers trained in various key occupations.

I began to develop relatively simple models that could be used in virtually any organization to analyse and predict turnover and estimate future requirements. This approach takes the view that it is critically important to have tight linkages between certain human resources planning functions—such as succession planning, recruitment, and training—and general business planning.

As my consulting group carried out this type of work in various companies, we recognized the need for better information on the future labour market supply of workers in certain strategic, high-skill occupations. As it turned out, other people were having the same thoughts. In late 1974, I was contacted by Neil A. Macdougall, the general manager of the Technical Service Council (TSC). The TSC was established in 1927 as a non-profit placement service and personnel consulting firm run by industry. At the time the TSC became one of my clients (1975), it was financed by over 500 industries, was used for recruiting by over 1500 firms, and had offices in all major Canadian cities. Over the 15 years my company served the TSC as a consultant, the council continued to grow. In 1988, it was financed by over 800 member organizations and was used by over 1600 firms.

Neil Macdougall was a tall, athletic man in his middle years. Trained as an engineer and highly goal-directed, he had two passions in life: flying his own plane and making the Technical Service Council the best organization of its type in Canada.

He had learned about my work by reading the publications of the Commission on Post-Secondary Education in Ontario. When we met, he came directly to the point. The Technical Service Council was interested in entering into a potentially long-term relationship with a consultant who could produce a series of supply and demand studies in various strategic occupational areas such as engineering, chemistry, business, and accounting. To be useful to the end users, the studies would have to contain detail for different industrial groupings and be periodically updated. I asked for three weeks to develop a detailed proposal. Macdougall agreed.

Forecasting labour market supply and demand uses some of the tools of demographic forecasting but goes considerably further because of the need to include various economic variables. Fortunately, my work at Princeton and subsequent self-study had given me a good grasp of the economic principles involved, but I was hardly an expert in macroeconomic modelling. To do the Technical Service Council work properly, I needed a partner

K.S.R. "Ram" Murthy, 2004.

who was. I made many enquiries and had the considerable good fortune to connect up with K.S.R. "Ram" Murthy, an economist and modelling expert at Trent University. Ram was involved in various federal government economic forecasting initiatives, so apart from his technical expertise he understood the dynamics of the applied setting.

Over the 15 years we worked together, Ram and I produced many labour market supply and demand trend briefings and papers for the Technical Service Council. In addition, we wrote five major monographs that were published and nationally distributed by the Council.[59] This, of course, led to other work. The various studies Ram Murthy and I conducted, and which the TSC so effectively disseminated, provided several thousand employers across Canada with occupational supply and demand information that was of direct practical use in planning and recruitment initiatives related to meeting critical skill needs. The studies also provided information useful to the educational and training institutions responsible for bringing on the required supply. The need for the Technical Service Council studies eventually faded as the federal government became more actively and effectively involved in occupational forecasting. I believe the groundbreaking work Ram Murthy and I did helped move this agenda forward.

Apart from his technical expertise, Ram Murthy is a person with a deep generosity of spirit. He trained me (and my long-time associate John Blakely) in a wide range of forecasting and modelling techniques we continue to use today.

* * *

The demographic forecasting I discussed earlier in this chapter is a highly useful tool when an organization is seeking to target its marketing and promotion activities more effectively. However, there are times when an organization wants to change its image and bring new products and services to the marketplace. My company has been involved in various studies relating to the latter objectives.

In the early 1980s, I was approached by a large Toronto-based credit union that required an analysis of its market and assistance with the design and implementation of a major membership drive. The credit union was operating in an increasingly competitive environment for financial institutions and was seriously concerned about lack of growth in its market share and the looming possibility of actual deterioration.

After two exploratory meetings with the senior management of the credit union, it became clear to me that a multi-phase project was required. First, it would be necessary to gather data on existing customers and potential customers with particular reference to what they were looking for in a financial institution. Second, using the customer and potential customer information, it would be necessary to come up with a strategy for redesigning the credit union's image and service profile. Finally, with these fundamentals in place, a membership drive could be designed and launched. I developed a proposal along these lines and it was accepted.

In addition to the senior management group, the credit union had a board of directors that was very much involved in the project. It soon became clear to me that management and certain influential directors did not always share the same definition of the problems at hand. Since the work could not go forward effectively in the absence of agreement, I found myself attending many joint management–directors meetings talking about the project in ways designed to build shared understandings that would provide the foundation for a go-forward consensus. The downside of this was that it delayed the organization's response to a challenging business situation. The upside was that once a working consensus was arrived at, there was a higher level of buy-in to the project and commitment to its successful conduct and implementation.

Given the nature of their business, financial institutions tend to be relatively effective in maintaining customer data and having a good idea of what their catchment areas are. The credit union was no exception, and I did not have great difficulty developing representative samples for surveys of existing customers and potential customers. As soon as the survey designs had been finalized, I hired some assistants and plunged into data gathering and analysis.

The survey data produced a number of important insights: (1) many existing customers were significantly underutilizing the credit union—in some cases because they didn't know the services were available and in other cases because they were getting the services at a different institution; (2) the credit union didn't have a credit card service, and this was perceived as a major disadvantage; (3) personal contact between customers and non-customers emerged as a vitally important mechanism for recruiting new customers to the credit union; (4) the credit union's image was perceived as too "low profile," and its promotional materials were viewed as being unattractive and not sufficiently informative.

A senior management and directors meeting was organized for me to present the survey results and implications for action. Various findings created quite a stir in the group, and some reactions were borderline emotional. I kept emphasizing how important it was that we now knew what the problems were and had a solid foundation for designing and implementing needed changes. Every consultant sooner or later experiences the "shoot the messenger" syndrome, and I was anxious for this not to happen on this occasion! My strategy was to be as patient as humanly possible while people ventilated and keep on reinforcing the positive perspective. I found this easy to do, since I firmly believed that now that we knew the problems, we could fix them. The meeting was long and, frankly, exhausting, but by the time it ended people had come around and the working consensus was still intact. I should add that this situation is not unique. Such meetings occur with great regularity in the consulting business, although they do vary in their level of intensity.

Phase 1 of the project was complete. Phase 2 involved redesigning the credit union's image and promotional materials. I now needed some assistance on the creative side. For a number of years, I met my creative requirements through Instructional Media Services—IMS for short—which was a unit located in the Faculty of Medicine of the University of Toronto. The primary mission IMS had was to supply the graphic materials extensively used in medical education. However, the IMS staff were available on a fee-for-service basis for other creative assignments, and I made frequent use of their services when the occasion arose. The credit union project required the development of a new logo for the organization, promotional brochures, display posters, and a new "membership kit." I provided the IMS creative people with the essential sociological dimensions that would have be represented in the material they prepared. These dimensions included: (1) communicating financial stability/solidity; (2) communicating a focus on people as well as business; (3) making the "full service" spectrum very clear and easily understandable; (4) ensuring gender and racial diversity in all pictorial materials. I provided the text, which I had written in light of what I had learned from the data gathering and analysis.

IMS provided me with initial mock-ups of the new materials, which I took to a meeting of the credit union's senior management and directors. After the Phase 1 meeting I described earlier, I was ready for anything. To my pleasant surprise, the draft materials developed by IMS received a positive reception, with only a few suggestions for minor changes. I proceeded to finalize with IMS the production of the materials the credit union would use as a central part of the new membership drive.

Working with the credit union on that membership drive consumed the final months of the project. I designed a number of campaigns, including a Members Recruit for the Credit Union Campaign, an Underutilizers Campaign, and a Non-Members Campaign. Creative use was made of mailers, computer-based marketing, and other innovative multi-method marketing approaches. Staff were trained at the credit union's various locations, so that they would become more effective in the marketing function when dealing with customers. I designed a monitoring and evaluation system, so that results could be tracked and performance assessed. In addition, a specific marketing function was set up in the organization and a marketing manager was hired. After one year of the membership campaigns, the credit union's growth rate was 90.2 percent better than in the preceding year.

The credit union project is a classic example of the steps a consultant goes through to reorient a client's business. As the following example shows, however, there are other approaches as well.

In the late 1990s, I was contacted by a well-known executive search firm that indicated they were acting for a major telephone and telecommunications company. I was advised that they had been retained to locate a consultant to work on some highly sensitive business matters for the company. I accepted an invitation to attend a meeting in a week's time. This was the first time I had ever been approached about a consulting assignment through a headhunter, an unusual practice.

The meeting was held in an office tower near the corner of King and Bay Streets in downtown Toronto. Apart from myself, there were four people present. One was the managing partner of the headhunting firm, his assistant, an executive vice-president from the telecommunications company, and his assistant. After a few introductory pleasantries from the managing partner, the executive V.P. took over the discussion. He explained that because of new competitive dynamics in the telephone and telecommunications industry, his company was facing a revenue challenge. If the company was going to continue to grow in an acceptable fashion, it had to develop new business areas, and quickly.

The executive V.P. had been put in charge of a corporate task force with the mission of identifying new product and service areas. He indicated that a highly confidential document had been prepared, which profiled and assessed the new business areas.

With some very strict conditions attached, this document would be provided to the consultant selected for the mission. The executive V.P. then addressed his central dilemma. Although the task force felt the new product and service areas were technically feasible to develop, they were far less sure of the extent to which the marketplace was ready for such new offerings. Conventional market research was not the immediate answer, because concepts—rather than established products and services—were being dealt with. The executive V.P. concluded by saying that what the task force wanted was an analysis of the changing sociological landscape and how this might affect receptivity to the new product and service lines being considered.

I was then invited to give my reactions. I had done consulting assignments in the telecommunications sector before and, although the work was mainly focused on human resources planning issues, I had developed a sense of the sector's culture and business operations. Also, before the meeting, I had taken the precaution of consulting various information sources—including the Internet—that helped bring me up to speed on sector developments.

As a starting point, I addressed the general principle that the development of new products and services is generally most cost-effective and rapid when the new offerings are closely linked to the company's existing business and technology platforms. I agreed with the executive V.P. that this principle, however important, could not be looked at in isolation. It was vitally important to obtain measures of market readiness; given his description of the situation, a sociological scan would be an appropriate starting point. I then outlined the steps I viewed as fundamental to the project. First, I would have to read the strategic business development document. Second, sociological scan work would have to be done for each proposed new product and service area. Third, the results of this exercise would be subjected to in-depth discussions with members of the corporate task force and other key corporate officials. Fourth, it would then be necessary to put the new product and service proposals into some form of priority order given various factors such as development costs, technical feasibility, time to market, and market readiness. Fifth, with this level of definition in place, the assessment of each product and service area would be tightened by factoring in any additional market research intelligence that could be obtained from corporate databases or other sources. In short, I was outlining a multi-factor strategy built from the foundation up.

We had some further general discussion around these ideas, I made a few brief comments about my consulting group and how it operated, and the meeting concluded. Next morning, I received a telephone call from the managing partner of the headhunter firm. The telecommunications company had decided to engage my consulting practice for the mission. He wondered if I could drop by his office fairly soon. He had a copy of the business development document for me, an undertaking of confidentiality form I would have to sign, and a retainer letter from the telecommunications company. He asked if I could give him, in three days' time, a one-pager outlining what my company would deliver, what it would cost, and what the timetable would be.

As I read the business development document later that evening, I could readily see the reasons for strict confidentiality. The material was *very* sensitive. As I got more deeply into the document, I could see the value of carrying out sociological scan work. However, I could also see that having this done by a single person was risky. Among other things, there were several proposed new product and service lines, each with their own set of sociological dynamics. I wanted to involve my University of Toronto sociology colleague Lorne Tepperman in the scan phase. Lorne and I had worked together on other projects, including corporate missions, and I had great respect for his ability to create highly imaginative but rigorous sociological analyses and link them to practical concerns. I telephoned the executive V.P., discussed the situation with him, and obtained approval to proceed with my plan.

With the telecommunications company's proposed new product and service lines very much in mind, Lorne and I scanned the sociological landscape in five areas: the new population, the new family, the new workplace, the new leisure, and the new social problems. I then took the lead on the in-depth sessions with corporate officials that led to prioritization of the proposed new product and service lines and the factoring in of additional market research intelligence.

Over the ensuing years, some of the new products and services have appeared in the marketplace. Others may still be in development or may have been abandoned, having been overtaken by new technological or competitive realities. Whatever the final outcome, the project clearly demonstrates that sociological knowledge can make practically useful contributions to the process of business adaptation and evolution.

My final example here tells the story of how one of sociology's longest established methods—survey research—helped a multinational computer company launch a new line of products in 1998. The company, which I had consulted to previously, had a new generation of servers and desktop and laptop computers it wanted to bring out in the Canadian market. It had a large-scale U.S. market research study that provided a great deal of information on different segments of the market and what people were looking for. The U.S. study also contained information on sources of information purchasers relied on, price point sensitivities, and competing products. The central problem facing the company's marketing decision makers was that it was by no means clear that the U.S. results were applicable to Canada.

I proposed a replication/validation survey. This meant gathering the same range of data in Canada as was done in the U.S. but carefully adjusting the methodology to take account of differences in the size of the Canadian market, the nature of the population distribution, and differences in Canadian industrial and economic structure. The client organization agreed to proceed in this direction.

As usual with private sector assignments, there was great pressure to complete the work very quickly—consistent, of course, with accurate results. I needed a partner.

I have known Kathleen Reil for over 24 years, going back to when she was a graduate student in my University of Toronto policy methods seminar. After graduating with her M.A., Kathleen entered employment with Ontario's environment ministry, where she was soon leading a series of environmental social impact studies. She remained at the ministry for a few years and then decided to open her own consulting firm with her sister, Jane, a lawyer by training. Although Kathleen specializes in environmental issues, she is highly expert in a wide range of areas, including survey research and statistical analysis. Over the years, we have collaborated on several projects, reports, and publications. Happily, she agreed to join forces with me on the replication/validation survey. We developed a nationally representative sample with regional and industrial detail, trained and supervised a staff of telephone interviewers, and analysed and reported the data.

The study met the client's needs. It showed which parts of the U.S. marketing plan could be used in Canada. Equally important, it showed which parts could not.

* * *

As I mentioned in Chapter 7, my interest in environmental issues led me to become involved in a number of environment-related projects, including social impact assessment studies. I carried out this work for the voluntary or advocacy sector, the public sector, and private sector corporations.

One early spring morning in 1975, I was sitting in my university office working on a faculty recruitment plan, one of my responsibilities as a department chair. The intercom on my telephone sounded and I picked it up. My secretary, Frances Knapp—a wonderfully efficient woman in her forties—advised me that a Dr. Wasyl Janischewskyj of the University of Toronto's Engineering Faculty was outside and hoped he might see me briefly. The name didn't mean anything to me, but I assumed it must have something to do with the engineering manpower supply and demand studies with which I was involved. Dr. Janischewskyj turned out to be a tall, grey-haired, and distinguished-looking man in his early fifties. He was polite almost to the point of courtliness and combined this with a genial manner. He started off by apologizing for coming by unannounced and explained that since he was in the area, he had decided to take a chance. He asked if he might have a few minutes of my time. I was still somewhat preoccupied with staffing formulae, but Dr. Janischewskyj had a personality that was hard not to like.

We started a discussion. It turned out that Dr. Janischewskyj had heard about my work in connection with an earlier environment-oriented project. He explained that he was an electrical engineer and was involved in research on the impacts of ultra-high voltage (UHV) electric power transmission corridors. I learned that the General Electric Company—in co-operation with the Electric Power Research Institute (a Palo Alto, California, think-tank)—had established in Pittsfield, Massachusetts, a large initiative called Project UHV. Project UHV included an experimental ultra-high voltage transmission line about a mile and a half long. This line, which had been constructed at huge cost, could be started up, shut down, and manipulated in various ways for the purposes of a wide range of engineering and medical studies that were ongoing. (This was my introduction to the body of work on the effects of electromagnetic radiation on human and animal health.) "But," Janischewskyj continued, "we're finding that many of the potential problems have social or psychological elements, things like UHV impacts on television reception. We need a social scientist to join the team." This meeting led to a seven-year-long working relationship.

Wasyl Janischewskyj had a modest and self-effacing way. It was from others I learned that he was not simply a professor of electrical engineering but one of North America's leading electric power researchers. Neither of us knew much about each other's fields. We both made the effort to obtain some basic understandings, but there is only so far you can go with this. Amazingly, it didn't seem to matter. We worked together as an effective team.

General Electric was required by U.S. law to do impact studies and, to the company's credit, had committed resources to leading-edge work rather than taking a basic compliance position. Wasyl Janischewskyj and I developed detailed specifications for a large-scale study that would examine the effects of ultra-high voltage electric power transmission lines on television picture quality. The project would require a sophisticated fusion of electrical engineering and social science knowledge and would involve complex logistics. After two months of specification development work, General Electric entered into a contract with my company.

The first step was to create two-and-a-half-hour-long three-quarter-inch videotapes of various types of program material uncontaminated by any type of interference or degradation. Since this material was going to be reacted to by various groups of human subjects in field trials, it was important that the material itself not contain any content that would be likely to induce

Part of the system used to experimentally contaminate television picture segments, Pittsfield, Massachusetts.

emotive responses (for example, images of a much disliked politician). In short, I was looking for material that was neutral or bland in nature. Putting these master tapes together took a lot of image selection and editing time. The next step was taking the master tapes and the videotape machine to Project UHV in Pittsfield, Massachusetts. I should add that this was before videotape machines became extensively miniaturized. "The Monster," as my associates and I called the project videotape machine, was three feet long, two feet wide, and seemed to weigh a ton. Getting it through both U.S. and Canadian customs was an interesting experience.

Once at Project UHV, the next task was to contaminate various segments with different types and levels of power line interference. Some segments would be left uncontaminated to serve as controls. Janischewskyj and I had worked out a detailed protocol that specified precisely how many segments should be contaminated by which type of interference, at what magnitude, and for how long. The actual process of contamination was hugely complex. The experimental UHV line had to be started, shut down, restarted, and manipulated in various ways to produce the required results. Sometimes we had to wait for the right ambient weather conditions.

We were almost there when an equipment failure wrecked the entire process. I had created a backup of the master tape, but it turned out that it couldn't be used because it was a second-generation tape and would not be experimentally acceptable. I returned to Toronto to commence the labourious task of creating a second master tape. This time, however, I had discussions with General Electric officials and obtained their agreement to increase the budget, so that a second videotape machine could be purchased. By wiring the two machines up in the right way, it would be possible to make two first-generation master tapes simultaneously. I should add that each of these machines cost over $3000, a fair sum in 1976.

When I eventually returned to Project UHV in Pittsfield, I had two uncontaminated master tapes and each of the two machines on which they had been prepared. I was also armed with letters for the customs officers testifying that I was a responsible researcher and not a videotape machine importer/exporter or worse. This time, the lengthy and complex process of tape contamination worked properly.

With the master tape and the machine used to create it back in Toronto, I began the process of producing the tape that would be used in the human trials. This tape would comprise 132 10-second segments of program material. Some of the segments were uncontaminated to serve as controls. The others had been contaminated by varying types and magnitudes of UHV power line interference. To avoid any systemic bias, the order in which the segments were presented was arrived at randomly. After each 10-second clip of program material, there were 10 seconds of blank tape during which the human subjects involved in the trials would rate the quality and acceptability of the preceding picture.

There were, on average, 10 human subjects in each test group, and they were selected with statistical care to ensure proper representation of the general population. Fifty-five trials were held at seven test sites in the U.S. and Canada. The sites were designed to replicate normal television viewing conditions.

During the years of my thoroughly enjoyable and effective collaboration with Wasyl Janischewskyj, we produced reports for

General Electric, published our results in refereed journals, and made many conference presentations.[60] Of central importance, the work built a bridge between what was learned about social impacts and the development of UHV power line engineering standards that would minimize or eliminate the effect of such impacts. This would not have been possible without the fusion of applied social research knowledge and electrical engineering knowledge.

The work carried out for the General Electric company was really about trying to deal with impacts before they became impacts. In other cases, however, impacts have to be assessed in situations where the people affected are already involved.

In late 1994, I was contacted by a major Canadian company with a subsidiary that was involved in extracting aggregates from gravel quarries in the Hamilton, Ontario, area. One of the quarries had been fully excavated some time ago and was now being used as a landfill site for non-toxic solid waste. Another quarry in the same general area had become depleted relatively recently, and the company was now proceeding with a proposal to develop it into a landfill site as well. The Ontario Ministry of Environment and Energy required that the company conduct and submit a complete environmental assessment before any authorization to proceed was issued. This environmental assessment was required to include a full social impact assessment study that would identify all such impacts, provide guidance to the development of impact management strategies, and ensure that the concerns of local residents were fully understood and properly taken into account.

It was clearly going to be a large-scale study. A considerable volume of data would have to be gathered and analysed. It would be necessary to work closely with company officials, who had a significant business interest at stake in the matter. Extensive consultations and briefings would also have to be conducted with the residents' committee and the lawyers and consultants representing their interests.

Given her broad experience with environmental matters and specific experience with social impact assessment studies, I decided to contact Kathleen Reil and propose that we join forces for the purposes of the project. We almost immediately agreed to do so, on a simple 50–50 basis. Because we were both experienced in social impact assessment studies, development of the proposal to the company was relatively straightforward. It was accepted within two day of its receipt.

Our first step was to arrange a meeting with company officials to scope out a number of project-related issues. In addition, we arranged a site visit to the quarry and surrounding area where the proposed landfill development would take place. Once we had done this, we were in a position to specify the data collection areas (that is, the geographical areas within the range of probable impact) and the types of data to be gathered. We decided that we would have to survey residents, agricultural operators in the area, non-resident property owners, and—finally—persons responsible for operating or managing social facilities in the area. With these decisions in place, it was now possible to develop statistically appropriate samples and design the various survey forms.

When all this work was complete—and the process took several weeks—we were in a position to make a detailed presentation to a public meeting of the residents' committee and their legal and technical advisers. In our experience, it is always best to come to such meetings with a clear plan but recognizing, of course, that changes may have to be made. The development of our plan had been guided by three objectives: we wanted the plan to be thorough, we wanted it to be easily understandable by lay people, and we wanted to ensure that resident concerns were fully and properly taken into account.

Our strategy proved to be sound. Sometimes public meetings on environmental issues can erupt with high levels of emotion and conflict, with the result that nothing is accomplished. The public meeting Kathleen and I addressed proceeded in an orderly way. We made a detailed presentation of the project methodology. Questions were asked and responded to fully. Suggestions were made and these were carefully noted. By being completely transparent with the residents' committee, we had established a foundation for the trust that was essential to the project going forward successfully and the results being accepted as a basis for action.

Two weeks later, we had our finalized methodology in place and approvals in hand from the client organization and the residents' committee. We now plunged into an extensive process of data gathering and analysis. Throughout this, we kept company officials and the residents' committee informed. This is the best strategy a consultant has to ensure that the tabled report is accepted by the various stakeholder groups.

Our final report contained 14 recommendations setting forward specific measures to ameliorate impacts and protect resident interests. All of the proposals flowed in a transparent way from the research results. The report was accepted by the residents' committee and the company and formed a central part of the full environmental assessment required by the Ministry of Environment and Energy. In due course, the company received permission to proceed with its project.

* * *

In Chapter 7, I discussed scanning of organizational operating environments as a classic example of a multi-method, applied, policy-oriented research method. This aspect of my consulting company's work grew out of a 1986 project my University of Toronto colleague Lorne Tepperman and I did for IBM Canada.

Over the ensuing years, I used this approach in various settings, both in the public and private sectors. As the so-called information explosion continued to expand, I found that the approach attracted increasing interest from private sector clients. This is because environmental scanning is essentially an information management tool designed to help a company identify what it really needs to know about its operating environment and then apply that knowledge to corporate action plans.

In my private sector environmental scanning work, I have found that client organizations are almost invariably focused on three things. First, they want to know about what is happening in the realm of government regulation—with particular reference to new developments and how to get a cost-effective response mechanism into place. Second, they want to know about anything that may affect their marketplace (e.g., demographics, technology, regulation, changing lifestyles, etc.), both in terms of new opportunities and new competitive challenges. Third, they are concerned about effective workforce management, which includes being able to meet critical skill needs, managing increasingly diverse workforce demographics, and coping with the complexities of employment law and regulation—both current and emerging.

The broad approach to environmental scanning does not vary that much from company to company. What does vary—often significantly—is the specific type of information relevant to a company's operations and effectively linking that information to practical corporate action plans. To do environmental scans effectively, the consultant must be able to comprehend many different types of corporate cultures and operating environments, be skilful at development of an overall conceptual situation analysis, and have an in-depth understanding of how to access data—and, by analysing it appropriately, extract the nuggets of corporately useful strategic intelligence they contain.

This type of work will become increasingly important in years to come as information proliferation—driven by technologies like the Internet—continues and organizational operating environments become more and more complex.

* * *

As I mentioned in Chapters 8 and 9, involvement in Judge Abella's Royal Commission on Equality in Employment led my consulting firm to become extensively engaged in the implementation and maintenance of employment equity programs. My company's private sector clients who proceeded with the implementation of employment equity were doing so for one of three reasons. Some were federally regulated industries (e.g., banking, radio and television, transportation) and were therefore regulated under the federal Legislated Employment Equity Program. Others did business with the federal government as suppliers of goods or services and were accordingly required to comply with the Federal Contractors Program for Employment Equity. A final category of organizations was affected by Ontario employment equity legislation. When the NDP won the 1990 Ontario election, the new government sent a strong signal to the province's employer community that legislated employment equity would be introduced. An Employment Equity Commission was formed and much study and consultation was carried out, culminating in Ontario's employment equity legislation receiving royal assent on December 14, 1993.

The companies to which my group provided employment equity consulting services varied widely. A broad range of industrial and business sectors were involved, including manufacturing, accounting, consulting, telecommunications, banks and financial institutions, high-technology enterprises in such fields as computer and advanced imaging systems, and energy and pipeline companies. The client companies also differed in size, ranging from organizations that were just over the 100 employee regulatory threshold to complex corporations with 60,000 or more employees. Another source of variation was the number of operating centres the client company had. In the case of smaller enterprises, this typically meant one or two offices in one or two cities. In the case of some large corporations, there were many locations, dotted across the country. The latter presented complicated logistical issues, particularly when dealing with the employment equity requirement that all members of an employer's workforce be surveyed to ascertain the representation levels of employment equity-designated group members. Client companies also differed in terms of the nature of their commitment to the employment equity implementation and maintenance process. Some were doing it solely because it was a regulatory requirement. Others proceeded because of regulatory requirements but also because senior management took the view that institutionalizing equity principles was sound human resources management practice.

A final source of variation was the nature of my consulting group's engagement with the client company. In some cases, we would set up an employment equity program and that would be the end of the story. In other cases, we would continue to work with the client company for years, updating equity data, improving data management systems, assisting with the production of reports, and periodically reviewing employment policies and practices to ensure that equity principles were being followed in a wide variety of areas, including recruitment, training, and promotion. In still other cases, equity-related work with a client company would lead to consulting involvement in other areas of human resources management practice, including benefits audits, conflict resolution systems, anti-harassment policies and programs, and developing strategies for the effective harmonization of work and family responsibilities.

As of 2004, work related to employment equity has been an important part of my consulting company's service profile for 19 years. Over this period, I would describe our experience as being characterized by two main dimensions. The first is successive waves of activity. The second relates to increasing diversification in the service mix we provide.

The work John Blakely and I did for Judge Abella's Royal Commission on Equality in Employment took place between 1983 and 1984. Even before legislation and contract compliance regulations came into place in 1986, many organizations took steps to commence the implementation of employment equity. In some cases, this was done because management decision makers had concluded that employment equity was an inevitable regulatory development. In other cases, such as those of the Ontario Public Service and the City of Toronto (discussed in Chapter 8), the implementation of employment equity reflected a desire to exhibit jurisdictional leadership and also to introduce employment practices that were increasingly viewed as sound human resources management.

My consulting company was strategically positioned to participate in this rapidly emerging market, and we were soon implementing employment equity programs in a wide variety of organizations. By 1990, employment equity programs had been implemented by most of the employers regulated under the federal employment equity legislation or the federal contract compliance program. In a number of cases, we continued to work with these organizations, assisting them with the ongoing maintenance of their programs. The second wave of new employment equity implementation work came along in 1990, when the NDP formed the government in Ontario. The Ontario approach to legislated employment equity was closely modelled after the federal system. This proved to be a strategic advantage for my consulting firm, given our several years' experience in the implementation of employment equity programs established in response to federal requirements.

The Conservatives formed the Ontario government in 1995 and, early in their mandate, repealed the Ontario Employment Equity Act. This development, however, did not preclude my consulting practice from becoming involved in a further wave of employment equity activity. By this time, we were working with a number of employers who had implemented employment equity, found it a desirable human resources management practice, and had no intention of dismantling their programs. This led to a third wave of consulting activity that had two main components. First, employers committed to employment equity wanted to know what they could do under the new regime. Second, by 1998, new external labour market comparison data—based on the 1996 census—were available. This meant that organizations with employment equity programs had to ensure that their employment equity data systems incorporated the new data, that new statistical reports were prepared on employment equity-designated group representation levels in the employer's workforce compared to the external labour market, and that plans for the achievement of employment equity goals and targets were reviewed in light of the new conditions.

Over the years, my consulting company's employment equity business became extensively diversified. Initially, my objective was to provide a leading-edge consulting capability in the implementation and maintenance of employment equity programs. That objective continues to this day but has been supplemented by other activities. In Chapter 7, I mentioned meeting, in late 1989, the lawyer and publisher Stephen Gibson. We started to work together in 1990. As a starting point, Stephen wanted to diversify his law-oriented publishing into human resources management. For my part, I wanted to develop venues for reaching a larger audience with the employment equity implementation and maintenance strategies my consulting company had developed. After several months of careful planning, we launched, in January 1991, the first issue of the monthly publication titled *The Employment Equity Review*.[61] The lead article in the inaugural edition had the prescient title, "NDP Government to Introduce Employment Equity Legislation."

The focus of the *Review*, which was mainly written by John Blakely and myself, was to present timely and accurate information on best practices in the field of employment equity. Encouraged by the enthusiastic take-up the new publication received, Stephen and I went on to plan and then carry out a series of employment equity conferences, which drew large audiences for several years. Both the publication and the conferences recruited many new clients seeking assistance in implementing and maintaining their employment equity programs.

At the beginning of 1996, Stephen and I changed the title of *The Employment Equity Review* to *Valuing Diversity*,[62] and John Blakely and I began to produce new types of content. This decision was motivated by our strong perception that an increasing number of employers were coming to view employment equity not in narrow, compliance-oriented terms but rather as a important part of effective human resources management in an era of change.

Our perception proved correct—*Valuing Diversity* did well. When, later in 1996, Stephen went to the U.S. to pursue new ventures, the publication was taken over by Emond Montgomery Publications, an organization run by Paul Emond, a highly capable law professor at York University's Osgoode Hall. In late 1999, Paul and I had discussions that led to a decision to migrate *Valuing Diversity* to *The Compensation Law Reporter*,[63] with an associated shift in content. *The Compensation Law Reporter* was acquired by Canada Law Book in late 2000 and continues to be based on the material John Blakely and I prepare.

In addition to expert opinion newsletter publication, I was interested in writing business-oriented books on employment equity and other human resources management issues. In 1987, I made contact with CCH Canadian Publishers, a leading Canadian publisher of legal works that was interested in bringing out more titles related to human resources management. In connection with my employment equity implementation work, I had assembled a considerable amount of briefing materials and other templates that I felt could be used as the basis for a book. CCH agreed and, in 1988, *Information Systems for Employment Equity: An Employer Guide*[64] was published. The book, which provided a practical, step-by-step guide to employment equity implementation, went into 12 printings and formed the basis for a long-term relationship with CCH Canadian.

Between 1990 and 2002, five more books were published. In the 1990 book, *Computing for Equity: Computer Applications for Employment Equity,*[65] John Blakely and I joined forces with Eric Severn, a computer programmer, to develop strategies for automating various types of employment equity statistical analysis and regulatory report preparation. The book was accompanied by a *Demonstration Workbook,*[66] which contained a sample software diskette and exercises the reader could work through in order to become familiar with the procedures. This book rapidly led to a number of assignments working on the employment equity data systems of various organizations.

It was at this point that I met Paul Boase and encouraged him to become associated with my consulting group. Paul had a master's degree in psychology combined with systems analysis and computer programming skills that were at a very high level. I had worked with computer specialists in the past who were technically very proficient but did not have much knowledge of or interest in the substance of the issues being addressed. That was not an issue with Paul. Until he left for Ottawa in 2000, he made a major contribution to the consulting group by regularly coming up with innovations that kept us competitive on the database development and systems solutions side of the business.

In 1996, John Blakely and I published *Information Systems for Managing Workplace Diversity*[67] with CCH Canadian. By now, CCH had established a presence in the U.S., the U.K., Europe, Australia, New Zealand, Singapore, and Japan. The company had also extensively revised its approaches to book promotion and distribution, which made it even more of a force in the increasingly competitive world of publishing. The *Managing Workplace Diversity* book was designed to fulfill the same general purpose as the 1988 *Employer Guide* book but took account of the many changes that had occurred over the intervening eight years.

Re-thinking HR Management: Strategies for Success in an Era of Change,[68] authored by John Blakely and myself, was brought out by CCH in 1999. This book reflected the increasing diversity of my consulting group's private sector practice. Drawing on an expanded base of experience, *Re-thinking HR Management* went beyond equity and diversity concerns to address such issues as the linkage between human resources plans and business plans, improving organizational effectiveness, and dealing with such matters as labour adjustment, work and family life, and telework. Less than a year later, John and I broke additional new ground with *Equal Pay*.[69] Published by CCH, the book was a practical guide to pay equity regulatory requirements and effective compliance strategies in all Canadian jurisdictions.

Our most recent CCH book—*Internet Solutions for HR Managers*[70]—also explored new territory by examining how rapidly evolving Internet technology can contribute to various areas of HR management, such as recruitment, benchmark development, environmental scanning, and networking. John and I were joined on this book by Katherine Lee, an outstanding graduate of the University of Toronto's master of industrial relations program and an expert on e-business and Internet applications. In keeping with the technology we were writing about, John and I never met Katherine in person. Her invaluable contribution to the authorship team was made entirely by e-mail and teleconferencing. Katherine is now completing an M.B.A. at York University's Schulich School of Business, and I have every expectation that I will meet her in person at some future York University social event!

* * *

As the foregoing shows, my consulting firm pursued several lines of business in the private sector. Over time, many of these activities became increasingly diversified. This diversification served two important purposes. First, it ensured that there was always business to be done. Second, it made the consulting practice infinitely more interesting.

A significant amount of the consulting group's work came through referrals, but network development was also important. The latter was fostered by speaking engagements and conferences. Also important was constant publication of practical, easy-to-understand, and immediately useful material on issues of current importance. A further key success factor was the ability to form and sustain strategic alliances with other consultants or professionals and being able to create fast response teams that can "hit the ground running" and work together effectively.

These principles are equally valid in public sector and broader public sector consulting, but I find them particularly crucial when working in the private sector environment.

Part III

Summation

The final part of the book contains only one chapter: "Taking Social Research to the Larger World." This chapter begins with a brief, summative account of some key events that have shaped my life and my career as a university professor and consultant. Setting aside personal experiences, I then examine some of the larger questions Canada faces in today's world and the contribution that can be made by applied, policy-oriented social research in understanding and coping with these questions and challenges. The last part explores issues and questions related to strategies for more effective training of applied social researchers.

CHAPTER 11

Taking Social Research to the Larger World

This book looks back over eight years of post-secondary education and 38 years of university professorship and consulting work. In cumulative terms, it accounts for more than two thirds of my life to date.

Like all careers, mine has had some trying moments, but most of it was—and continues to be—vastly enjoyable and productive of sustained personal growth. How did this happen? I was born ahead of the baby boom—a career-long timing advantage—but not born into an era ravaged by world war or economic depression. Quite the contrary. I and many others like me were enormous beneficiaries of sustained economic growth in the 1950s and 1960s and expansionary government policies that promoted growth in education and economic opportunity. Although I would never have admitted it in my youth, I was probably lucky to be born in Victoria, British Columbia, Canada. Although a small city, Victoria had a disproportionately high share of very interesting and gifted people, some of whom I had the good fortune to meet.

I started my university education at a small but good place—Victoria College—where small classes provided a chance to work closely with professors (learning what post-secondary education was all about) and form enduring friendships with classmates. It was also because of Victoria College that, in 1961, I met my wife, Lorna Marsden, who has always supported my life and career as I have tried to support hers.

I lived in England and Europe for a year at a point in my life when the maturity- and character-building elements of the experience were maximized. I met Kaspar Naegele at the University of British Columbia, and I am still in awe of the selfless contribution he made to my intellectual and personal development. I was

Avie Bennett (chancellor emeritus of York University), Lorna R. Marsden, and Edward B. Harvey.

intelligent enough to follow his advice and accept Princeton over other universities for my doctoral studies. From start to finish, I was at Princeton for only two years and seven months. But during that short time, I was given a lifetime foundation.

I was exceptionally fortunate to return to Canada in 1966, when this energetic, civil, and inherently decent country was in the process of transformative changes that would build a better nation and create previously non-existent opportunities for people with my kind of training. I benefited and grew from association with those colleagues, students, and research assistants who shared my view of the importance of applied, policy-oriented work and enthusiastically engaged with me in pursuit of the mission.

I was given the chance to work on initiatives of national importance and see some of my ideas work their way into public policy. As a way of life, it has been—and continues to be—characterized by an exciting diversity of work, a fascinating range of contacts, and ongoing opportunities for new experiences and personal growth.

* * *

Setting personal experiences aside, I want to explore two broad questions. First, in today's world, is there an important role for applied, policy-oriented social research in our society? Second, is such work a valuable specialization to foster and grow within the broader context of sociology in general?

I think the answer to both these question is yes.

For my generation of applied social researchers, the important policy areas included health care, education and training, employment and labour markets, immigration, and equality of opportunity. The new generation of applied social researchers will find that these policy areas continue to be of importance, but that the questions that need to be investigated have taken some twists and turns.

In the 1960s and 1970s, the challenges included working out policy and program frameworks that would respond to the huge number of young people in need of education and employment. As we start the twenty-first century in Canada, the demographics have shifted dramatically. Now we have an aging population and all the implications that reality holds for health care costs, social security programs, and a declining labour force. The changing face of immigration over the past four decades has also produced new policy challenges of how to balance diversity and social cohesion. And, in today's world, Canada faces unprecedented global and internationalization pressures that present opportunities but also pose complex questions of how we will maintain our institutional and societal identity.

The new generation of applied, policy-oriented social researchers will have much to do, including the following.

As a nation, Canada has realized significant economic and social benefits from immigration. In 2001, 250,346 immigrants came to Canada. Of this number, 62 percent were economic immigrants, 27 percent fell into the family reunification category, and 11 percent were refugees.[71]

Worldwide, most advanced industrial nations are experiencing population aging, and Canada is no exception in this regard. An aging population presents various social and economic policy challenges. And although there is no single solution to these complex issues, immigration plays an important role in mitigating the effects of Canada's low birth rate and declining labour force.

To realize the full benefits of immigration, we have a significant national interest in ensuring that immigrants achieve successful social and economic integration in as timely a manner as possible. This does not always happen, as was shown in my Chapter 9 discussion of various immigration policy studies in which I have been involved. In the present environment, policy and program thinking is very much focused on such areas as improving credential assessment and recognition processes and providing immigrants with better opportunities to acquire work-related English-language skills. These are appropriate emphases in the present context, but the nature and composition of immigration to Canada will continue to change in the future and, in so doing, pose new policy and program challenges. The formulation of effective responses to these challenges needs the insights applied social research can provide.

The trend of immigration ensures that Canada will become an even more multicultural society in the future. Such diversity culturally enriches the nation but also raises complex policy questions about how a functional level of social cohesion is to be maintained. Addressing this increasingly significant issue presents policy makers with a difficult balancing act. Canadian policy does not support forced assimilation and explicitly recognizes the value of maintaining ethnocultural roots and solidarities. However, citizenship brings with it certain responsibilities as well as rights. A coherent and functional society requires that its members share and observe some common precepts and understandings about such responsibilities and rights, which, to complicate matters further, change and evolve over time. Educational institutions—particularly at the K to 12 level—will play a key role in this ongoing process. The curriculum will have to balance ethnocultural heritage concerns with the needs of citizenship education. Once again, the understandings of applied social research can provide a foundation for better policy and program development.

The aging of the population has policy implications that go well beyond immigration. For several decades now, Canada has witnessed a sustained increase in the proportion of its population that is employed. That increase, combined with technology and education-driven improvements in productivity, has been the central cause of improvements in our national standard of living.

In Canada today, retirement at the age of sixty-five is still enforced in many jurisdictions, although it is coming under increasing attack with associated proposals for legislative change. In fact, for many years now, there has been a growing trend for Canadians to retire earlier. In the next decade, members of the baby boom generation will be retiring in huge numbers. If the retirement age patterns described above continue to prevail, then the proportion employed in the population will either plateau or fall. Such a development will have a direct effect on the nation's economic standard of living.

Given life expectancy trends, it also means that workers will have to make unprecedented financial arrangements to cover their living costs during long years of retirement. Social security entitlement programs will come under increasing pressure, and it is difficult to see how tax increases can be avoided.

What I have just described is a function of a life course pattern that begins with an extended period of educational preparation, is followed by a work phase that typically lasts a bit less than half of a person's life, and is followed by an increasingly long retirement phase. In an era of rapid change, this life course pattern is becoming less and less appropriate. The growth of the knowledge economy means that many more workers will have to accommodate to lifetime learning. This raises important policy and program questions about how lifetime learning is designed and delivered, who benefits from it and who doesn't, and what are the causes of successful versus unsuccessful outcomes.

As for mandatory retirement, it is a policy that is increasingly at variance with the new realities. These new realities include the fact that an increasing proportions of retired persons have economically valuable skills and the health to deliver them effectively in work settings. The linkages between education, employment, and retirement require significant policy rethinking. Applied social research can make a vital contribution to that process.

The forces of globalization or internationalization continue to expand at a rapid pace and, in so doing, affect every aspect of our lives—social, cultural, and economic. My work on North

American issues, described in Chapter 9, raised my consciousness about the many complex policy challenges arising from coping with international competitive pressures and effectively engaging new opportunities while preserving certain values and practices that are central to maintaining the institutional distinctiveness of Canadian society. The areas of concern are many and include education, trade, border relations and security, migration, and cultural influences and change. In many of these areas, applied social research has an important contribution to make to the policy debate and policy development process.

* * *

There will be many opportunities for applied, policy-oriented social researchers in the years to come. I would go further and argue that an increasing proportion of the policy challenges we face has important sociological dimensions. Should university departments of sociology position themselves to take maximum advantage of these opportunities?[72]

My answer, for three reasons, is yes. The new policy challenges facing Canada need practical, usable sociological intelligence as part of the solution-building process. By engaging the issues in this way, the discipline of sociology would be empowered by greater relevance in real terms. This would counteract the often-encountered view that sociologists are part of the problem, not part of the solution. Finally, moving in this direction would give sociology students a richer intellectual experience and open new career opportunities.

Some university departments of sociology provide support, in varying degrees, for applied work. But, generally speaking, applied, policy-oriented social research is not a well-established specialization within the discipline. What are its future prospects in departments of sociology? To explore this question, I have to return to personal experience. This experience, although extensive, is not comprehensive. Put another way, I know a certain amount about other departments in other universities, but most of my direct experience is centred around the sociology departments of the University of Toronto and the Ontario Institute for Studies in Education of the University of Toronto (OISE/UT).

I have taught graduate-level "practitioner preparation" courses at OISE/UT that focused on such issues as equity and diversity management. Typically, the courses had robust enrolments—attracting students from sociology but also from various other departments and faculties. The students' motivations were, by and large, very clear: it was a topical area, they considered the course to be useful career preparation, and they viewed me as a person with considerable practical experience in the field.

At OISE/UT and the University of Toronto sociology department, I have also taught more general courses focused on the issues of applied social research and policy studies. Compared to "practitioner preparation" courses, enrolment in these courses tended toward the lower end of the spectrum, particularly at the University of Toronto sociology department.

In both the OISE/UT courses (graduate students) and the University of Toronto sociology department courses (senior undergraduates and graduate students), virtually none of the students enrolled had any work experience or had taken other courses that would have raised their awareness of what policy is and of the role that applied social research can play in its shaping. In part, this was due to the lack of a program or set of inter-related courses that would have helped build such a perspective. Some of the students (a minority) engaged with the ideas, and some of them went on to work with me. With respect to the latter group, I found that even they did not develop an operationally effective understanding of applied, policy-oriented research until they had the experience of working on actual projects. In applied, policy-oriented social research, courses are important to the development of understandings and technical skills, but an apprenticeship component is also essential.

When the idea of an applied sociology program was first introduced in the University of Toronto sociology department, some colleagues on the left wing of the political spectrum attacked the proposal aggressively, condemning it as a form of co-optation in the service of corporate and state elites. Over time, this opposition faded, but the program never really took root. Periodically, a small number of faculty would meet to discuss what might be done. These discussions did not lead to sustained substantive change, largely because of the absence of a clearly and strongly defined program structure supported by a set of interrelated courses and related practical project experience opportunities.

Although there are colleagues and students who are important exceptions to this, I think that generally the culture of sociology departments is not highly congenial to applied work. In some cases, the negative views are based on notions that applied social research is atheoretical (quite mistaken, in my view) or somehow pedestrian. In other instances, the opposition is based on political or ideological perspectives that applied work cannot be critical and simply serves to prop up unjust societal and institutional practices. Thinking back to some of the examples discussed in this book on royal commissions and task forces, I do not think this is a fair or reasonable allegation. Nor do I think it pedestrian to be concerned with the state of policy in such critical institutional areas as health, education, employment, immigration, and equality of opportunity.

Part of the problem in many sociology departments is that some colleagues and students do not make an adequate distinction between institutions and the status quo. I am quite prepared to agree that much in the status quo is a legitimate target for critical scrutiny and change. Indeed, much has changed over the years and more will change in the future. Debates over whether the change is "too little" or "too much" are inherently political and, in the nature of political differences in Canada, largely worked out in an institutionalized framework. It is mistaken to characterize—or even demonize—institutions as orchestrated instruments by which powerful elites maintain the status quo. Institutions provide order and continuity in our societal arrangements, but they also are subject to change—that is what royal commissions and task forces are all about, not to mention much general policy work in the public sector.

A considerable amount of sociological thinking fosters the development of strongly ideological world views. Ideology is inherently hostile to compromise, at least at the level of its central precepts. (Practice is another matter, as the history of the Soviet Union suggests.) But having said this, the process of advancing policy change in an institutionalized context almost invariably involves the making of operational compromises. This is not the same as compromising one's values. Another seductive feature of ideology is its apparent simplicity. By embracing an ideological "solution," one does not necessarily have to engage with the hard, incremental work that is the essence of policy development and implementation.

I find a central irony in the situation I have been describing. Many sociologists sincerely want to work toward a better world. But many elect to pursue this in ways that virtually ensure they will have no impact. There is too often a total disconnect between inherently good values and flawed or simply infeasible strategies for change.

What does all this imply for the prospects of developing strong applied and policy-oriented social research programs in university departments of sociology? First, I want to make a distinction between different types of programs. For example, the School of Policy Studies at Queen's University offers a master of public administration degree, a one-year interdisciplinary program that provides advanced skills in policy analysis and management for students seeking policy-making careers in both the public sector and the private sector. The program does a good job of preparing students to become informed *users* of policy-oriented information and working it into various types of policy applications. The work of applied, policy-oriented social research is different from this. It is concerned with *producing* information that feeds into the policy development and shaping process. In order to do this properly, a doctoral degree is required.

I do not think it is impossible to establish such programs in university departments of sociology, but I certainly don't think it is easy. Several conditions need to be present. The program needs to have clear definition and a committed coordinator. Students need to be recruited specifically to the program and have a clear understanding of what it means to train to be an applied, policy-oriented social researcher. Core courses and core faculty are required, as is the working out of arrangements with other departments to ensure that students receive interdisciplinary training in such areas as policy economics and policy-oriented demography. Arrangements need to exist so that students have ongoing opportunities to work in team situations on practical, case-study projects. The best results will be obtained if there is constant interaction between the practical work experience and the taking of courses.

* * *

Institutionalized programs aside, I have known and worked closely with a number of students who, in the absence of having access to a well-defined applied social research program, have nonetheless succeeded in becoming effective applied, policy-oriented social researchers. For this to happen, I believe that three sets of conditions have to be present.

First, certain personal values or predispositions are helpful to success in this type of work. The person needs to have an interest in going beyond criticism and working toward change in an institutionalized context. It is a definite help to have a pragmatic outlook that includes a willingness to entertain reasonable compromise and accept that, in a country like Canada, most social and institutional change is incremental in nature. It is a further benefit not to have a doctrinaire perspective on theoretical frameworks and methodological strategies but instead be inclined to work with a variety of appropriate approaches, often in combination with one another. It is valuable to have an entrepreneurial point of view and a way of thinking that sees opportunities rather than impediments.

Second, it is important to select courses of study in such a way that they add up to an interrelated set of understandings and skills. This is equally true whether one is talking about undergraduate or post-graduate education. Of course, actual choices may well be limited or structured by the types of courses available or specific requirements attached to the student's program of study. Having said that, however, there are certain areas of study that make a major contribution to developing competency in applied, policy-oriented social research.

It is important to take courses that provide an understanding of how organizations and institutions work, for these are the settings in which much applied, policy-oriented social research proceeds. It is also essential to acquire an understanding of how social change works and, through theory courses, develop an ability to think conceptually about problems and processes. An effective applied social researcher has to have a sophisticated understanding of statistical and research methods. It is important that both quantitative and qualitative approaches be studied and an understanding developed of how these different perspectives can be used to support one another. Given the multi-factorial nature of most policy issues, it is of central importance to obtain some interdisciplinary exposure, particularly in such areas as economics and demography. Finally, the student needs to learn how to write well, present effectively, and develop a high level of computer literacy.

Third, practical experience is at the core of becoming an applied, policy-oriented researcher. It is ideal if the practical experience can be ongoing and interwoven with the coursework. This way, the two types of learning inform and energize one another. There are large competency-building gains to be realized if the practical experience takes place in team situations and involves persons with different disciplinary and experiential perspectives. As I observed in Chapter 7, there are important aspects of doing applied, policy-oriented research that are not found in the textbooks. These understandings are acquired largely through experience.

* * *

In this book, I have written about various circumstances and experiences that led me to become a university professor and a consultant—a person with two careers. This is not a typical model. Is it a desirable model?

I think it to be a desirable model for reasons that are both personal and societal in nature. As for the personal side, doing what I did produced some material benefits but, far more important, it brought the psychological rewards of highly varied and interesting work, the opportunity to work with people in many sectors of Canadian society (and sometimes internationally), and the sense of efficacy that I frankly enjoyed when, from time to time, I saw my ideas making a difference in policy and program thinking.

On the societal side, I fundamentally and strongly believe that sociology has large contributions to make to the shaping of more enlightened and effective public policy. Whatever problems the discipline has with ideology and politicization (and they are far from trivial), there is a core of ideas and techniques with high relevance to understanding and acting upon complex societal, institutional, and organizational issues. That relevance will be even greater in the Canada of the future.

Having said that, I want to make it clear that I am not some sort of advocate for making all sociologists into applied, policy-oriented social researchers, even if that were possible—and, of course, it is not. I am arguing that sociologists have a lot to bring to the table and that by facilitating the process to do this—for those who want to do it—we would be adding value to our society, the policy process, the discipline, and those who study and plan to work in the field.

I do not think that any of this is easy to do, but given the current era of rapid social change and increasing social complexity, it has never been more important to keep on trying.

Introduction to Appendices

In writing this book, I have deliberately avoided putting in a large number of endnotes. I have reserved their use for direct references to people or publications or for when I have quoted from other sources. For the most part, this book is about the work I have done in the context of the university and as a consultant. Part III includes three appendices that provide details on that work. Appendix A sets out the papers, monographs, and books I have written, many of them co-authored. Appendix B provides details on selected speeches and other public presentations. Finally, Appendix C lists for my company, Urban Dimensions Group, Inc., a selection of the reports for projects where I served as lead consultant. For client confidentiality reasons, this list omits a number of private sector assignments.

This section also includes the list of photographs and drawings used in the book, and the endnotes.

APPENDIX A

Papers, Monographs, and Books of Edward B. Harvey

* Asterisk denotes publication in refereed journal.

*1. "Some Implications of Value Differentiation in Pharmacy," *Canadian Review of Sociology and Anthropology* (February 1966), pp. 23–27.

*2. "Psychological Rigidity and Muscle Tension," *Psychophysiology* (October 1966), pp. 224–26.

*3. "Social Change and the Jazz Musician," *Social Forces* (September 1967), pp. 34–42.

*4. "Decision Makers in Conflict," *The Business Quarterly* (Autumn 1967), pp. 23–27.

*5. "Technology and the Structure of Organizations," *American Sociological Review* (April 1968), pp. 247–59.

6. *Practitioners and Specialists: Some Factors Producing Career Variation* (London, Ont.: Faculty of Medicine, University of Western Ontario, November 1969).

7. With L.R. Marsden, *A Comparison of Specialists and Non-Specialists in Ontario Medical Practice* (London, Ont.: Faculty of Medicine, University of Western Ontario, July 1970).

8. *Pharmacy Student Manpower in Canada* (Toronto: Commission on Pharmaceutical Services, June 5, 1970).

9. *Pharmacy Student Manpower in Canada: Some Major Differences between English and French-Speaking Students of Pharmacy* (Toronto: Commission on Pharmaceutical Services, July 1970).

10. *General Practice on the Urban-Rural Scene* (London, Ont.: Faculty of Medicine, University of Western Ontario, September 1970).

11. With L.R. Marsden, *Practices, Attitudes and Backgrounds of Specialists in Ontario* (London, Ont.: Faculty of Medicine, University of Western Ontario, November 1970).

12. With R. Mills, "Patterns of Organizational Adaptation: A Political Perspective," in M. Zald, ed., *Power in Organizations* (Nashville, Tenn.: Vanderbilt University Press, 1970), pp. 181–213.

*13. "Robert Dreeben/The Nature of Teaching," *Interchange* (Toronto: Ontario Institute for Studies in Education), vol. 1, no. 2 (1970), pp. 108–11.

*14. With L.R. Marsden, "Adolescence, Social Class and Occupational Expectations," *Canadian Review of Sociology and Anthropology*, vol. 7, no. 2 (1970), pp. 138–47.

15. With L.R. Marsden, *Some Salient Attitudes of Medical Educators toward the Health Delivery System* (London, Ont.: Faculty of Medicine, University of Western Ontario, October 1971).

16. With J. Lennards, *The Changing Nature of Post-Secondary Education: Attitudes, Costs and Benefits* (Toronto: Commission on Post-Secondary Education, 1971).

*17. With L.R. Marsden, "Equality of Educational Access Reconsidered: The Post-Secondary Case in Ontario," *Interchange* (Toronto: Ontario Institute for Studies in Education), vol. 2, no. 4 (1971), pp. 11–26.

18. With R. Fetterly, "Pharmacy Student Manpower in Canada," *Canadian Pharmaceutical Journal* (January 1971), pp. 12–14.

19. With J. Bulcock and L.R. Marsden, "Language Barriers to Modernization: African Examples," in E.B. Harvey, ed., *Perspectives on Modernization: Essays in Memory of Ian Weinberg* (Toronto: University of Toronto Press, 1972), pp. 182–97.

20. Editor, *Perspectives on Modernization: Essays in Memory of Ian Weinberg* (Toronto: University of Toronto Press, 1972).

21. *Education and Employment of Arts and Science Graduates: The Last Decade in Ontario* (Toronto: Commission on Post-Secondary Education in Ontario, 1972).

22. "University Degrees and Jobs," *Orbit* (Toronto: Ontario Institute for Studies in Education) (April 1972), pp. 7–10.

23. *A Report on the Feasibility of a Canadian National Study of Fertility Knowledge, Attitudes and Practices* (Ottawa: National Department of Health and Welfare, 1972).

24. *Post-Graduate Education and the Labour Market* (Toronto: Ontario Institute for Studies in Education, January 1972).

25. With L.R. Marsden, *The Attitudes of Ontario Medical Students toward Their Training and Future Careers* (London, Ont.: Faculty of Medicine, University of Western Ontario, May 1972).

26. *Education and Employment: Experiences and Expectations* (Toronto: Ministry of Colleges and Universities, February 1972).

27. *Alternative Occupational Futures and the Social Science Graduate* (Ottawa: Canada Department of Manpower, 1973).

28. With T. Corl, *The Development of an Evaluation Methodology for the Neighbourhood Improvement Program* (Ottawa: Ministry of State for Urban Affairs, 1973).

29. With J. Lennards, *Key Issues in Higher Education* (Toronto: Ontario Institute for Studies in Education, 1973).

30. *Education Systems and the Labour Market* (Don Mills, Ont.: Longman Canada, 1973).

31. *The Air We Perceive* (Toronto: York-Toronto Tuberculosis and Respiratory Disease Association, 1973).

32. With T. Corl, *Outline for a General Review of the Highly Qualified Manpower Survey* (Ottawa: Ministry of State for Science and Technology, 1973).

*33. "The Vanishing Practitioner," *Journal of Medical Education*, vol. 48 (August 1973), pp. 718–24.

34. With T. Corl, *A Review of the University Student Information System* (Ottawa: Statistics Canada, February 12, 1974).

35. With T. Corl, *Commentary on the Proposed Study of the Aspirations of Canadian Youth* (Ottawa: Statistics Canada, 1974).

*36. "Canadian Higher Education and the Seventies," *Interchange* (Toronto: Ontario Institute for Studies in Education), vol. 5, no. 2 (1974), pp. 42–52.

37. With L.R. Marsden, *Recycling: Attitudes and Outlooks* (Toronto: Atkinson Foundation, 1975).

38. With V.L. Masemann, *Occupational Graduates and the Labour Force* (Toronto: Ministry of Education, 1975).

39. With V.L. Masemann and A. Kazanjian, *An Evaluation of the Student Guidance Information Service* (Toronto: Ministry of Education, 1975).

40. With M. Slaght and V.L. Masemann, *An Evaluation of the Career Development Credit Course* (Toronto: Ministry of Education, 1975).

41. With A. Kazanjian, *Education and Employment of Arts and Science Graduates: The Class of 1972* (Toronto: Ministry of Colleges and Universities, May 1975).

42. *Industrial Society: Structures, Roles and Relations* (Homewood, Ill.: Dorsey Press, 1975).

43. With K.S.R. Murthy, *Supply of and Demand for New Graduates* (Toronto: Technical Service Council, 1975).

*44. With I. Charner, "Social Mobility and Occupational Attainments of University Graduates," *Canadian Review of Sociology and Anthropology*, vol. 12, no. 4 (November 1975), pp. 385–405.

*45. "Training and Transition," *Training* (Ottawa: Manpower and Immigration) (Fall 1975), pp. 28–35.

46. With T. Corl, *Highly Qualified Manpower Survey: Analysis and Recommendation* (Ottawa: Ministry of State for Science and Technology, 1975).

47. With Stewart Goodyear, *Education and Employment of Post-Secondary Graduates: A Longitudinal Study* (Toronto: Ministry of Colleges and Universities, November 1975), vols. 1–3.

48. With K.S.R. Murthy, *Engineering Manpower Demand and Supply* (Toronto: Technical Service Council, 1976).

49. "Dimensions of a Decade: Canadian Higher Education in the Sixties," in G. McDiarmid, ed., *From Quantitative to Qualitative Change in Ontario Education* (Toronto: Ontario Institute for Studies in Education, 1976), pp. 1–27.

*50. "Demographics and Future Marketing," *The Business Quarterly*, vol. 41, no. 2 (Summer 1976), pp. 61–65.

51. Editor, with L.R. Marsden, *Canadian Population Concerns* (Toronto: Population Research Foundation, 1977).

*52. "Managerial Manpower: Surpluses and Shortages," *The Business Quarterly*, vol. 42, no. 1 (Spring 1977), pp. 52–58.

*53. With L.R. Marsden, "Medical Educators and Community Physicians: Parallel Roads in Search of an Interchange," *Bulletin of the New York Academy of Medicine*, vol. 53, no. 5 (June 1977), pp. 409–21.

54. "Accessibility to Postsecondary Education—Some Gains, Some Losses," *University Affairs* (Ottawa: Association of Universities and Colleges of Canada) (October 1977), pp. 10–11.

*55. "Forecasts for Training," *Adult Training* (Ottawa: Manpower and Immigration), vol. 3, no. 1 (1977), pp. 41–47.

56. "Education for What?" in S. Berkowitz and R. Logan, eds., *Canada's Third Option* (Toronto: Macmillan of Canada, 1978), pp. 206–19.

57. *Barriers to Employer Sponsored Training: A Conceptual Assessment and Review of Literature* (Toronto: Ministry of Colleges and Universities, September 1978).

58. With L.R. Marsden, *Fragile Federation: A Study of Social Change in Canada* (Toronto: McGraw Hill Ryerson, February 1979).

59. With K.S.R. Murthy, *Supply of and Demand for Accounting Professionals in Canada* (Toronto: Technical Service Council, 1979).

60. *National Study of the Employment Patterns of 1976 B.A. and B.Sc. Graduates* (Ottawa: Canadian Employment and Immigration Commission, May 1980).

61. *Program and Organizational Review of Secondary School Occupational and Vocational Programs* (Toronto: Board of Education for the Borough of Etobicoke, August 1980).

62. With W. Janischewskyj, *Human Response to Interference with TV Picture Quality* (Palo Alto, Calif.: Electric Power Research Institute, October 1980).

63. With K.S.R. Murthy, *Supply of and Demand for Engineers in Canada* (Toronto: Technical Service Council, 1980).

64. *Barriers to Employer-Sponsored Training in Ontario* (Toronto: Ministry of Education, 1980).

*65. With S. McShane, "Employer Sponsored Training for Industrial Skills: Current Practices and Future Directions," *Interchange* (Toronto: Ontario Institute for Studies in Education), vol. 11, no. 3 (1980–81), pp. 23–32.

*66. With W. Janischewskyj and M. Comber, "Power Line Interference and Assessment of Television Picture Quality," *IEEE Transactions on Power Apparatus and Systems*, vol. PAS-102, no. 5 (May 1983), pp. 1039–49.

*67. With R. Kalwa, "Occupational Status Attainments of University Graduates: Individual Attributes and Labour Market Effects Compared," *Canadian Review of Sociology and Anthropology*, vol. 20, no. 4 (November 1983), pp. 435–53.

*68. "The Changing Relationship between University Education and Inter-generational Social Mobility," *Canadian Review of Sociology and Anthropology*, vol. 21, no. 3 (August 1984), pp. 275–86.

69. With J.H. Blakely, "Human Capital: New Skills for New Jobs," *Ideas on Innovation*, vol. 1, no. 3, pp. 1–2.

*70. With J.H. Blakely, "Managing Technological Change in the Workplace," *Canadian Journal of Public Health* (May/June 1985), pp. 55–57.

71. With J.H. Blakely, "Strategies for Establishing Affirmative Action Goals and Timetables," *Research Studies of the Commission on Equality in Employment* (Ottawa: Minister of Supply and Services, 1985), pp. 115–29.

*72. With J.H. Blakely, "Education, Social Mobility and the Challenge of Technological Change," *Western Economic Review*, vol. 4, no. 2 (July 1985), pp. 30–45.

73. "The Practice of Applied Sociology," in L. Tepperman and J. Richardson, eds., *The Social World: An Introduction to Sociology* (Toronto: McGraw-Hill Ryerson, 1986), pp. 59–79.

74. With L.R. Marsden, "Excellence and Equality: The Contradiction in Science Teaching in America," in A.B. Champagne and L.E. Hornig, eds., *Science Teaching: The Report of the 1985 National Forum for School Science* (Washington, D.C.: National Science Foundation, 1985), pp. 126–47.

75. With J.H. Blakely, "Maximizing Use of Human Resource Information Systems (HRIS)," in S.L. Dolan and R.S. Schuler, eds., *Canadian Readings in Personnel and Human Resource Management* (St. Pauls: West Publishing Co., 1987), pp. 444–60.

76. "Science, Technology and Economic Development: Some Reflections on Canadian Society," in L. Tepperman and J. Curtis, eds., *Understanding Canadian Society* (Toronto: McGraw-Hill Ryerson, 1988), pp. 289–312.

*77. With J.H. Blakely, "Technology and Employment in Canada," *Science and Public Policy* (February 1988), pp. 53–66.

*78. With J.H. Blakely, "Socioeconomic Change and Lack of Change: Employment Equity Policies in the Canadian Context," *Journal of Business Ethics*, vol. 7 (1988), pp. 133–50.

79. *Information Systems for Employment Equity* (Toronto: CCH Canadian Publishers, 1988).

*80. With J.H. Blakely, "Market and Non-Market Effects on Male and Female Occupational Status Attainment," *Canadian Review of Sociology and Anthropology*, vol. 25, no. 1 (1988), pp. 323–40.

81. "Employment Equity and Ontario Schoolboards," *Orbit* (Toronto: Ontario Institute for Studies in Education), vol. 19, no. 3 (October 1988), pp. 3–5.

*82. With K.S.R. Murthy, "Forecasting Manpower Supply and Demand, A Model for the Accounting Profession in Canada," *International Journal of Forecasting*, vol. 4 (1988), pp. 551–62.

83. "Critical Approaches to Pay Equity," *Pay Equity Guide*, vol. 1, no. 11 (November 1988), pp. 73–80.

84. With K.S.R. Murthy, *Engineering Supply and Demand, 1988–1998* (Toronto: Technical Service Council, 1988).

85. With L. Tepperman, *Selected Socio-economic Consequences of Disability for Women in Canada*, Statistics Canada, Catalogue 82–615 (Ottawa: Minister of Supply and Services, 1990).

86. With E. Severn and J. Blakely, *Computing for Equity: Computer Applications for Employment Equity* (Toronto: CCH Canadian Publishers, 1990).

87. With E. Severn and J. Blakely, *Computing for Equity: Demonstration Workbook* (Toronto: CCH Canadian Publishers, 1990).

*88. With J. Blakely and L. Tepperman, "Toward an Index of Gender Equality," *Social Indicators Research*, vol. 22 (1990), pp. 299–317.

89. *The Underutilization of Women in the Canadian Economy and Intervention Points for Public Policy* (Toronto: Council of Ministers of Education, 1990).

90. *Socioeconomic Comparisons among Employment Equity Visible Minority Sub-Groups and the Reference Population* (Ottawa: Employment and Immigration Canada, 1991).

*91. "Population of Persons with Disabilities: The Health and Activity Limitation Survey," *Publications of the Interdepartmental Working Group on Employment Equity Data* (Ottawa: Statistics Canada, March 1992).

92. "No Pre-packaged Solution Yet Available for Employment Equity Data Management," *Employment Equity Review*, vol. 2, no. 4 (April 1992), pp. 27–34.

*93. With N. Scott Wortley, "Factors Influencing Socioeconomic Disadvantage among Selected Ethnic Groups, Canada, 1986: A Multiple Regression Analysis," Working Paper 4.16 of the Employment Equity Data Program (Ottawa: Statistics Canada, April 1992).

94. "How to Effectively Manage the Employment Systems Review," *Employment Equity Review*, vol. 2, no. 6 (June 1992), pp. 43–48.

95. "Why Information Technology Is Essential to Employment Equity Compliance," *People and Information*, vol. 1, no. 7 (July 1992), pp. 8–12.

96. "Employment Opportunities and Challenges in Canada in the Forest Sector: The New Context for Human Resource Planning," in *Training for Canada, Proceedings of the Canadian Council of Forest Ministers Forum on Human Resource Needs of the Forest Sector in the 1990s, Vancouver, March 12–14, 1991* (Ottawa: Forestry Canada, 1993), pp. 15–16.

*97. With N. Scot Wortley, "Patterns of Socioeconomic Disadvantage for Selected Ethnocultural Groups, Canada, 1986," Working Paper 4.15 of the Employment Equity Data Program (Ottawa: Statistics Canada, February 1993).

98. With J. Blakely, "Employment Equity in Canada," *Policy Options*, vol. 14, no. 2 (March 1993), pp. 3–8.

*99. With J. Blakely, "Employment Equity Goal Setting and External Availability Data," *Social Indicators Research*, vol. 28 (1993), pp. 245–66.

*100. With J. Blakely, "Implementing and Managing Employment Equity," *Canadian Labour Law Journal*, vol. 2, no. 1 (Summer 1993), pp. 245–66.

101. With J.W.P. Veugelers, "Educational Equity: The Next Steps," *Policy Options*, vol. 14, no. 9 (November 1993), pp. 19–23.

102. With J. Blakely, "Present Conditions and Problems of Human Resource Development in Canada," in *Proceedings of the International Seminar on Industrialization and Human Resource Development in the Asia Pacific Region, 8–9 December 1993, Tokyo, Japan* (Tokyo: Institute of Developing Economies, 1993), pp. 103–08.

103. With J.H. Blakely, "Building Opportunities for People," in *Proceedings of the 69th Annual Congress of the Association of Worker's Compensation Boards of Canada, Saint John, N.B., June 11–14, 1995* (Mississauga, ON: Association of Workers' Compensation Boards of Canada, 1995), pp. 132–53.

104. With J.H. Blakely, *Information Systems for Managing Workplace Diversity* (Toronto: CCH Canadian Publishers, 1996).

105. With Bobby Siu, "Knowing Your Neighbours: Four Ways to Use Census Data for Insight into the Ethnic Mix in Your Trading Area," *Marketing Magazine* (November 18, 1996), p. 18.

106. With J. Blakely, "Strategic Directions in Managing and Valuing Diversity," *Valuing Diversity*, vol. 8, no. 9 (September 1998), pp. 66–72.

107. With J. Blakely, *Re-thinking HR Management: Strategies for Success in an Era of Change* (Toronto: CCH Canadian Publishers, 1999).

108. With K. Reil and B. Siu, "Aboriginal Peoples Continue to Face Economic and Employment Hardship," *Windspeaker* (May 1999), p. 10.

*109. With B. Siu and K. Reil, "Ethnocultural Groups, Period of Immigration and Socioeconomic Situation," *Canadian Ethnic Studies*, vol. 31, no. 3 (1999), pp. 95–103.

*110. With L. Lo, V. Preston, S. Wang, K. Reil, and B. Siu, "Immigrants' Economic Status in Toronto: Rethinking Settlement and Integration Strategies," Working Paper #15 (Toronto: Centre of Excellence for Research on Immigration and Settlement, March 2000).

111. With J. Blakely, "HR Management and the HR Challenge," *Canadian Industrial Relations and Personnel Developments* (Toronto: CCH Canadian Publishers), no. 21 (2000), pp. 541–45.

112. With John Blakely, *Equal Pay* (Toronto: CCH Canadian Publishers, 2000).

113. With John Blakely, "Millennium Issues in Compensation and Diversity Management," *Compensation Law Reporter*, vol. 1, no. 1 (January 2000), pp. 1–8.

114. With B. Siu, "Immigrants' Socioeconomic Situation Compared, 1991–1996," *INSCAN* (International Settlement Canada), vol. 15, no. 2 (Fall 2001), pp. 1–3.

115. "Family-Friendly Policies in the Canadian Context," *The Compensation Law Reporter*, vol. 2, no. 6 (August 2001), pp. 57–64.

116. *Increasing Community College Participation in Mobility Initiatives Including Strategies to Increase Private Sector Involvement*, Alliance for Higher Education and Enterprise in North America, AHEENA Working Papers Series NA 0901 (Toronto: AHEENA, 2001).

117. With John Blakely and Katherine Lee, *Internet Solutions for HR Managers* (Toronto: CCH Canadian Publishers, 2002).

118. With Richard Liu, *North American Linkage Activity in Canadian and U.S. Institutions of Higher Education*, Alliance for Higher Education and Enterprise in North America, AHEENA Report NA 0802 (Santa Fe, NM: North American Institute, 2002).

119. With Richard Liu, *North American Higher Education Collaboration: Post Wingspread Developments*, Alliance for Higher Education and Enterprise in North America, AHEENA Report NA 0902 (Ottawa: Department of Foreign Affairs and International Trade, September 2002).

120. With Richard Liu, *North American Linkage Activity in Canadian Institutions of Higher Education*, Alliance for Higher Education and Enterprise in North America, AHEENA Report NA 1002 (Toronto: AHEENA, 2002).

121. With Richard Liu, "North American Linkage Building by Canadian and U.S. Institutions of Higher Education," *Policy Options*, vol. 24, no. 8 (September 2003), pp. 46–49.

122. "Building North American Higher Education Linkages: Canadian Universities and Community Colleges Compared," *College Quarterly* (Winter 2003), pp. 1–10.

Selected Speeches and Public Presentations of Edward B. Harvey

1. "The Changing Social Mobility and Occupational Attainment Patterns of University Graduates," guest lecture at Mount Saint Vincent University, Halifax, N.B., January 23, 1975.

2. "Supply and Demand: New Graduates in Engineering," 8th Annual APEO Undergraduate Conference: Forecast for Engineers, Kingston, Ont., January 23, 1976.

3. "Environmental Impact of High Voltage Transmission Lines," Annual Meeting of the Cage Club, held at the University of Toronto, Toronto, May 17, 1976.

4. "Occupational Opportunities for Chemical Professionals," 50th Chemical Conference of the Chemical Institute of Canada, London, Ont., June 8, 1976.

5. "Current Priorities in Canadian Manpower and Education Policy," paper delivered to members of Canadian Studies Program, St. Lawrence University, Canton, N.Y., November 17, 1976.

6. "Post-Secondary Education in Canada: Problems and Possibilities," Urban Affairs Symposium, Toronto and District Liberal Association, Hotel Toronto, November 20, 1976.

7. "The Current and Future Labour Market," Annual Meeting of the University and College Placement Association, Sheraton Centre, Toronto, December 9, 1976.

8. "The Aging Baby Boom: Future Socioeconomic Impacts on Canadian Society," Second Conference of the Canadian Association for Future Studies, Queen's University, Kingston, Ont., June 1977.

9. "Changing Relationships among Education, Employment and Social Mobility," Higher Education Colloquium Series, Ontario Institute for Studies in Education, Toronto, October 25, 1977.

10. "Manpower Planning and the Baby Boom," Ontario Society for Training and Development, Toronto, November 14, 1977.

11. "Strategies for the Psychoacoustical Assessment of Transmission Line Audible Noise," IEEE Symposium on Transmission Line Audible Noise, South Bend, Ind., September 19, 1977.

12. "Employment Creation and Industrial Strategy," 25th Annual Meeting of the University and College Placement Association, Toronto, June 11, 1978.

13. "Labour Force Patterns, Problems, Policies," Liberal Caucus Conference, Elgin House, Muskoka, Ont., September 8–10, 1978.

14. "Industrial Strategy, Job Creation and Product Development," National Design Council Conference, Vancouver, B.C., September 29, 1978.

15. "Supply and Demand for Accounting Professionals in Canada," Annual National Meeting of Partners of Thorne Riddell and Company, Montebello, P.Q., September 19, 1979.

16. "Prospects for Employer Sponsored Industrial Training in Ontario," Technology and Human Development: A Challenge for the 80s, conference co-sponsored by Women's Canadian ORT and the Ontario Institute for Studies in Education, Toronto, January 27, 1980.

17. "Employment Opportunities in the Eighties," Lakehead University Career Week Conference, Thunder Bay, November 5, 1980.

18. "Education: Meeting the Needs of the Workplace in the Eighties," Coping with the Skilled Manpower Crisis: Canadian Professional Conferences, Toronto, March 16, 1981.

19. "Perspectives on Human Resource Planning," Meeting of the Section on Industrial/Organizational Psychology of the Ontario Psychology Association, Toronto, October 21, 1982.

20. "Equality of Educational Access: Emerging Conceptual and Policy Issues," Participation Study Steering Committee Conference, Alberta Advanced Education, Banff, Alta., October 21, 1983.

21. "The Greying World: Challenges and Risks," 11th Annual Conference of the Older Adult Centres' Association of Ontario, London, October 25, 1984.

22. "Critical Occupations in Ontario's Technological Advancement," Senior Staff Development Seminar of the Ontario Women's Directorate, Toronto, June 22, 1984.

23. With John H. Blakely, "Managing Technological Change in the Workplace," Beyond Health Care Conference, Toronto, October 11, 1984.

24. "Critical Occupations in Ontario's High Technology Labour Market," Annual Conference of the Ontario Association of Educational Administrative Officials, Toronto, November 1, 1984.

25. "Technological Change and Emerging Occupations: Implications for Women," Jobs for the Future: Women, Training and Technology, a conference organized by the Office of the Deputy Premier, Ontario, Toronto, November 28 and 29, 1985.

26. "Internal Demographics: Making Maximum Use of Human Resource Information Systems," Survival of the Fittest: Organizations and People, Canadian Human Resource Planners Symposium, Toronto, October 1, 1985.

27. "Excellence and Equality: The Contradiction in American Science Teaching," First Annual National Forum for Social Science, sponsored by the American Association for the Advancement of Science, The Shoreham Hotel, Washington, D.C., October 10, 1985.

28. "Outlook on Jobs and Incomes in the High Technology Sector," Collective Bargaining and Professional Employees Conference, sponsored by the Federation of Engineering and Scientific Associations, Ascot Inn, Rexdale, Ont., November 16, 1985.

29. "Multiculturalism and Canada's Institutional History," guest lecture, Stong College, York University, January 15, 1986.

30. "Supply and Demand Patterns for Professionally Trained Persons in Canadian Agriculture, 1985–1989," Agricultural Institute of Canada Conference, Skyline Hotel, Ottawa, January 31, 1986.

31. "The Status of Women in Toronto," City of Toronto Institute on Women and Work Conference, City Hall, Toronto, November 26, 1987.

32. "How to Successfully Design and Implement an Employment Equity Plan," EquiNet Employment Equity Conference, Prince Hotel, Toronto, June 30, 1988.

33. "Employment Equity, External Availability and Data on Persons with Disabilities," Toronto Employment Equity Practitioners Workshop on Employment Equity and Persons with Disabilities, Westbury Hotel, Toronto, September 22, 1988.

34. "The Dimension of Pay Equity," EquiNet Pay Equity Conference, Bristol Place Hotel, Toronto, October 4, 1988.

35. "Current Trends in Employment Equity," Personnel Association of Ontario Conference, Sheraton Hotel, Toronto, March 8, 1989.

36. "Employment Equity: Resources for Results," Ontario Women's Directorate Resources for Results Conference, Delta Chelsea Inn, Toronto, May 25, 1989.

37. "Persons with Disabilities: Data Resources for Employment Equity," Toronto Employment Equity Practitioners Association Conference, Delta Chelsea Inn, Toronto, May 31, 1989.

38. "Trends in the Canadian Labour Force," Annual Conference of the Canadian Vocational Association, Downtown Holiday Inn, Toronto, June 12, 1989.

39. "The Military as an Agent of Social Change," Minister's Conference on Social Change and National Defence, Canadian Forces College, Toronto, February 22, 1990.

40. "Why Employment Equity Will Be the Major Human Resources Issue of the 1990s," Third Annual EquiNet Spring Conference on Pay Equity and Employment Equity, The Old Mill, Toronto, May 31, 1990.

41. "The New Context for Human Resource Planning," Canadian Council of Forest Ministers Forum on Forest Sector Human Resource Needs in the 1990s, New World Harbourside Hotel, Vancouver, B.C., March 13, 1991.

42. "How to Design and Implement the Specifics of Employment Equity," Fourth Annual EquiNet Fall Conference on Employment Equity and Pay Equity, The Old Mill, Toronto, November 19, 1991.

43. "Demystifying Technical Aspects of Employment Equity," Employment Equity Forum, University of Toronto, November 26, 1991.

44. "Reconciling Information Technology and Employment Equity," Canadian Association of Human Resource Systems Professionals Conference, Skydome Hotel, Toronto, March 25, 1992.

45. "Employment Equity Systems Review," Toronto Employment Equity Practitioners Association Conference, Sheraton Centre Hotel, Toronto, June 2, 1992.

46. "Mandatory Features of the Proposed Ontario Employment Equity Legislation," Retail Council of Canada Conference, Toronto, October 8, 1992.

47. "Ontario Employment Equity Legislation and the Role of the Employment Systems Review," Noranda Canada Employment Equity Group Conference, BCE Place, Toronto, October 22, 1992.

48. "Implications for Ontario School Boards of Impending Employment Equity Legislation," Metropolitan Toronto School Board Employment Equity Seminar, North York, Ont., January 19, 1993.

49. "Employment Equity Policy: Responses to Patterns of Ethnocultural Disadvantage in Canadian Society," Department of Sociology & Canadian Studies Centre Colloquium Series, Duke University, Durham, N.C., March 1, 1993.

50. "Overview of Employment Equity Planning," Canadian Manufacturers' Association Employment Equity Conference, Days Inn, Toronto Airport, September 24, 1993.

51. "Conducting an Employment Systems Review," The 1993 Annual Provincial Employment Equity Conference for School Boards, Colleges and Universities, Ramada Renaissance, Don Valley, Ont., November 15–16, 1993.

52. "The Employment Equity Survey: How to Do It Properly," The 1993 Annual Provincial Employment Equity Conference for School Boards, Colleges and Universities, Ramada Renaissance, Don Valley, Ont., November 15–16, 1993.

53. "Present Conditions and Problems of Human Resource Development in Canada," International Seminar on Industrialization and Human Resource Development in the Asia Pacific Region, Institute of Developing Economies, Tokyo, December 8, 1993.

54. "Developing the Employment Equity Critical Path," The Ontario Hospitals Employment Equity Network Conference, St. Joseph's Health Centre, Toronto, January 21, 1994.

55. "Globalization and Labour Force Change: Policy Options and International Linkages," The North-South Institute, Senior Staff Seminar, Ottawa, March 8, 1994.

56. "Keys Steps in Employment Equity Implementation," Canadian Manufacturers' Association Conference on Employment Equity, Toronto, Days Inn Toronto Airport, November 1, 1994.

57. "Toward Effective Employment Systems Review Strategies," Ontario Library Association Employment Equity Conference, Toronto, Westin Harbour Castle Hotel, January 13, 1995.

58. "Systematic Approaches to Employment Equity Compliance," Canadian Manufacturers' Association Conference on Employment Equity, Toronto, The Canadian Manufacturers' Association, May 11 and 18, 1995.

59. "Building Opportunities for People," 69th Annual Congress of the Association of Workers' Compensation Boards of Canada, Saint John, N.B., June 13, 1995.

60. With Christine Minas, "School Performance and Catchment Area Characteristics: A Study of English Writing Test Outcomes within an Urban School Board," Canadian Sociology & Anthropology Association Meetings, Memorial University of Newfoundland, St. John's, Nfld., June 10, 1997.

61. With John Blakely, "The Demise of Employment Equity in Ontario: A Case Study of the Changing Public Policy Context," Eighth Conference

on Canadian Social Welfare Policy, University of Regina, Regina, Sask., June 26, 1997.

62. With B. Siu, K. Reil, and John Blakely, "Socioeconomic Status of Immigrant Men and Women in Selected Ethnocultural Groups in Canada," 3rd National Metropolis Conference, Vancouver, B.C., January 15, 1999.

63. With B. Siu and K. Reil, "The Economic Status of Chinese Immigrants: A Comparison of Native-Born and Foreign-Born Canadians," Chinese Canadian National Council's National Conference, Metro Hall, Toronto, April 9, 1999.

64. With K. Reil and B. Siu, "Settlement and Socioeconomic Experiences of Immigrants to Canada: Some Implications of Gender, Race and Period of Immigration," Society for the Psychological Study of Social Issues (SPSSI), International Conference, Toronto, August 13, 1999.

65. With K. Reil, "Foreign Credential Recognition and the Canadian Economy," Qualification Recognition Conference, Westin Harbour Castle Hotel, Toronto, October 13, 1999.

66. "Education, Training and Project Development: The Tripartite Alliance for Education and Business in North America," 11th Biennial Congress of the Inter-American Organization for Higher Education (IOHE), Hotel Hilton, Quebec City, P.Q., October 12, 1999.

67. With K. Reil, "An Analysis of Socioeconomic Situation, Ethnocultural Groups, Period of Immigration and Gender for Toronto and Canada," OCASI Conference, Geneva Park, Ont., October 22, 1999.

68. "The Alliance for Higher Education and Enterprise in North America: A Briefing," Consortium for North American Higher Education Collaboration (CONAHEC) Sixth Annual North American Higher Education Conference, Universidad Veracruzana, Veracruz, Mexico, October 28, 1999.

69. "The Systematic Approach to Employment Equity Implementation," Forum for Managers, The Public Service Commission, Government Conference Centre, Ottawa, January 18, 2000.

70. "Patterns of Immigrant Integration," Immigrant Settlement Working Group Conference, COSTI, Columbus Centre, Toronto, January 28, 2000.

71. "The Role of Educational Mobility in North American Economic Development," Canada–Mexico Business Retreat, Four Seasons Hotel, Punta Mita, Nayarit, Mexico, February 19, 2000.

72. With K. Reil, "Socioeconomic Differences by Ethnocultural Groupings and Period of Immigration," Fourth National Metropolis Conference, Metropolitan Hotel, Toronto, March 23, 2000.

73. With L. Lo, V. Preston, S. Wang, K. Reil, and B. Siu, "Immigrants' Economic Status in Toronto: Rethinking Settlement and Integration Strategies," Fourth Annual Metropolis Conference, Metropolitan Hotel, Toronto, March, 25, 2000.

74. "Foreign Trained Professionals and Workers: Patterns of Underemployment," Foreign Professional and Skilled Workers Forum, York South Simcoe Training and Adjustment Board, Sheraton Parkway Hotel, Toronto, March 30, 2000.

75. "Employment Equity Goal Setting," Conference on Employment Equity Implementation for Public Service Managers, Treasury Board of Canada, Government Conference Centre, Ottawa, April 4, 2000.

76. With B. Siu, "Settlement, Racism and Poverty," National Settlement Conference: Building Our Settlement Vision, Queen's University, Kingston, Ont., June 18, 2001.

77. With B. Siu, "Is the Socioeconomic Situation of Immigrants Getting Better?" Accessible Community Counselling and Employment Forum, Metro Hall, Toronto, February 7, 2002.

78. "The Underemployment of Visible Minority Immigrants," 2002 Brain Gain Conference: Bridging the Demographic Gap, Conference Board of Canada, Weston Prince Hotel, Toronto, March 27, 2002.

79. "The Costs of Discrimination in the Canadian Labour Market," Human Resources Development Canada Senior Staff Seminar, Promenade du Portage, Hull, P.Q., November 22, 2002.

Selected Consulting Reports of Urban Dimensions Group, Inc. (Projects Led by Edward B. Harvey)

Note: For reasons of client confidentiality, a number of private sector projects led by Edward B. Harvey have been omitted from this listing.

1. *Family Practice Manpower Requirements in Canada.* A report prepared for the College of Family Physicians of Canada, January 24, 1975.

2. *Public Library Needs in the East End of Toronto.* A report prepared for the Toronto Public Library Board in cooperation with Information Consultants, Toronto, May 1975.

3. *The Frontier Community.* A report prepared for Design Canada, a subdivision of Industry, Trade and Commerce (Canada), November 1975.

4. *The Family Physician in the Emergency Department.* A report prepared for the College of Family Physicians of Canada, November 1975.

5. *Culture and Recreation Facilities in Ontario: Supply and Demand; Management Summary.* A report prepared for the Ministry of Culture and Recreation in Ontario; March 31, 1976.

6. *Cultural and Recreational Facilities and Activities in Ontario: Supply and Demand.* A report prepared for the Ministry of Culture and Recreation in Ontario, March 31, 1976.

7. *Resources and Counselling: A Project Search Report.* A report prepared for the Counselling Foundation of Canada, May 1976.

8. *Neighbourhood Improvement Program Delivery System Evaluation: Research Design.* A report prepared for Central Mortgage and Housing Corporation, August 1976.

9. *Neighbourhood Improvement Program Delivery System Evaluation: Procedures for Gathering Background Data.* A report prepared for the Central Mortgage and Housing Corporation, 1976.

10. *Neighbourhood Improvement Program Impact Evaluation: Research Design.* A report prepared for Central Mortgage and Housing Corporation, September 1976.

11. *Neighbourhood Improvement Program and Residential Rehabilitation Assistance Program: Delivery System and Impact Evaluation; Case Study: Kingston, Ontario.* A report prepared for Central Mortgage and Housing Corporation, December 1976.

12. *Neighbourhood Improvement Program and Residential Rehabilitation Assistance Program: Delivery System and Impact Evaluation; Case Study: Charlottetown, PEI.* A report prepared for Central Mortgage and Housing Corporation, December 1976.

13. *Neighbourhood Improvement Program and Residential Rehabilitation Assistance Program: Delivery System and Impact Evaluation; Case Study: Niagara Falls, Ontario.* A report prepared for Robert Mills Associates, Ltd., Toronto, December 1976.

14. *Neighbourhood Improvement Program and Residential Rehabilitation Assistance Program: Delivery System and Impact Evaluation; Case Study: Dartmouth, NS.* A report prepared for Robert Mills Associates, Ltd., Toronto, December 1976.

15. *Neighbourhood Improvement Program and Residential Rehabilitation Assistance Program: Delivery System and Impact Evaluation; Case Study: Halifax, NS.* A report prepared for Robert Mills Associates, Ltd., Toronto; December 1976.

16. *Neighbourhood Improvement Program and Residential Rehabilitation Assistance Program: Delivery System and Impact Evaluation; Case Study: Hamilton, Ontario.* A report prepared for Robert Mills Associates, Ltd., Toronto, December 1976.

17. *The Effects of High Voltage Line Corona Discharge on T.V. Picture Quality.* A report prepared for the Department of Communications, Ottawa, December 1976.

18. *A Report of the Evaluation of the Residential Rehabilitation Assistance Program.* A report prepared for the Central Mortgage and Housing Corporation, June 1977.

19. *A Comparison of RRAP Users and Non-Users.* A report prepared for the Central Mortgage and Housing Corporation, July 1977.

20. *An Evaluation of the Human Environment Sector Long-Term Research Program Draft.* A report prepared by the Alberta Oil Sands Environmental Research Program, July 28, 1977.

21. *Proposals for More Effective Evaluation of the Affirmative Action Program in the Ontario Public Service.* A report prepared for the Research Branch of the Ontario Ministry of Labour, August 1, 1977.

22. *Review of "Human Environment System Research Report: Draft III" and "A Theoretical Perspective for Conducting Social Research on the Oil Sands Project."* A report prepared for the Alberta Oil Sands Research Program, October 1977.

23. *An Urban RRAP Quality Study.* A report prepared for Robert Mills Associates, Ltd. Toronto, October 17, 1977.

24. *Determining the Future for Family Physicians in Canadian Health Care: Roles and Requirements.* A report prepared for the College of Family Physicians of Canada, November 1977.

25. *Employment Opportunities in Product Development: Operations Manual.* An operations manual prepared for Kelly, Gairns and Connolly, Ltd., Ottawa, in connection with the organization and delivery of the Employment Opportunities in Product Development Program, January–June 1978.

26. *A Review of "The Probability of Advertising Exposure Report #5," a Research Report on Five National Medical Publications conducted for the* Medical Post *of the MacLean-Hunter Research Bureau.* A report prepared for the Canadian Medical Association, April 1978.

27. *A Study of Multi-lingual Library Needs in Ontario; Phase One: A Report on Sociodemographic Characteristics of the Fourteen Planning*

Regions in Ontario. A report prepared for the Directors of Ontario Regional Library Systems, April 15, 1978 (revised edition: June 15, 1978).

28. *A Pilot Study of the Affirmative Action Program in the Ministry of Labour.* A report prepared for the Ministry of Labour (Ontario), June 1978 (revised: November 1978).

29. *A Review of a Report Entitled "Longitudinal Study of Personal Adjustment and Social Conditions in the Fort McMurray Area."* A report prepared for the Alberta Oil Sands Environmental Research Program, October 1978.

30. *Some Implications of Re-organization and Redundancy Procedures for the Affirmative Action Program.* A report prepared for the Women's Crown Employees Office, Ministry of Labour (Ontario), November 1978.

31. *Final Evaluation of the Employment Opportunities in Product Development Program.* A report prepared for Kelly, Gairns and Connolly, Ltd., Ottawa, March 1979.

32. *A Conceptual Model for Study of Impacts of Oil Sands Development in the Fort McMurray Area.* An interim report prepared for the Alberta Oils Sands Environmental Research Program, March 1979.

33. *A Review of a Document Entitled: "First Interim Report: A Study of Human Adjustment in the Fort McMurray Area" by John W. Gartrell, Thames Research Group, Inc.* A report prepared for the Alberta Oil Sands Environmental Research Program (Human System), April 1979.

34. *Field Operations Manual for Client Service Representatives Study: Central Mortgage and Housing Corporation.* A report prepared for Kelly, Gairns and Connolly, Ltd., Ottawa, June 1979.

35. *Progress Report on the Analysis of Field Data Gathered by Client Service Representatives of the Central Mortgage and Housing Corporation.* A report prepared for Kelly, Gairns and Connolly, Ltd., Ottawa, September 1979.

36. *Project: Progress Research Operations Manual.* An operations manual prepared for the Canadian Library Association in Connection with Project Progress, October 1979.

37. *Analysis of Field Data Gathered by Client Service Representatives of the Central Mortgage and Housing Corporation.* A report prepared for Kelly, Gairns and Connolly, Ltd., Ottawa, December 1979.

38. *A Conceptual Framework for the Identification of the Socio-Economic Impacts of Oil Sands Development in the Fort McMurray Area.* A draft final report prepared for the Alberta Oil Sands Environmental Research Program, April 1980.

39. *A Conceptual Framework for the Identification of the Socio-Economic Impacts of Oil Sands Development in the Fort McMurray Area: Additional Tabulations.* A report prepared for the Alberta Oil Sands Environmental Research Program, April 1980.

40. *Project Progress: A Study of the Canadian Public Libraries.* A report prepared for the Canadian Library Association, Ottawa, January 1981.

41. *Specification of Immigration and Information Requirements for Policy and Priority Development.* A report prepared for the Minister's Task Force on Immigration Practices and Procedures, January 1981.

42. *Gathering and Organization of Data on Selected Immigration Issues.* A report prepared for the Minister's Task Force on Immigration Practices and Procedures, February 1981.

43. *Policy Analysis and Interpretation of Selected Immigration Issues.* A report prepared for the Minister's Task Force on Immigration Practices and Procedures, March 1981.

44. *Report of the Research and Analysis Group of the Opportunities in Mining Project.* A report prepared for the Canadian Public Affairs Consulting Group, July 1981.

45. *An Evaluation of the Opportunities in Mining Conference: Vancouver, B.C., April 27–29, 1981.* A report prepared for the Canadian Public Affairs Consulting Group, July 1981.

46. *Presentation Guidelines Manual for Project Progress Seminar Series.* A report prepared for the Canadian Library Association, November 18, 1981.

47. *Occupational and Educational Plans of Canadian Youth as They Impact on ROTP Subsidized Educational Opportunities: Phase One Report.* A report prepared for the Department of National Defence (Canada), December 28, 1981.

48. *Occupational and Educational Plans of Canadian Youth as They Impact on ROTP Subsidized Educational Opportunities: Phase Two Report.* A report prepared for the Department of National Defence (Canada), May 20, 1982.

49. *Occupational and Educational Plans of Canadian Youth as They Impact on ROTP Subsidized Educational Opportunities: Phase Three (Final) Report.* A report prepared for the Department of National Defence (Canada), September 14, 1982.

50. *The Shortage of Skilled Workers and the Ontario Educational System; Opportunities and Barriers for Women: A Summary Report.* A report prepared for the Ministry of Labour (Ontario), March 31, 1983.

51. *Market and Network Study of the Arts and Culture Studies and Reports of the Department of Communications.* A report prepared for the Department of Communications (Arts and Culture Sector) Ottawa, June 17, 1983.

52. *Strategies for Establishing Affirmative Action Goals and Timetables.* A report prepared for the Royal Commission on Equality in Employment, October 1983.

53. *A Quality of Working Life Trial at Canadian Forces Supply Depot 25: Phase One Report.* A report prepared for the Department of National Defence (Canada), December 1983.

54. *QWL Trial at CFSD 24: Number One Monitoring Results.* A report prepared for the Department of National Defence (Canada), February 1984.

55. *Sample Survey Study of Ontario Firms on Emerging and Critical Occupations.* A report prepared for IDEA Corporation, February 15, 1984.

56. *An Evaluation of "Participation Patterns Study of Alberta Post-Secondary Students: Report of the Steering Committee."* A report prepared for Alberta Advanced Education, June 1984.

57. *A Planning Process for the Calgary Public Library.* A report prepared for the Calgary Public Library, July 1984.

58. *QWL Trial at CFSD 25: Effects of Changes in the Sample Base During the Trial.* A report prepared for the Department of National Defence (Canada), August 1984.

59. *QWL Trial at CFSD 25: Number Three Monitoring Results.* A report prepared for the Department of National Defence (Canada), August 1984.

60. *Program Evaluation Skills for Military Personnel.* A training course developed for the Department of National Defence (Canada), August 1984.

61. *Professional Manpower Planning for Canadian Agriculture: Phase One Report.* A report prepared for the Agricultural Institute of Canada, September 24, 1984.

62. *Evaluation of QWL Trial at CFSD 25: Final Report.* A report prepared for the Department of National Defence (Canada), December 1984.

63. *QWL Trial at CFSD 25: Number One Post Trial Monitoring Results.* A report prepared for the Department of National Defence (Canada), December 1984.

64. *QWL Trial at CFSD 25: Number Two Post Trial Monitoring Results.* A report prepared for the Department of National Defence (Canada), December 1984.

65. *A Critical Assessment of Existing SVP and GED Methodology.* A report prepared for National Occupational Analysis and Classification Systems-Research, Employment and Immigration Canada, January 1985.

66. *Alternative Scales and Procedures for the Measurements of SVP and GED.* A report prepared for National Occupational Analysis and Classification Systems-Research, Employment and Immigration Canada, February 1985.

67. *Development of a Post-Abella Strategy for the Canadian Human Rights Commission.* A report prepared for the Canadian Human Rights Commission, February 1985.

68. *Alternative Scales and Procedures for the Measurement of SVP and GED: Part II.* A report prepared for National Occupational Analysis and Classification Systems, Employment and Immigration Canada, March 27, 1985.

69. *Computerized Human Resource Information System (CHRIS) and Data Needs for Equal Opportunity/Affirmative Action Planning, Implementation and Evaluation.* A report prepared for the Equal Opportunity Division, City of Toronto, April 24, 1985.

70. *Organizational Analysis as a Prelude to QWL Design and Implementation.* A report prepared for the Department of National Defence (Canada), June 1985.

71. *Organizational Analysis at CSFD 25: Overview Report.* A report prepared for the Department of National Defence (Canada), June 1985.

72. *Developing a Goals and Timetables Package for Equal Opportunity Planning and Monitoring in the City of Toronto Workforce.* A report prepared for the Equal Opportunity Division of the City of Toronto, September 1985.

73. *Demand and Supply Trends for Agricultural Professionals in Canada.* A report prepared for the Agricultural Institute of Canada, October 1985.

74. *Excellence and Equality: The Contradiction in Science Teaching in America.* A report prepared for the American Association for the Advancement of Science, October 1985.

75. *Continuing Assessment of Technology Skills for Ontario: The New Jobs in Technology.* A report prepared for IDEA Corporation, November 1985.

76. *The Gender Equality Index for Ontario: Feasibility Study.* A report prepared for the Ontario Women's Directorate, December 1985.

77. *Specifications for a Survey of Racial Minorities, Disabled Persons and Francophones in the Ontario Public Service.* A report prepared for the Civil Service Commission (Ontario), February 1986.

78. *Educational Strategies to Maximize Service Sector Opportunities in Ontario.* A report to the Task Force on Ontario's Service Sector, February 1986.

79. *Pay Equity and Ontario's Small Business Sector.* A report prepared for Small Business Advocacy, Ontario Ministry of Industry, Trade and Technology, June 1986.

80. *Environmental Scan Study.* A report prepared for IBM Canada Ltd., June 1986.

81. *A Canadian Forces Social Demographic Trends Information System: Design Phase.* A report prepared for the Department of National Defence (Canada), July 1986.

82. *The Gender Equality Compendium: A Prototype for Ontario.* A report prepared for the Ontario Women's Directorate, October 1986.

83. *Study of Social, Cultural and Economic Barriers to Employment Opportunities for Women in Toronto: Phase I Report.* A report prepared for the City of Toronto, October 1986.

84. *A Canadian Forces Social Demographic Trends Information System: Data Assembly Phase.* A report prepared for the Department of National Defence (Canada), November 1986.

85. *The Gender Equality Index for Ontario: An Empirical Test.* A report prepared for the Ontario Women's Directorate, November 1986.

86. *Analysis and Interpretation of Ontario Public Service "I Count" Census Returns.* A report prepared for the Human Resources Secretariat (Ontario), November 1986.

87. *Employment Equity Self-Identification Survey Strategy for Canadian Banks.* A report prepared for the Canadian Bankers' Association, September 1986.

88. *Analysis and Interpretation of Ontario Public Service "I Count" Census Returns: Technical Appendix.* A report prepared for the Human Resources Secretariat (Ontario), November 1986.

89. *A Canadian Forces Social Demographic Trends Information System: Implementation Phase.* A report prepared for the Department of National Defence (Canada), February 1987.

90. *HRS Employment Equity Database: Technical Documentation.* A report prepared for the Human Resources Secretariat (Ontario), March 1987.

91. *Canada Post Workforce Census: Final Report of Computer-Based Analysis of Data.* A report prepared for Canada Post Corporation, June 1987.

92. *Equal Opportunity Goals and Timetables Action Planning: Technical Assistance Materials.* A report prepared for the Equal Opportunity Division, City of Toronto, June 1987.

93. *HRS Downsized Employment Equity Database: Technical Documentation and Tests.* A report prepared for the Human Resources Secretariat (Ontario), August 1987.

94. *We All Count Census: Analysis and Recommendations.* A report prepared for the Liquor Control Board of Ontario, August 1987.

95. *Goals and Timetables Made Easy.* A report prepared for the Equal Opportunity Division, City of Toronto, September 1987.

96. *Employment Standards in Small Firms in Ontario.* A report prepared for the Small Business Branch, Ministry of Industry, Trade and Technology (Ontario), October 1987.

97. *The Status of Women in Toronto: An Overview.* A report with accompanying audio-visual presentation prepared for the Institute on Women and Work, Toronto, November 26–28, 1987.

98. *Pay Equity Commission Database: A Feasibility Study.* A report prepared for the Pay Equity Commission, July 1988.

99. *Pay Equity Commission Database: Survey Design Materials.* A report prepared for the Pay Equity Commission, September 1988.

100. *Growth of the Contingent Workforce in Ontario: Structural Trends, Statistical Dimensions, and Policy Implications.* A report prepared for the Ontario Women's Directorate, February 1989.

101. *Selected Socioeconomic Consequences of Disability for Women in Canada Aged Fifteen and Over.* A report prepared for Statistics Canada, March 1989.

102. *An Inner City School Index for the Toronto Board of Education.* A report prepared for the Toronto Board of Education, June 1989.

103. *The Institute on Women and Work: Directions for Action.* A report prepared for the Equal Opportunity Division, City of Toronto, June 1989.

104. *The Gender Equality Review: Ontario, 1990.* A report prepared for the Ontario Women's Directorate, March 1990.

105. *The Socioeconomic Situation of Women Compared to Men: Toronto, 1990.* A report prepared for the Institute on Women and Work, Toronto, June 1990.

106. *The Underutilization of Women in the Canadian Economy and Intervention Points for Public Policy.* A report prepared for the Council of Ministers of Education (Canada), June 1990.

107. *A "B Scale" for the Toronto Board of Education.* A report prepared for the Toronto Board of Education, October 1990.

108. *An Evaluation of the Strengthening Community Health Program (SCHP).* A report prepared for the Health Promotion Directorate, Health & Welfare Canada, February 1991.

109. *Socioeconomic Comparisons Among Employment Equity Visible Minority Sub-Groups and the Reference Population.* A report prepared for

the Employment Equity Branch, Employment and Immigration Canada, May 1991.

110. *Population of Persons with Disabilities Reported under the Employment Equity Act.* A report prepared for the Employment Equity Branch, Employment and Immigration Canada, May 1991.

111. *Population of Persons with Disabilities: The Health and Activity Limitation Survey.* A report prepared for the Employment Equity Branch, Employment and Immigration Canada, May 1991.

112. *Canadian Forces (CF) Internal Survey on Homosexual Issues.* A report prepared for the Department of National Defence (Canada), June 1991.

113. *Social Marketing Strategies and the Ontario Environment.* A report prepared for the Ministry of Environment (Ontario), August 1991.

114. *Hypothetical Policy Impacts of Pay Equity Regulatory/Legislative Change.* A report prepared for the Ministry of Labour (Ontario), September 1991.

115. *Population of Persons with Disabilities: The Health and Activity Limitation Survey.* A report prepared for the Interdepartmental Working Group on Employment Equity Data, March 1992.

116. *What Is Success in Employment Equity? A Regression Based Analysis of Factors Influencing the Representation of Designated Groups in Varying Employment Situations.* A report prepared for the Employment Equity Branch, Employment and Immigration Canada, June 1992.

117. *Patterns of Socioeconomic Disadvantage for Selected Ethnocultural Groups, Canada, 1986.* A report prepared for the Interdepartmental Working Group on Employment Equity Data, June 1992.

118. *Improvements in the Occupational Status of Women.* A report prepared for the Ontario Women's Directorate, January 1993.

119. *Social Marketing to Change Environmental Attitudes and Behaviours.* A report prepared for the Ministry of the Environment (Ontario), January 1993.

120. *Toward an Integrated Employment Equity Implementation Strategy for Metropolitan Toronto School Boards.* A report prepared for the Metropolitan Toronto School Board, May 1994.

121. *Review of Employment Policies and Practices.* A report prepared for George Brown College, September 1994.

122. *A Comparison of Three Allocation Algorithms for Use with the Metropolitan Toronto School Board Inner City Scale.* A report prepared for the Metropolitan Toronto School Board, November 1994.

123. *Review of Employment Policies and Practices.* A report prepared for the Scarborough Board of Education, March 1995.

124. *A Review of Employment Policies and Practices at York Board of Education.* A report prepared for the York Board of Education, May 1995.

125. *A Review of Employment Policies and Practices at North York Board of Education.* A report prepared for the North York Board of Education, May 1995.

126. *Employment Systems Review: Results of the Focus Groups.* A report prepared for the Scarborough Board of Education, June 1995.

127. *Review of Employment Policies and Practices.* A report prepared for the Ontario Public Service Employees Union, June 1995.

128. *Review of Employment Policies and Practices.* A report prepared for the Toronto Board of Education, June 1995.

129. *Review of Employment Policies and Practices.* A report prepared for the East York Board of Education, June 1995.

130. *External Availability of Employment Equity Designated Group Members for Typical School Board Jobs.* A report prepared for the Metropolitan Toronto School Board, September 1995.

131. *Breakdown Analysis of Employment Systems Review Survey Results.* A report prepared for the East York Board of Education, November 1995.

132. *George Brown College Employment Equity Database: Documentation and Reports.* A report prepared for George Brown College, March 1996.

133. *Key Issues for Action.* A report prepared for the Toronto Board of Education, March 1996.

134. *Analytical Commentary on "High Yield" and "Low Yield" Strategies for Removing Barriers to Employment Equity.* A report prepared for the Toronto Board of Education, May 1996.

135. *Employment Systems Review: Results of the Focus Groups.* A report prepared for the East York Board of Education, May 1996.

136. *Ontario Public Service Employees Union Employment Equity Database: Documentation and Reports.* A report prepared for the Ontario Public Service Employees Union, June 1996.

137. *Sources of Variation in School Scores in the 1991–1992 Provincial Review of Writing in Grade 12 English: A Pilot Study of the Toronto Board of Education Schools.* A report prepared for the Toronto Board of Education, June 1997.

138. *Representation Levels for Employment Equity Designated Groups by Employment Equity Occupational Groups (EEOG) for the Total Organization and the Departments of the Organization.* A report prepared for the Bank of Canada, September 1997.

139. *Information Resources for Linkage Development: The Wingspread Project.* A report prepared for Vista Inc., November 1997.

140. *Representation Levels of Employment Equity Designated Group Members at the Bank of Canada.* A report prepared for the Bank of Canada, March 1998.

141. *Employment Equity Occupational Group (EEOG) Representation and Gap Analysis.* A report prepared for the Bank of Canada, April 1998.

142. *Personnel Movement Patterns by Employment Equity Designated Groups.* A report prepared for the Bank of Canada, May 1998.

143. *Strategies for Policy/Program Oriented Research Applications of the International Migration Database (IMOB).* A report prepared for Citizenship and Immigration Canada, May 1998.

144. *Employment Equity Designated Group Representation Levels in the George Brown College Workforce.* A report prepared for George Brown College, November 1998.

145. *A Review of the Survey Instruments and Methodology Used in the Government of Ontario's College Accountability Framework.* A report prepared for Centennial College, May 1999.

146. *Employment Equity Designated Group Representation Levels in the George Brown College Workforce.* A report prepared for George Brown College, March 2000.

147. *Project Partnership Areas Involving the Commission for Environmental Cooperation and the Alliance for Higher Education and Enterprise in North America.* A report prepared for the Commission for Environmental Cooperation, September 2000.

148. *Overview of Data on Persons with Disabilities Aged 15–64 Years: Estimates for 1996.* A report prepared for the York South Simcoe Training and Adjustment Board, November 2000.

149. *Socioeconomic Situation of Immigrants: Variations by Immigrant Attributes and Implications for Losses to the Canadian Economy.* A report prepared for the Maytree Foundation, February 2001.

150. *Mining, Petroleum and Forestry Industry Views on Carbon Emissions Trading Regime Strategies.* A report prepared for the Commission for Environmental Cooperation, March 2001.

151. *A Study of the Characteristics and Experiences of Immigrants Seeking Employment in Regulated Professions in Ontario.* A report prepared for the Access to Professions and Trades Unit, Ministry of Training, Colleges and Universities (Ontario), September 2001.

152. *The Costs of Discrimination: Women and the Canadian Economy.* A report prepared for Human Resources Development Canada, March 2002.

153. *The Costs of Discrimination: Visible Minorities and the Canadian Economy.* A report prepared for Human Resources Development Canada, March 2002.

154. *Skill Shortages and Training Needs in the York Region.* A report prepared for the York South Simcoe Training and Adjustment Board, April 2002.

155. *A Compensation Benchmark Study of Superintendents, Deputy Superintendents and Operational Managers in the Ontario Adult Corrections Sector.* A report prepared for the Ministry of Public Safety and Security, Ontario, January 2003.

List of Photographs and Drawings

Page 24: Edward B. Harvey, off to a high school graduation event, 1957. Source: author's collection.

Page 34: The approach to Victoria College with the Young Building in the background; drawing by Edward Goodall, circa 1959. Source: image used courtesy of the estate of Edward Goodall. (The author would particularly like to thank Edward Goodall's son, Richard, for his kindness and generosity in providing copies of various works by his father.)

Page 35: An idyllic setting: students outside Victoria College's landmark Young Building, circa mid-1950s. Copyright University of Victoria.

Page 37: Edward B. Harvey's MG TC sports car, parked in front of the Pacific Ocean, Victoria, B.C., circa late 1950s. Copyright author.

Page 39: Issue 2 (1958) of *Evergreen Review*, with an inscription (written in 1998) by the *Review's* publisher, Barney Rosset. Source: author's collection; gift from Barney Rosset, 1998.

Page 40: Charles Mingus in concert, Victoria College, 1961. Source: *The Tower* (Victoria College Yearbook), 1960–61.

Page 42: The Honourable Lester B. Pearson speaking at Victoria College, 1961. Source: *The Tower* (Victoria College Yearbook), 1960–61.

Page 48: Kaspar D. Naegele, in his University of British Columbia office, 1964. Source: University Archives, University of British Columbia Library, neg. #1.1/4134-1. Used with permission.

Page 61: "President Kennedy Assassinated," Victoria *Daily Times* Bulletin Board, November 22, 1963. Source: University of Victoria Archives, copyright J.J. Philion.

Page 66: Holder Hall, Princeton University. A fine example of Princeton architecture. Source: Brian Rose, New York.

Page 69: Valerie Ayer, Princeton, 1966. Source: author's collection.

Page 75: Wilbert E. Moore, professor of sociology at Princeton University and sociologist at the Russell Sage Foundation, 1966. Source: American Sociological Association, Washington, D.C. Used with the permission of the American Sociological Association.

Page 89 and cover: Dr. Edward B. Harvey, as co-director (with Dr. Andrew T. Hunter) of the Ontario Medical Manpower Commission, 1967. Source: author's collection.

Page 96: S.D. Clark, Chair, Department of Sociology, University of Toronto, 1963–1969. Source: University of Toronto.

Page 126: Lorna R. Marsden, president and vice-chancellor of York University, 1997–present. Source: Office of the President, York University, copyright Doug Hall Inc.

Page 143: John H. Blakely, circa 2002. Source: John H. Blakely.

Page 154: (Left to right) Lloyd Axworthy and Edward B. Harvey, 2002. Source: author's collection.

Page 158: Madam Justice Rosalie S. Abella, Ontario Court of Appeal. circa 2003. Appointed to the Supreme Court of Canada, 2004. Source: Madam Justice Abella.

Page 170: (Left to right) Edward B. Harvey and Barbara Kasinska, Syncrude Alberta Oil Sands Development Site, northern Alberta, 1979. Copyright author.

Page 188: Hon. David R. Peterson, P.C., Q.C., Premier of Ontario, 1985–1990. Used with the permission of Mr. Peterson.

Page 195: Members of the board of directors of the Alliance for Higher Education and Enterprise in North America, with President Ernesto Zedillo of Mexico and Canadian Prime Minister Jean Chrétien on the occasion of the prime minister's state visit to Mexico, April 8–9, 1999. Source: Office of the Prime Minister, Ottawa.

Page 204: K.S.R. "Ram" Murthy, 2004. Source: Dr. K.S.R. Murthy.

Page 214: Part of the system used to experimentally contaminate television picture segments with ultra-high voltage electrical interference, Project UHV, Pittsfield, Massachusetts, 1976. Copyright author.

Page 230: (Left to right) Avie Bennett, chancellor of York University; Lorna R. Marsden, president and vice-chancellor of York University; and Edward B. Harvey; Toronto, 2003. Copyright author.

Back cover: (left to right) Edward B. Harvey, Lorna R. Marsden, Margaret Trudeau, Prime Minister Pierre Elliott Trudeau; 24 Sussex Drive, Ottawa, Summer, 1975. Source: Office of the Prime Minister, Ottawa, Canada.

Endnotes

1. F.H. Leacy, *Historical Statistics of Canada* (Ottawa: Statistics Canada and the Social Sciences and Humanities Research Council of Canada, 1983), pp. B1–14.

2. Daniel Kubat and David Thornton, *A Statistical Profile of Canadian Society* (Toronto: McGraw-Hill Ryerson, 1974), p. 104.

3. C. Wright Mills, *White Collar: The American Middle Classes* (New York: Oxford University Press, 1953).

4. Books by Simon Marinker include *Beyond the Citadel* (Victoria: Trafford Publishing, 1999) and *Assassination, Preparation & Consequences* (Victoria: Trafford Publishing, 2002).

5. Conversation with Herbert Siebner, *circa* 1994.

6. Barney Rosset will be best remembered as a radical thinker who revolutionized how Americans thought about literature during the time he controlled Grove Press and through trailblazing publications like *Evergreen Review*. The second issue of *Evergreen Review*, published in 1958 and titled "San Francisco Scene," broke new ground with its presentation of works by Miller, Rexroth, Ginsberg, Kerouac, and Ferlinghetti.

7. Books by Wayson Choy include *The Jade Peony* (New York: Picador, 1997) and *Paper Shadows: A Chinatown Childhood* (Toronto: Penguin, 2000).

8. Edward B. Harvey, "The Professions and Sociology: Some Implications for Pharmacy," *Western Druggist* (July 1963), pp. 21–22.

9. Talcott Parsons, *The Structure of Social Action* (New York: The Free Press of Glencoe, 1937).

10. Talcott Parsons, *The Social System* (New York: The Free Press of Glencoe, 1951).

11. Sigmund Freud, *On Creativity and the Unconscious: Papers on the Psychology of Art, Literature, Love and Religion* (New York: Harper & Row, 1958).

12. Karl Menninger, *Man against Himself* (New York: Harcourt Brace & World, 1938).

13. Erving Goffman, *Asylums: Essays on the Social Situation of Mental Patients and Other Inmates* (New York: Anchor Books, 1961).

14. W. Stuart Hughes, *Consciousness and Society: The Reorientation of European Social Thought, 1890–1930* (New York: Vintage, 1958).

15. Erik H. Erikson, "Identity and the Life Cycle," *Psychological Issues*, vol. 1, no. 1 (1959).

16. Cyril Belshaw, *Under the Ivi Tree: Society and Economic Growth in Rural Fiji* (Berkeley: University of California Press, 1964).

17. Howard Engel, *Crimes of Passion* (Toronto: Key Porter Books, 2001), pp. 153–58.

18. Dan Oberdorfer and J.T. Miller, *Princeton University: The First 250 Years* (Princeton: Princeton University, 1996).

19. Ben Rogers, *A.J. Ayer: A Life* (New York: Grove Press, 1989).

20. Charles H. Page, *Fifty Years in the Sociological Enterprise: A Lucky Journey* (Amherst: University of Massachusetts Press, 1982), pp. 151–68.

21. R.H. Cyert and J.G. March, *A Behavioral Theory of the Firm* (Englewood Cliffs, N.J.: Prentice Hall, 1963).

22. Edward B. Harvey, *Structure and Process in Industrial Organizations* (Princeton: Princeton University Doctoral Dissertation, 1967).

23. Lorna R. Marsden and Edward B. Harvey, *Fragile Federation: Social Change in Canada* (Toronto: McGraw-Hill Ryerson, 1979).

24. Obituary of Kaspar D. Naegele, 1923–65, written by Theodore Mills and Frank Jones. The eight-page typescript is undated and no indication is given of its intended place of publication. I discovered the document when going through the Naegele materials provided to me in the summer of 1965.

25. Marion J. Levy, *The Family Revolution in Modern China* (Cambridge, Mass.: Harvard University Press, 1949).

26. Marion J. Levy, *The Structure of Society* (Princeton: Princeton University Press, 1952).

27. Edward B. Harvey, "Some Implications of Value Differentiation in Pharmacy," *Canadian Review of Sociology and Anthropology* (February 1966), pp. 23–27.

28. Edward B. Harvey, "Psychological Rigidity and Muscle Tension," *Psychophysiology* (October 1966), pp. 224–26.

29. Lorna R. Marsden, *Doctors Who Teach* (Princeton: Princeton University Doctoral Dissertation, 1972).

30. Parsons, *The Social System*.

31. Edward B. Harvey, "Social Change and the Jazz Musician," *Social Forces* (September 1968), pp. 34–42.

32. Edward B. Harvey, "Decision Makers in Conflict," *The Business Quarterly* (Autumn 1967), pp. 23–27.

33. Edward B. Harvey and J.H. Blakely, *Information Systems for Managing Workplace Diversity* (Toronto: CCH Canadian Publishers, 1996).

34. Edward B. Harvey and J.H. Blakely, *Re-thinking HR Management: Strategies for Success in an Era of Change* (Toronto: CCH Canadian Publishers, 1999).

35. Edward B. Harvey, J.H. Blakely, and Katherine Lee, *Internet Solutions for HR Managers* (Toronto: CCH Canadian Publishers, 2002).

36. Edward B. Harvey, "Technology and the Structure of Organizations," *American Sociological Review* (April 1968), pp. 247–59.

37. Edward B. Harvey, *Industrial Society: Structures, Roles, and Relations* (Homewood, IL: Dorsey Press, 1975).

38. Edward B. Harvey, *Education and Employment of Arts and Science Graduates: The Last Decade in Ontario* (Toronto: Commission on Post-Secondary Education in Ontario, 1972).

39. Edward B. Harvey, *Education Systems and the Labour Market* (Don Mills, Ont.: Longman Canada, 1973).

40. Edward B. Harvey and J. Lennards, *The Changing Nature of Post-Secondary Education: Attitudes, Costs and Benefits* (Toronto: Commission on Post-Secondary Education, 1971).

41. Edward B. Harvey and J. Lennards, *Key Issues in Higher Education* (Toronto: Ontario Institute for Studies in Education Press, 1973).

42. Lorna R. Marsden, *Population Probe: Canada* (Toronto: Copp Clark, 1972).

43. Edward B. Harvey and Lorna R. Marsden, eds., *Canadian Population Concerns* (Toronto: Population Research Foundation, 1977).

44. *Pharmacy in a New Age*, report of the Commission on Pharmaceutical Services, Toronto, 1972.

45. Rick Helmes-Hayes, ed., *Forty Years: 1963–2003*, a history of the University of Toronto Sociology Department (Toronto: Canadian Scholars' Press Inc., 2003), pp. 56–57.

46. Helmes-Hayes, *Forty Years*, p. 65.

47. Edward B. Harvey, ed., *Perspectives on Modernization: Essays in Memory of Ian Weinberg* (Toronto: University of Toronto Press, 1972).

48. Edward B. Harvey, "The Vanishing Practitioner," *Journal of Medical Education,* vol. 48 (August 1973), pp. 718–24.

49. *The Employment Equity Review*, Toronto, Pay Trends Inc., vol. 1, no. 1 (January 1991) to vol. 5, no. 12, (December 1995).

50. Marsden and Harvey, *Fragile Federation*, p. 6.

51. Edward B. Harvey, "Dimensions of a Decade: Canadian Higher Education in the Sixties," in G. McDiarmid, ed., *From Quantitative to Qualitative Change in Ontario Education* (Toronto: Ontario Institute for Studies in Education, 1976), pp. 1–27.

52. E. Earl Wright and Rodger S. Lawson, *Policy Considerations for Female Affirmative Action Programs* (Kalamazoo, Mich.: W.E. Upjohn Institute for Employment Research, April 1974), p. 4.

53. Marsden and Harvey, *Fragile Federation*, p. 47.

54. For an introduction to social marketing, see Philip Kotler and Eduardo L. Roberto, *Social Marketing: Strategies for Changing Public Behavior* (New York: The Free Press, 1989).

55. Edward B. Harvey, B. Siu, and K. Reil, "Ethnocultural Groups, Period of Immigration and Socioeconomic Situation," *Canadian Ethnic Studies*, vol. 31, no. 3 (1999), pp. 95–103.

56. Edward B. Harvey, L. Lo, V. Preston, S. Wang, K. Reil, and B. Siu, "Immigrants' Economic Status in Toronto: Rethinking Settlement and Integration Strategies," Centre of Excellence for Research on Immigration and Settlement (CERIS), March 2000, Working Paper 15.

57. Edward B. Harvey and Richard Liu, "North American Linkage Building by Canadian and U.S. Institutions of Higher Education," *Policy Options* (September 2003), pp. 46–49.

58. Edward B. Harvey and Richard Liu, "Building North American Higher Education Linkages: Canadian Universities and Community Colleges Compared," *College Quarterly* (Winter 2003), pp. 1–10.

59. The five monographs, all of which were co-authored by Edward B. Harvey and K.S.R. Murthy were: *Supply of and Demand for New Graduates* (Toronto: Technical Service Council, 1975); *Engineering Manpower Demand and Supply* (Toronto: Technical Service Council, 1976);

Supply of and Demand for Accounting Professionals in Canada (Toronto: Technical Service Council, 1979); *Supply of and Demand for Engineers in Canada* (Toronto: Technical Service Council, 1980); *Engineering Supply and Demand, 1988–1998* (Toronto: Technical Service Council, 1988).

60. Edward B. Harvey and Wasyl Janischewskyj, *Human Response to Interference with TV Picture Quality* (Palo Alto, Calif.: Electric Power Research Institute, October 1980). Also see Edward B. Harvey, Wasyl Janischewskyj, and M. Comber, "Power Line Interference and Assessment of Television Picture Quality," *IEEE Transactions on Power Apparatus and Systems*, vol. PAS-102, no. 5 (May 1983), pp. 1039–49.

61. *The Employment Equity Review*, Toronto, Pay Trends Inc., vol. 1, no. 1 (January 1991) to vol. 5, no. 12 (December 1995).

62. *Valuing Diversity* was published on a monthly basis from January 1996 to December 1999.

63. *The Compensation Law Reporter* commenced monthly publication in January 2000 and is continuing.

64. Edward B. Harvey, *Information Systems for Employment Equity: An Employer Guide* (Toronto: CCH Canadian Publishers, 1988).

65. Edward B. Harvey, J.H. Blakely, and E. Severn, *Computing for Equity: Computer Applications for Employment Equity* (Toronto: CCH Canadian Publishers, 1990).

66. *The Demonstration Workbook* was published with *Computing for Equity*.

67. Edward B. Harvey and J.H. Blakely, *Information Systems for Managing Workplace Diversity* (Toronto: CCH Canadian Publishers, 1996).

68. Edward B. Harvey and J.H. Blakely, *Re-thinking HR Management: Strategies for Success in an Era of Change* (Toronto: CCH Canadian Publishers, 1999).

69. Edward B. Harvey and J.H. Blakely, *Equal Pay* (Toronto: CCH Canadian Publishers, 2000).

70. Edward B. Harvey, J.H. Blakely, and Katherine Lee, *Internet Solutions for HR Managers* (Toronto: CCH Canadian Publishers, 2002).

71. Private communication with officials of Research and Policy Branch, Citizenship and Immigration Canada, 2003.

72. In writing this section of the book, I had discussions with Richard Liu and Karen Myers, two University of Toronto sociology department graduate students with an interest in applied, policy-oriented social research. Their views were most helpful. I assume full responsibility for any conclusions drawn.